UNDERCURRENTS

THE HIDDEN WIRING OF MODERN MUSIC

EDITED BY ROB YOUNG

WIRE
WWW.THEWIRE.CO.UK

continuum
LONDON • NEW YORK
www.continuumbooks.com

First published 2002 by **Continuum**
The Tower Building, 11 York Road, London SE1 7NX
15 East 26th Street, New York, 10010

Reprinted 2003

British Library Cataloguing-in-Publication Data
A catalogue record for this book is available from the British Library
ISBN 0-8264-6450-5

Typeset by Non-Format (www.non-format.com)
Printed and bound in the UK by MPG Books Ltd, Bodmin

CONTENTS

ACKNOWLEDGEMENTS

Undercurrents could not have come about without the combined efforts of my colleagues at *The Wire*. Tony Herrington, the magazine's publisher (and editor between 1994-2000), gave the green light to the idea when it was proposed as a series in late 1998, and he, Chris Bohn and Peter Shapiro provided invaluable work in shaping, editing and proofing the final results. Anne Hilde Neset made additional suggestions and comments; Ben House, Andy Tait and Phil England took good care of the magazine's business end. Special thanks are due to the contributors to this volume, all of whom help to elevate the daily routine at *The Wire* into such a stimulating exchange of ideas, month after month. Our Art Directors, Kjell Ekhorn and Jon Forss, designed the cover and typeset the interior with their usual imagination and finesse. Felix Cemmel assisted in compiling the Bibliography and Discography.

Thanks to David Hayden at Continuum for his initial enthusiasm for the book project, and to Janet Joyce, Angela McMahon and Veronica Higgs for overseeing the later stages of production.

Arne Neset pinpointed the Thoreau quotations in "Worship The Glitch". La Monte Young and Marian Zazeela, Sri Karunamayee, Henry Flynt and Catherine Christer Hennix gave invaluable help with "The Eternal Drone". Assistance with both sections of "The Ragged Trousered Anthologist" was given by John DeFore at Revenant, Rani Singh at The Harry Smith Archives, Brenda Dunlap at Smithsonian Folkways, Brian Doherty, M Henry Jones, Martha Blegen and Nick Amster.

Chapters 1-4, 6, 9-12, 14, 16 and 19 were first published in edited form in *The Wire* during 1999; 7 and 8 in 2000; 15 and 17 in 2001. Chapters 5, 13 and 18 appear for the first time in this volume.

INTRODUCTION

THE HIDDEN WIRING

BY ROB YOUNG

At the beginning of 1999, with the millennium finally visible on the horizon, *The Wire* magazine decided to take a stab at commemorating the wider picture of modern music with a monthly series called Undercurrents. The brief was to pick 12 themes or conceptual approaches: detectable narrative strands which are often alluded to in reviews or features but never elaborated with anything more than a swiftly turned journalistic locating phrase. The original series threw up an expansive range of ideas, from the occult origins of recorded sound itself through the ancient belief in cosmic resonance, to the various, often ramshackle solutions to problems of new performance practices thrown up by new technologies such as electronic music or interactive software. When the year 2000 broke, we continued the series of 'thinkpieces' under the heading Tangents. This volume collects all the original 12 Undercurrents pieces, some of them in uncut or substantially revised versions, adds the highlights of the subsequent Tangents series, and stirs in three more essays specially commissioned for this book.

These essays offer stepping stones towards an understanding of the forces that have shaped, and continue to shape modern music. Although by no means definitive, these collected essays emerge as a series of accounts of ingenious creativity, often in the face of hostility, oblivion, incredulity and cynicism. Some paint portraits of heroic folly that have come to represent beacons and touchstones; attempts to express fundamental truths – scientific, emotional, mystic, spiritual and erotic – through wind, wire, electricity and song.

Sometimes the articles overlap, interlock and strike sparks off each other. Drone based musics, ascribed therapeutic aspects in Marcus Boon's "The Eternal Drone", become an ideological battleground in "Slapping Pythagoras". A John Cage turntable experiment mentioned in Christoph Cox's "The Jerrybuilt Future" will become a central tenet of Peter Shapiro's "Deck Wreckers", an examination of the ways in which the gramophone/record player has attained usage more than just a playback device – a perfect illustration of William Gibson's assertion that "the street finds its own use for things". In fact, Cage appears passim; a philosopher and musical liberator whose tidal influence has surged into rock, pop and jazz as much as avant garde composition.

These narratives form continuities that conventional music discourse rarely bothers to involve itself with. A record such as The Grateful Dead's *Anthem Of The Sun*, constructed using methods that echo the concrète tape cut-ups of French composers Pierre Schaeffer and Pierre Henry 20 years previously, is likely to be critiqued solely in the context of late 60s Californian narcotics and hippy culture. Separate camps such as avant garde music and rock 'n' roll are held, from a media perspective at least, to view each other with mutual suspicion. In fact musicians themselves tend to be less prone to generic empire building.

Out of all these various takes on modern music, two especially strong currents materialise in the stream of information. One is what composer and author Joel Chadabe has called (in a useful but not terribly wieldy phrase) "the great opening up of music to all sounds". John Cage's piece *4'33"*, often mocked for its apparent contempt for traditional performance, deserves to be placed alongside Marcel Duchamp's R Mutt urinal as a great, playful, psychedelic artefact. Often misnamed *Silence*, *4'33"* is actually a tabula rasa permitting music to open up to ambience and contingency. The second is the transforming effect of the electronic revolution, which has affected not only the distribution, recording and reception of music and sound but also fundamentally rewired the way musicians approach the sharp-end activity of making music.

The book's first section, 'Electrification', traces out the moment that sound, speech and music were able to be converted and transmitted over any distance via electromagnetic impulses. The inventors who made this possible were Alexander Graham Bell, inventor of the telephone, and Thomas Edison, whose phonograph stands as the model on which so many contemporary music metaphors now rest. In its mechanism of repeated revolution allied with the needle's dimension of forward temporal travel along the groove, coupled with the manoeuvrability of the vinyl object on the turntable, an industry, a new way of thinking about time itself, and an enhanced selfconsciousness about the performance and recording of music, were born.

As well as infiltrating the distribution of the recorded artefact, and opening up many more worlds of sound to be consumed and experienced than ever before, electricity, in the form of amplification, altered performers' relationships with their instruments and with their audiences.

The microphone, as outlined in Ian Penman's "On The Mic", enabled singers to think about their craft in entirely new ways, that had nothing to do with traditional notions of 'projection', communication and public utterance. The extreme sensitivity of the microphone to the minutest of sounds lent a new intimacy to sound works and music which paved the way for ambitious, phantasmagoric studio constructions that dealt more with interior states of mind and psychological intensity than the narration of a story in song, or a straight recital of a predestined set of notes.

There is a book still to be written about the role of the producer as artistic mediator in the development of 20th century music: Phil Spector, George Martin, Lee 'Scratch' Perry, Trevor Horn, Giorgio Moroder, Hank Shocklee, Van Dyke Parks, Teo Macero, Bill Laswell, Rudy Van Gelder and Steve Albini, to name a few, have finessed an art that may be on the decline as music moves away from the expensive recording studio to the realm of the DIY digital home set-up. But that sense of the homemade is not an entirely late 20th century approach.

Christoph Cox's "The Jerrybuilt Future", outlining the inventions and gizmos and happenings that emerged from the activities of several music groups of the 1950s and 60s in America and outside, including The Sonic Arts Union, ONCE Group, Musica Elettronica Viva, et al, illuminates groups of musicians with more of a sense of humour than most academic classical composers, but who had little interest in the archaic and received structures that have become ossified in classical music: the sonata, symphony, concerto. Instead, expressing deep unrest with contemporary political life, and with the destructive forces unleashed in modern warfare (and picking up on notions of 'Electronic Disturbance' propounded by William S Burroughs), these experimental groups were forced to invent a customised instrumental tools, amplification systems and performance scenarios. Electronic music's difficulty in reaching large audiences is partly a consequence of it being 'in the can' before the evening has begun. Playback over a sound system in a public auditorium remains problematic – although the problem is one of context and demographics, as the worldwide spread of reggae, dance music and DJ culture has made a social nexus of the act of spinning a record over a sound system in public space. Less dancefloor-friendly electronica has inevitably become a more private experience, created by solipsists, not as a music of social interaction, but as a nocturnal, personal playback experience, tending to reflect more microscopic detail than grand sweep. The myriad of information compacted into the digital musics discussed in "Worship The Glitch" represents one millennial extreme.

The section entitled 'Occultism' looks at instances where musical science from antiquity has remained alive in the fabric of contemporary musical argument. Ancient cultures in Asia and the Americas placed greater emphasis upon the power of acoustics than European tradition acknowledges. Western art music (ie classical composition) has been more focused on issues of narrative structure, emotionalism and formalism. The scientific building blocks of acoustics, from the drone to the intervals between notes that, arranged in different ways, give the different scales, have come to be of greater importance to those concerned with volume, noise, improvisation, the physical immediacy of sound, such as the amplified assaults of rock groups like The Stooges or Swans, the hymnal jazz of John Coltrane, or the droneworks of La Monte Young. John Szwed's biography of the great American cosmic jazz bandleader Sun Ra contains several instances where the keyboard player would be approached after a concert by an anonymous onlooker, astounded that Ra had discovered 'forbidden' chords and warning him of the dangerous forces he was tampering with.

Sun Ra's own 'space ritual', conducted as an elaborate pantomime involving a big band dressed in glittering finery and, in his 1974 film *Space Is The Place*, appearing on earth by climbing out of a spaceship, is celebrated by Ken Hollings in "The Solar Myth Approach", in which he surveys the other instances of space ritual in modern music, teasing out the incredibly close parallels between Ra's heliocentric worlds and those of German composer Karlheinz Stockhausen, both of whom seemed in the early 60s to be treading in each other's footsteps as they claimed extraterrestrial origins.

In 'Mechanism', we are exposed to the effects of 20th century industrialisation on the production of sound. David Toop's essay "Humans, Are They Really Necessary?" examines the rich but untold history of musical automata and sound sculptures – in other words, devices which produce sound of their own accord once set in motion. From late Renaissance contraptions to modern day cybernetics, this is a trend more and more in evidence – there are now, especially in cities like Berlin and New York, art galleries devoted entirely to exhibiting sound pieces. The ensuing sequence of essays examine the impact of mechanical industrialisation on pop music. In "Automating The Beat", Peter Shapiro traces the mechanization of rhythm from early New Orleans marching bands via the machinery of funk drumming right up to the robotics of the drum machine, which has taken over as the industry standard for creating rhythm in rock and pop music (in the studio, even live drummers are often sampled and sequenced in order to keep the beat mathematically on the one). Biba Kopf's "The Autobahn Goes On Forever" takes up the thread, observing and evoking the myth of the road as it appears in German motorik acts like Kraftwerk, Neu! and Harmonia, using the 1970s road movies of Wim Wenders as a parallel text. Edwin Pouncey's "Rock Concrète" shows how even the last bastion of 'real' music, rock 'n' roll, has been subjected to a kind of plastic surgery in the wake of the development of more academic forms of electronic music. Finally, Peter Shapiro returns with an overview of the turntable, initially the vehicle by which recorded music was brought into early century homes, now the key tool of DJ and cutting-edge experimentalist alike in the manipulation and distortion of prerecorded sounds.

Finally, the 'Freedom' section takes on board a number of influential ideas and art movements. Futurism is a key movement here, not least because its progenitors such as the Italian Luigi Russolo were among the first to celebrate Noise for its own sake, and who wished to overthrow conventional music in favour of an approach that took into account the noise if the city, of the urban centre, of warfare, and of the supreme horrors inflicted by modern dictatorships. No wonder Futurism, even more than dada, remains an attractive point of reference for so many of today's younger experimental musicians and theorists. Mark Sinker's "Destroy All Music" offers a timeline of the development of Futurism and unearths a gallery of forgotten composers and works that seem unlikely to see the light of day. Julian Cowley expands on the Lettrist content by providing a compact account of Sound Poetry, a little known genre which was, for much of the 1950s and 60s, disseminated only through a subterranean network of cassettes and low-circulation publications such as *Revue OU*.

Through essays on chance music and improvisation respectively,

Andy Hamilton and David Toop take different tangents into the methods players and composers alike have utilised in order to liberate the creative consciousness from received ideas, tradition and cliche. In the 20th century, for the first time, musicians would sit down to begin playing music with no notion of how the resulting piece would actually end, nor indeed what might happen during the course of it. In the entire history of music, this approach to artistic practice is unprecedented. 'Total' or 'free' improvisation is one of the core innovations in modern music, even though for much of the century, even in African-American swing and jazz, to improvise was to remain within certain scalar, temporal or chromatic boundaries. As David Toop points out in "Frames Of Freedom", it is surprising to note how late the Surrealist concept of automatism was applied within a musical framework, even though it had affected the course of painting and poetry for decades up until the abstract expressionists.

Tom Roe's "Generation Ecstasy" is placed as a coda: the one essay here that descends to street level to engage with musicians in the midst of plying their trade. By picking up vibrations at the hub of New York's loft jazz scene, Roe's evocative piece shows how real lives – of musicians, audiences, communities, neighbourhoods – can be affected and transformed by the uncompromised activities of free musicians, and that the impulse to create without boundaries can be improbably strong, even in the face of financial hardships. Roe traces that continuity over a period lasting roughly one third of a century. Moreover, his depictions of musical activity promiscuously fusing across genre divides such as rock, jazz and composition are absolutely the stuff which *The Wire* has thrived on in its coverage of music's energy flashes and border crossings.

All this activity takes place at what are still generally viewed as the margins of culture, even more so in the age of instant celebrity and accelerated media saturation. But the 'obscurity' of these music activities need not be taken as a measure of their irrelevance. Chart return graphs and airplay minutes do not tell the entire picture. At the opening of the 21st century, the independent record industry appears to be rudely healthy; there has been a staggering proliferation of small labels, alternative distribution networks, international festivals and events encouraging uncompromising artists and approaches. As the accumulated weight of these articles demonstrates, the fringes are where the white heat of invention can be found at boiling point, where music retains the excitement and ferocious energy that has made it party to a number of social revolutions. *Undercurrents* serves to suggest how these forces have percolated up into mainstream culture, albeit in distorted and diluted forms, and presents enough evidence of inventive activity at the coal face to show that globalisation is far from eradicating music's pioneer spirits.

London
October 2002

PART ONE

ELECTRIFICATION

RECORDING ANGELS

THE ESOTERIC ORIGINS OF THE PHONOGRAPH

BY ERIK DAVIS

Though sound and music are essentially incorporeal aspects of human experience, they are dependent on the latent potentials of matter: bamboo tubes, stretched animal skin, throat-flesh. Even more fundamentally, sound rests upon vibration, the analogue fluctuations of that vaporous fluid we call air. But in the late 19th and early 20th centuries, that ocean of vibration became *electrified*. Just as traditional instruments can be seen as alchemical transformations of earth and air, woods and metals, so can the revolutionary sonic media that followed in the wake of the telegraph – telephone, phonograph and radio, not to mention theremins, Moogs and Roland 303s – be regarded as creative transmutations of the new 'elements' that would come to undergird the 20th century's cultural consciousness: electricity and electromagnetism.

"I am electrical by nature," wrote Ludwig Van Beethoven. "Music is the electric soil in which the spirit lives, thinks and invents." The old man's curious quip introduces us to what I like to call 'the electromagnetic imaginary': the mythic, animistic and just plain weird cultural dimensions of electricity and electromagnetism, those cosmic forces which carry an imaginative load as powerful for us as air, earth, water and fire were for the ancients. The word 'electricity' first entered the English tongue in a 1650 translation of a treatise on the healing properties of magnets by Jan Baptist Van Helmont, a Flemish physician and Rosicrucian who worked, significantly, on the borderline between natural magic and modern chemistry. Indeed, many of the earliest books on electricity described the force in distinctly alchemical terms, dubbing it the 'ethereal fire', the 'quintessential fire', or the 'desideratum', the long-sought universal panacea. Emerging from the gap between biology and physics, matter and the unseen ether, electricity is a liminal force that inevitably carries a powerful imaginative load.

In the 18th and 19th centuries, electricity also catalyzed the kind of heady enthusiasm that data devices do today. One of these electrogeeks, a failed American painter named Samuel Morse, was blessed with a formidable insight in the 1830s: if electric current could be squeezed through a wire, then "intelligence might... be instantaneously transmitted by electricity to any distance". After convincing Congress to plough $30,000 into his project, Morse strung up a wire between Baltimore and Washington DC. The first official message to career along the line, in

1844, was a strangely oracular pronouncement: "What hath God wrought!" This message reads as much like an anxious question as a cry of glee, and today we know the answer: what God wrought, or rather, what men wrought in their God-aping mode, was the information age.

Morse's system was not just electrical (and hence, effectively instantaneous); it was digital. The electric current that ran along telegraph wires was an analogue medium, flowing in the undulating waves that everywhere weave the world. But by regularly breaking and reestablishing this flow with a simple switch, and by establishing a code to interpret the resulting patterns of pulses, Morse chopped the analogue dance into discrete digital signs. But these signs were also electro-metallic *beats*, a rat-a-tat that foreshadowed the frenetic rhythms of the coming machine age. With Morse code in hand, railroads improved their ability to move goods over America's vast distances, newspapermen sped up the perceived pace of historical events, businessmen upped their managerial control (and their stress), and stock markets started pulsing in sync. In Nathaniel Hawthorne's *The House Of The Seven Gables*, the character Clifford asks a question at once ironic and prophetic of all the electromania to come: "Is it a fact – or have I dreamt it – that, by means of electricity, the world of matter has become a great nerve, vibrating thousands of miles in a breathless point of time?"

Writing about the telegraph in *Understanding Media*, Marshall McLuhan also argued that "whereas all previous technology (save speech itself) had, in effect, extended some part of our bodies, electricity may be said to have outered the central nervous system itself". For McLuhan, Morse's electric ganglion was only the first in a series of media that served to dissolve the logical and individualistic mindframe hammered out by alphanumeric characters, the printing press and Renaissance perspective drawing. The telegraph sparked the "electric retribalization of the West", a long slide into an immersive electronic sea of mythic participation and collective resonance. But McLuhan also saw this "outering" as the technological roots of the age of anxiety. "To put one's nerves outside," he wrote, "is to initiate a situation – if not a concept – of dread."

Because the self is partly a product of its communications, new media technologies remould the boundaries of being. As they do so, the shadows, doppelgängers and dark intuitions that haunt human identity begin to leak outside the self as well – and some of them take up residence in the emerging virtual spaces suggested by the new technologies. Spiritualism, for example, was bound up from the start with the telegraph: the knocks and rappings that passed back and forth between the Fox sisters and the dead pedlar in their Hydesdale cottage in 1848 – the spooky communiques which first sparked the popular religion of mediumship – were spectral echoes of the dots and dashes then hurtling through wires across the land. During the 1950s, the movement's most popular newspaper was called *The Spiritual Telegraph*, and Spiritualists like Allan Kardec and scientists like Michael Faraday both looked to electricity to explain the raps, creaks and table-hops that occurred during seances. By the 1860s and 70s, mediums had become the professional pop stars of the Victorian era; the attendees were treated to occult sideshows, as tables rapped and danced across the room, gooey ectoplasm materialised out of thin air, and musical instruments played creepy jigs in the dark – apparently all by themselves.

Sound clearly plays a privileged role in both manifesting and mystifying electricity. According to one contemporary account, the 'Finale' of a Boston lecture given by representatives of the Edison Company in 1887 was nothing less than a seance. "Bells rung, drums beat, noises natural and unnatural were heard, a cabinet revolved and flashed fire, and a row of departed skulls came into view." And when Alexander Graham Bell and Thomas Watson gave demonstration lectures for the telephone, the two men also conjured up tricks that delivered all the thrills and chills of a magic show.

The telephone always possessed a kind of shadow side. Though Bell came up with the notion of translating the vibrating pressures of the human voice into an electrical signal that could pass along a wire, Watson actually built most of the man's early devices. Like a lot of the electrical hackers of the time, Watson combined loads of practical know-how with weak and frequently wacky theories about the mysterious fluid itself – electricity is an experience before it is a fact, a dream before it is a science. In Watson's case, electrical theories were mixed up with spiritualist notions. Watson treated Spiritualism as a non-mystical science, and he initially concluded that, just as "a telegraph instrument transforms pulsations of electricity into the taps of the Morse code", so too did mediums transform energetic radiation into raps and knockings. He also believed spirits from the other side were helping the telephone along. And why not? We associate sentient life with what communicates, and here was an inert thing full of voices. As the emperor of Brazil exclaimed when he first heard the gadget: "My God, it talks!"

A similar shock, impossible for us to reconstruct, awaited folks first confronted with the phonograph. The telephone had already transformed sound waves into the fluctuations of an electric current, but in 1877 Thomas Edison discovered that changing an electric current in a stylus changed the amount of friction the stylus exerted on a rotating cylinder – which could therefore become a medium of sonic inscription. Though Edison himself was a most practical man, he was also something of a techno-spiritualist, and later attempted to build a radio device capable of capturing the voices of the dead. Such desires would persist, sublimated and not, throughout the 20th century. The Swedish researcher Konstantin Raudive claimed that magnetic tape recordings of silence often turn out, on repeated listening, to contain distinct voices, and contemporary devotees of 'Electronic Voice Phenomenon', a parapsychological hobby loosely inspired by Raudive's researches, have tuned into similar murmurs on non-broadcast radio frequencies, some of which are interpreted as messages from beyond the veil.

These dreams and sonic phantasms are not just kookery; they arise in the virtual spaces carved out by electrical media. By siphoning a bit of the 'soul' into an externalised device, such technologies triggered the ancient dread of the doppelgänger, that psychic simulacrum of the self that moves through the world of its own eerie accord. Freud dubbed the dread produced by the doppelgänger "the uncanny", which he connected to the queer feelings one gets from dolls and automata. It seems important to note that when Edison was imagining possible applications for his new device, one of his first notions, alongside producing platters of music, was to make dolls "speak, sing, cry and make various sounds".

Electricity had other tricks up its sleeve. In the 1830s, the great British experimental scientist Michael Faraday discovered that changing the electrical current in a wire coil somehow induced an energetic fluctuation in a nearby coil. This decidedly bizarre action-at-a-distance, which came to be called electromagnetic induction, is the driving force behind electrical power plants to this day. For his part, Faraday explained the mysterious force connecting the two coils as a "wave of electricity". Pointing to the strange patterns that iron filings create around the end of a magnet, Faraday also suggested that electromagnetic "fields" consisted of "lines of force", vibrating patterns that spread throughout space. Though Faraday initially considered these undulating images of fields and lines of force as nothing more than useful fictions, he gradually accepted them as a basic description of reality.

In the 1860s, James Clerk Maxwell translated Faraday's experimental findings into the language of mathematics, synthesizing optical, magnetic and electrical phenomena into four magnificent equations that governed the whole of electromagnetic reality. In doing so, Maxwell predicted the existence of the electromagnetic spectrum whose waves we now exploit for everything from broadcasting pop music to reheating food to analysing the chemical composition of Alpha Centauri. Einstein later called Faraday and Maxwell's work the "greatest alteration in the axiomatic basis of physics – in our conception of the structure of reality". Their electromagnetic universe set the stage for the final deconstruction of atomic materialism: the dissolution of the ether, the emergence of Einsteinian space-time, and ultimately the arrival of quantum mechanics and its colossal oddities. The corporeal cosmos melted into an immense sea of vibrations and insubstantial forces.

Metaphorically speaking, Faraday and Maxwell's model was also intensely musical, though its music was very different from the tonal structures of Western music – structures which, perhaps not coincidentally, began to dissolve just as the new model of the universe entered popular consciousness. Towards the end of the century, wireless hackers like Marconi and Tesla made direct technological contact with the invisible radio waves theoretically limned by Maxwell. In 1899, after five years of fiddling around with induction coils, batteries and primitive aerials (some of which he hung from balloons), Guglielmo Marconi equipped two ships with radio gear that issued speedily telegraphed reports on the yacht race for the Americas Cup. This little sports thrill captured the world's imagination, and the 20th century can be said to have started on a wireless note. Wireless telegraphy also served as a kind of sonic prophecy: those monotone Morse beep-beep-beeps that once signified news sound like post-Techno dance music.

Marconi's wireless flowered into radio, which in its first few decades reproduced a pattern of intense technical development and prophecies about world peace and democratic communication that sound eerily familiar in the wake of the Internet boom and bust. Moreover, early radio attracted legions of hackers, teenage and otherwise, who endowed their homebrewed crystal sets with an undeniable charge of experiment and anarchic play. For the first few decades of radio's life, hobbyist hams across the globe chatted up a storm while making important discoveries about the spectrum, especially on the shortwave side of things. By the 1920s, federal and commercial interests began stringing barbed wire across the many-to-many spectrum, professionalising and segmenting the formerly free-range medium.

Even as the airwaves were filling up with ads for laundry soap, radio freaks continued to hear some seriously otherworldly stuff in their primitive headphones. Thomas Watson got an early taste of these unearthly transmissions late at night in Bell's lab, when he would listen to the snaps, bird chirps and ghostly grinding noises that popped up on a telephone circuit: "My theory at this time was that the currents causing these sounds came from explosions on the sun or that they were signals from another planet. They were mystic enough to suggest the latter explanation but I never detected any regularity in them that might indicate they were intelligent signals." As Avital Ronell points out, "Science acquires its staying power from a sustained struggle to keep down the demons of the supernatural with whose visions, however, it competes." Watson may have been the first person to *listen to noise*. Though the sounds he heard may well have had terrestrial origins (the 'sferics' that radio hounds continue to hunt today), Watson made the crucial recognition that human ears could now directly register cosmic vibrations.

Watson was by no means the only electrohead to believe he was picking up play-by-play reports from other planets. During the summer of 1899, when inventor Nikola Tesla manufactured lightning and dreamed of broadcasting wireless power across the globe, he also started picking up regular signals on his 200 foot radio tower in Colorado, and tentatively concluded that he was "the first to hear the greeting of one planet to another". For decades, many early radio operators continued to pick up powerful, persistent and seemingly unexplainable signals, some of which were reported to be rather Pynchonesque repetitions of the Morse code for 'V'. Marconi himself claimed to have received such signals on the low end of the longwave spectrum, and in 1921 flatly declared that he believed they originated from other civilizations in space. On 24 August 1924, when Mars passed unusually close to the earth, civilian and military transmitters voluntarily shut down in order to leave the airwaves open for the Martians; radio hackers were treated to a symphony of freak signals.

These popular passions may seem corny in retrospect, but that is because the sublime and visionary edge of technology is always changing, opening up new virtualities that then become integrated into business as usual. For aeons, the hardwired side of human perceptions has been limited to our own unique sensory apparatus, an apparatus that partly determines the apparent nature of the world. New technologies of perception unfold new worlds of sublimity and threat, worlds which challenge us to reconfigure the limits of ourselves and to shape the meaning of the new spaces we find ourselves in. When ocular instruments extended human sight into Galileo's heavens and Robert Hooke's microscopic cellular regimes, they installed new explanatory spaces for the universe, spaces which reorganised the meaning of the cosmos and the actors in it.

But what kind of 'space' does our expanded encounter with electricity and the electromagnetic spectrum lead us into? Though the spectrum includes the wavelengths of visible light, and X-rays, ultrasound and radio astronomy can all be used to illuminate new dimensions of the universe, the essence of electromagnetism is invisible. In one of his more suggestive intuitions, Marshall McLuhan argued that electronic technologies were installing an "acoustic space" in the place of an earlier "visual space" – the linear, logical and sequential conception of the world that had dominated Western consciousness for many centuries. McLuhan believed that electronic media eroded this crisp and objective grid of facts, dissolving it into a psychic, social and perceptual environment that resembles the kind of space we hear: multi-dimensional, resonant, invisibly tactile, "a total and simultaneous field of relations". Though

McLuhan used "acoustic space" as an analogy for a psycho-social process that did not necessarily tickle the bones of the inner ear, his oceanic vision of acoustics does foreground the central role that music – and its electromagnification – would play in mapping and constructing pleasure and perception in the first fully technological century.

This secret sympathy between music and the electromagnetic imaginary was first intuited in the 17th century by the Jesuit polymath Athanasius Kircher, who identified certain vibrating musical tones as 'magnetic'. Kircher also invented the glass harmonica, an instrument that exploited the resonant tones produced by rubbing glass tumblers filled with water. Kircher's researches were carried on by the animal magnetist Franz Anton Mesmer, known today either as the king of charlatans or the man whose healing journeys into the netherworlds of the mind inadvertently spawned psychoanalysis. Mesmer believed that animal magnetism was "communicated, propagated and intensified by sound", and, as the liner notes to Ash International's 1995 compilation CD *Mesmer Variations* point out, he used to improvise on a version of Kircher's glass harmonica in order to set the mood in his healing salons. One visiting Viennese doctor described the "shiver through my nerves caused by the instrument", and suggested that "many of the phenomena of magnetism must have been brought out by the extremely penetrating tones of this music".

For us, Mesmer might serve as a utopian figure – half comic, half cosmic, experimental and underground – for the continued promise of electroacoustic phenomena in a world ravaged by technologies with far more violent and banal issue. Along with cinema, 20th century music has become one of the principal aesthetic zones where humans have used innovative gadgetry to make sense – and nonsense – of their own increasingly technologized souls. Musicians and composers both highbrow and pop have twiddled and tweaked electronic and electrical instruments, as well as electromagnetic recording and broadcasting technologies, in order to tune into new sonic, compositional and expressive possibilities. In so doing, they have also gone a long way toward reimagining the scrambled boundaries of subjectivity as it makes its way through the invisible landscapes – both dreadful and sublime – that make up the acoustic space of electronic media.

The uncanny undercurrent of electromagneticism also helps explain why electronic tones and timbres have, throughout the 20th century, frequently been associated with outer space, mysticism and cosmic consciousness. These connections run throughout both popular and experimental genres, encompassing Hollywood soundtracks, acid rock, the avant garde, lounge, Ambient, dub, Techno, jazz, funk and Trance. From Stockhausen and Subotnick to George Clinton and Juan Atkins, from Sun Ra and Klaus Schulze to Les Baxter or Goa Trance, electrical tones have operated as both cosmic signifiers and vibratory portals into altered states and spaces.

These associations speak to the deep legacy of the electromagnetic imaginary, a legacy that, as we've seen, goes back to Mesmer, alchemy and German nature philosophy. But it's important to suggest that these associations are not merely cultural constructions. The expressive power of electronic sounds is intimately linked with timbre, and one of the most fundamentally electronic timbres we know – the eerie metallic moan of the theremin – is not simply a quirk of technology or an aesthetic decision on the part of its inventor, Léon Thérémin. Theoretically, the theremin's tone is a pure sinewave. Though in practice a variety of non-harmonic effects can intrude delightfully, the fact remains that the theremin's haunting sound is not a product of synthesis, but of the fundamental conditions of electromagnetic reality. It is more like an Aeolian harp than a Casio beatbox, but the winds it rides are electromagnetic ones, stretching from here to the edges of the universe.

ON THE MIC

HOW AMPLIFICATION CHANGED THE VOICE FOR GOOD

BY IAN PENMAN

How did the 20th century begin? Listening in.

A middle aged, bourgeois psychoanalyst in Vienna takes the time to listen, that's all, and it blows our world apart. And how did our world – of songs and CDs, singers and samplers – begin? With a man in a room, talking to himself about the devil? Maybe. With Alexander Graham Bell's poignant "Come here, Watson, I want you"? Or that carnal Frankenstein wrought in the alchemical crucible of a studio named Sun? Perhaps. Definitely with something plucked out of the air. All in all, with something *overheard...*

The microphone stands in for the analyst's calm, promiscuous ear: neutral, forgiving, open to everything, the slightest trace or stammer or spoken mark. What we hear plucked out of the air sounds like outposts of innermost feeling – an outposting of our intangible inner murk. The first field recordings head out to the other side of the tracks, to dirt roads, cheap hotels, juke joints; other islands, other worlds. Culture was hitherto used (pronounce the word both ways) to look for things to hear in concert halls, recitals, the hierarchy of the 12 tone scale like a chastity belt or Victorian stays, pinning the singing, ringing diaphragm inside prior circumscription: a certain predefined aspiration. Microphonics and psychoanalysis – these new phantom sciences – make tremors speak from the invisible Inside, where we can neither see nor want the very thing we have always been scared to have revealed. Other voices.

Sigmund Freud; the field recording; the nascent pop studio – all perform similar functions. Freud listens for things no one has noted before. Previously, physicians considered only the cast of external symptoms. Freud, in a cautious and canny act of suspended hearing, listens for things between the word: dot-dash series of phonemes, swallowed rhythms, repressions, omissions. Listening out for some other thing: the unconscious, its beady silence or askew telepathy. Listening for what speaks in places we don't expect to find it. *We* don't speak, as Lacan will later say: *it* speaks. What is called our interior world finds itself exteriorised, and in fact such clear distinctions are rendered dubious by the new gramophonic circuitry, by the new grammatologies of analysis and amplification. Recording equipment, like Freud's new science, produces new takes, topologies, topographies. It's no coincidence that one of the first uses for microphonic equipment is field recordings, hermetic coils and dials used in the service of an opening distance. What might one day be called a vocal democracy: tongues untied, archived, allowed. Songs once considered below the belt, beyond the pale, grey room, black night songs. Itinerant blue shamans. Haitian ceremony. Hawaiian unheimlich. The advent of electricity means that such black spots and blue articulations became more than a local event. Such hand-held recordings now sound the way old silent films look: monochrome, brittle, haunted – a new mourning. Listen to early blues recordings and you can hear muffed chord changes, the buzz of tired strings, a myriad of local accents (the soft purr of Mississippi John Hurt or the apocalyptic bark of Blind Willie Johnson). Strangely enough, this 'X' factor has survived, lives on reformed, reknotted, in the spooky lo-fi of Will Oldham and Royal Trux, and the tragic last testaments of Kurt Cobain and Jeff Buckley.

Freud's theories and the coming remix of studio muzik together shatter the founding illusion of our centrifugal 'I'. The song becomes a viral dissemination: technologised, broadcast, relayed, replayed, addressed to everyone and no one. Recording projects the voice into a nowhere of a future, where it can listen back, say "that's not quite right" (according to what unspoken index?), and correct itself. In its procession, modern recording becomes a science of grafts and sleights. Far from our own spontaneous voice (a mongrel we can't always make do what we wish, make speak what we want), the Song soon becomes a technological paradigm: something which can be turned up, levelled out. Far from truthful, the microphone can record lies, doubts, concealments, allowing manipulative 'takes' of the voice from which a certain tone can be synthesized in the studio console. Thus, the presumed truth of the voice (as in some scene of confession or gospel gnosis) cannot be thought of as immutable, as the voice is always now – via recording – at a remove from itself, allowing the singer a certain overview or vantage they never possessed before. Each song becomes a history of the making of song.

The microphonic song is a trace taken out of the air and made monumental. Pre-microphone, the song was a performance with its place in a social continuum – now it is abstracted, sent into the everywhere air. When the singer first starts to sing into – and more crucially *for* – the microphone, it was assumed that what was being captured were moments of immortal truth: the record of a performance which would exist whether the microphone had been there or not. But the microphone is like a syringe, which can put in as much as it takes out, filling the singer's head with hallucinatory notions. Outsiders slip through now, because the microphone is a short cut (like the telephone) which repays a more economical delivery, honouring the whisper as much as a holler. The most obvious effect of the microphone is that the usual paradigm of the overarching reach of the voice as signifier of higher truth – as in gospel and opera – could be overturned, allowing the new conversational song of singers like Billie Holiday, Chet Baker, Frank Sinatra. (Just as the 'theatrics' of the hysteric, under Freud's beneficent care, are replaced by a more truthful murmur.) Later, multitracking will allow a 'singer' like Brian Wilson – no voice at all in the old way of things – to pull off the assumption of a choral grandeur: his neurasthenic 'I' raised, remade, multi-plied.

There exists a fascinating document: a recording of Billie Holiday in the studio between takes, vamping, chattering, just rapping, jes' signifyin'... loving the sound of her own voice. She sounds like an angel, a grumpy big cat, a schizo; stoned, drunk; serrated, seraphic; a man, a wind instrument; or here and there something like Linda Blair in *The Exorcist* crossed with Neal Cassady. And then she says this: "I'm tellin' you – me and my old voice, it just go up a little bit and come down a little bit. It is not LEGIT. I do not got a legitimate voice." Right there the unconscious speaks, speaks a truth more pinpointed than any analysis to come. There's also another revelatory scene in her (dubious, co-authored) autobiography *Lady Sings The Blues*, when she describes pressing her ear up against the parallel ear of a new gramophone to hear Louis Armstrong for the first time. Inaugural revelation, a preverbal dawn: "It was the first time I had ever heard anybody sing without using any words, [but] 'Ba-ba-ba-ba-ba-ba-ba' had plenty of meaning for me."

This idea that someone singing a song not their own, an apparently banal song, or a wordless song, can say as much as any 'important' authored song, goes against the tenets of rock's critical wisdom. James Baldwin amplifies the meaning of the young Billie's revelation when he writes: "It was Bessie Smith, through her tone and cadence, who helped... reconcile me to being a 'nigger'." Tone and cadence, mark you – not any incendiary or explicit lyric.

Lyrical 'authenticity' has been consistently over-valued in the dominant (white) discourse, so much so you'd think it was virtually immaterial whether there was a microphone there or not, and a mouth to sing into it. Such phallogocentric criticism cannot bring itself to imagine that, say, the 'softest' song in the world might equally bear the harshest truths. The microphonic song insinuates encoded, bodily truths in a code often so subtle (with such infinite gradation of tone) as to be almost inaudible. We rub up against a wider 'political' disourse here, too, in relation to what Flannery O'Connor once called the black person's "very elaborate manners and great formality, which he uses superbly for his own protection and to insure his own privacy".

We can see here that Song is a 'survival' in at least two or three senses, a living on, an echo of something unsaid. (In some cases something which, if it was said out loud, might get the speaker jailed or lynched.) Billie Holiday's real 'autobiography' was her Song, and this revolutionary fact – that you don't need to pen your own words to make clear all the pain and pleasure, sense and ambivalence of a life – is an incredible thing, which births a properly 'microphonic' singing. When I think about Billie Holiday I think about a massive appetite; when I think about her drug habit I think of someone trying to fill themselves with a huge tranche of dispossessed land, all the space they have been denied in 'real' life – the spacy ease of a Sunday walk without constraint, worry or woe, free to drift with the lightest of steps. (Insert advert voice: "Only narcotics can do this!") In the Holiday song you hear a Brechtian balancing act (which isn't also painful and preachy on the ear), whose lyrics paint a more or less normative picture but where, if you listen – really listen – to the voice, you know things are otherwise.

It is often said of Holiday and Sinatra that they give an 'intimate' performance – but intimate for whom? With whom? The 'intimacy' of microphonic singing is also the distanced 'take' of recording and, thereby, transmission and reception at a distance. Intimacy is also the first step toward the promiscuous impersonality of a record buying public; of both the homogenous 'they' of popular reception and the Song's pivotal and ambiguous 'you'.

Even via the impersonality of disc, it was presumed that what you bought was the 'true' voice or persona of the singer. Presumption twice over: the listener's assumption of their 'own I', and, in turn, the singer's assumed truth-at-a-distance. However, as theorist Frances Dyson puts it, the voice is always already caught up in a prior symbolism: "Prior to any utterance, it is already caught within particular circuits, switchboards or 'machines' which both literally and figuratively encode, transmit and give meaning to vocal acts." Which is to say, we always expect specific things of singers – we always expect something more. No one expects a guitar to embody truth: it is a fleeting temporal act (run, riff, solo) rather than an eternal verity. Yet despite the ravages and inroads of modernism, something about the sung still primes us for self evident truth. The singer's voice, escaping embodiment, paradoxically embodies – and the microphone simply raises this paradox to a new pitch, a new economy of absence-presence in its neoteric circuitry. Thus with Holiday no one concerns themselves overmuch with what manner of truth resides in the supposedly 'trite' lyrics she is given to sing. The spell of truth is presumed to come from her personalised enunciation – voice as re-presented experience – as though the song were itself a body, replete with cuts, tracks and bruises: traces of the lived. In fact, Holiday spent half her time in song happily aswing. (Other instances of such fatal attraction-confusion are easily found: Kurt Cobain interpreted as apotheosis of a certain generational nihilism... when he may have been fatally sincere, almost childlike in his innocent hopes and dreams, heroin the only thing which could maintain him in his baby-frail hurt, keeping him endlessly in utero.) The lesson of this is: the minute we begin to garland the singer with projective imagery, something singular in the song dies. Unable to deal with the untrammeled mourning peal of the sung, we appliqué the prophylactic gleam of image, myth, caricature. And in a way, put the singer to death.

To accord hospitality to that which is absolutely foreign or strange, but also, to try to domesticate it, to make it part of the household and have it assume the habits, to make us assume new habits. This is the movement of culture.
Jacques Derrida

And this is precisely what happens. This is the history of our culture. All our favourite voices – slothful, wracked, diabolical, ethereal – brought into our sitting rooms to play. The recording studio and the analyst's room and our own new gramophonic hearth: simultaneously at home and beyond the homely, at once a room and an escape route where we can play hide and seek with our fears. The advent of the stylus/gramophone makes of our home a new spatio-temporal realm where we can shape our own deeply subjective timeframe in track-by-track increments. Where we can repeat the singer's experience, along a full range of Freudian response.

Freudian analysis, microphonics and voodoo have at least this in common: they arrange a spectral meeting (a coming to terms) with our lost voices and lamented others. We sing along with this body electric, suddenly inhabited by forgotten ancestors, speak with their voices, repeat their compulsions, do their bidding.

The question of a speculative realignment with dead family – with 'difficult' fathers or mourned mothers, lost brothers, dead twins, absent friends, longed for sisters – resonates all down our days. Hear it in Elvis and Billie; in Brian Wilson and Bob Dylan; and then nearer our own time in Lydia Lunch, Nick Cave, Diamanda Galas, Henry Rollins, Jeff Buckley, Kurt Cobain. Singers who scorn the easy lures of therapy culture, but who come to some account of their own in sound, in song. It is perhaps no coincidence that many of these same people will have problems themselves assuming the settled roles of family and home, of rootedness. As if once they had tasted the nomadic flight of song, the ground seems like a wanting place.

With the advent of full blown multitrack microphonia in the 60s, recordings definitively cease to be 'records' of any single event in space and time. The recorded voice is no longer the sure and certain residue of a 'performance', but the shifting centre of a collage of a thousand micro-performances, spaced out across different times and spaces. Différance made sublime, made hook, made hit. Divorced from any need to perform, the new studio song is a quantum event; the studio is a sounding board, be it for experiments in ego-transcendent sound (Brian Wilson) or ideological articulation (James Brown) or a strange, skewed admixture of both (Hendrix, The Doors, Love's Arthur Lee).

What would Freud have made of Brian Wilson? The Wilson who was such an unstable mixture of will and illness (but never ill will)? The Brian who can sum up all of Freud's "Mourning And Melancholia" in one piercing phrase: *"I'm waiting for the day that you can love again."* Like Freud, this is Brian's life: waiting, and listening. Brian knew. (Like so much of our century's 'lower class' or marginal geniuses, he *knew* without the cumbersome apparatus of over-educated knowledge.) *"I can hear so much in your sighs..."* Brian as radiophonic two-way ear. *Pet Sounds* not one more 'concept' album (in competition with kitsch piffle like *Sgt Pepper*) but as true, moving otobiography. Brian of that sublime moment in "Don't Talk (Put Your Head On My Shoulder)" when the line *"let me hear your heart beat"* is sung-softened-stirred-dissolved into *"being here with you..."*. Beat and being commingled. Brian making a mother's sun of himself in silent opposition to the castrating paternal eye. In his whispered *"listen"* you can hear a glistening 'son' finally reclaimed, sublimated, sublimed, sent into a glorious bodyless ether/afterlife of sound where he can be how he hears: littoral sun not literal son, a merman raised by the Enochian tablet of the studio console into a polyphonic congress with mescaline nymphs and stereo sprites and a whole undulant sonic seascape... stoned, immaculate.

Once there is a microphone, no more canons. Anyone can break into this room with a breath; whisper into its waiting ear. Although not everyone can survive an encounter with the forbidding metallic thereness of this strange passive thief, the microphone. Go on, approach it: see how it makes your whole posture change, your throat tremble, your whole being turn in on itself. In the much-told Robert Johnson tale, for instance, no one seems to have noticed that the devil he met was microphone shaped. A microphone, moreover, that he never even sought out, which came to him, and but for which we might never have known his name, his dread, his glory.

After the microphone, no self-contained lineages. Only ghost minglings, unprecedented grafts, insane translations. From now on, Song will be an aetherial, porous space in which voices lose their demarcation; in which the ordinary is made uncanny; in which the dead speak, in which anyone can speak, or sing, or be surprised. The history of the microphone in this century includes not just blues and pop and C&W and so on, but Richard Nixon, the Reverend Jim Jones and Charles Manson's songbook. And the recordings which seem almost too powerful to listen to are invariably those least tampered with. Artaud in 1947 with his apocalyptic radio 'song', "Pour En Finir Avec Le Jugement De Dieu" (itself a call to abandon pious constraint and let the body truly speak); Maya Deren's groundbreaking explorations in Haiti; Bob Dylan's *The Basement Tapes*; Peter Brötzmann's late 60s free jazz blast *Machine Gun*. Take your pick, make or fake your own lineage... no more canons.

How will this century end? Listening for the final toll. Waiting for the dead to speak.

We may already have heard our definitive eschatological Song – in works such as Scott Walker's nonpareil *Tilt* (1995) and Diamanda Galas's *Plague Mass* (1991). Some will doubtless object that such works take the Song too far, onto unrecognisable terrain. But that is just the chance and the dare of our song's survival. . . and why, too, we must constantly, vigilantly and mercilessly refuse any facile claims of an 'End' or 'Death' of the Song. Beware false prophets who come bearing essays which announce the 'end' of something: it usually marks little more than the exhaustion of their own resources – intellectual or financial. We need to think about not the end of song but the ends of song. Each singer must find their own end, their own will, their own way. In this way, song might be just beginning to truly speak... in the revivifying breath of a new mourning.

If a work like Walker's *Tilt* is in some part 'unlistenable', as its detractors claim, perhaps that's because our world, too, is now in sum unlistenable. One of the things that *Tilt* seems to suggest is, if we could hear everything in our post-Einstein, post-Auschwitz world – all the screams in the air, all the irrevocable negations of technology, all the ghosts – just a single moment of it, we would surely go mad from grief.

A switch is thrown and suddenly our 'blues' are global or cosmic, not individual. Such a feeling might destroy; might be too much for one fragile soul to take. We have indeed come a long way from Robert Johnson's moan, or Artaud's scream. Or sometimes, it seems, no way at all (listen to Diamanda Galas's resurrection of blues standards on *The Singer* and elsewhere). This is one of the reasons *Tilt*'s song is literally in ruins: as though a normal song were not strong enough to hold what Walker is pouring into it. For tapping into the business of mourning is no simple affair. What forces must such songs contain? Elemental, transmogrifying, tectonic. And just as the unwary magician can be rent asunder by calling down spirits too big for his talents, so the ill-equipped singer (and I mean this literally: a singer whose only equipment is illness, fragility, sickness) can suffer fatal combustion from going it alone into certain regions; from being our sole channel. Remember, songs are not displaced onto an instrument: they take place as a whorl of alchemy IN the singer's body (and ours). At times, it must feel as if the microphone is like some looming S&M master demanding more each time: each take, take it further, make yourself more of an object, more pain, your transcendence awaits...

How did the century end? Haunted, and haunted by its song.

THE JERRYBUILT FUTURE

THE SONIC ARTS UNION, ONCE GROUP AND MEV'S LIVE ELECTRONICS

BY CHRISTOPH COX

The sound is dirty. The needle trudges through the gnarled grooves of 30 year old vinyl. Under a sheet of hiss and crackle, the sound of amplified pots and pans being beaten with a pipe. A murmuring crowd and the sound of footsteps across a stage are signs that this document records only the audible traces of a largely visual, theatrical event. Aided by the photographs printed on the insert, one can dimly imagine the scene recorded here: tangled in wires, a troupe of scruffy hippies on their hands and knees rub odd objects together or twiddle the knobs of jerry-built consoles. "Live Electronic Music Improvised", the cover reads, "From Rome: MEV, From London: AMM".

The scene is worlds apart from those images that illustrate stock accounts of electronic music's origins: photos of technicians in suits and ties grinning beside shiny behemoths deep inside private universities or state-owned radio stations. As the traditional histories tell it, electronic music's founding opposition was the struggle between musique concrète and elektronische Musik, between the devotees of found sound and the advocates of sonic synthesis. But within a few years this tension had been resolved and replaced by a new and deeper one: the opposition between the studio and the stage, between crafted electronic composition and live electronic improvisation. This is the great divide, the rift between the founding fathers and their unruly children, the break between the twilight of modernism and the dawn of postmodernity ushered in by a federation of maverick electronic collectives, among them The ONCE Group, The Sonic Arts Union, AMM, Musica Elettronica Viva...

The first electronic music studios had been set up in the 1950s, funded by foundations and corporations interested in the development of communication and information technology. Musically, the studios were led by a cadre of academic serialists who saw electronic sound synthesis as a means of increasing control over their musical product. By building and programming tones from scratch, the composer could regulate and serialise every parameter of the musical field, from pitch to rhythm and dynamics. Responding to the dwindling audience for their music, 'total serialists' like Herbert Eimert, Milton Babbitt and Pierre Boulez took to the studios hoping to dispense with performance altogether and to forge a post-human music that no longer had to concern itself with the competencies and tastes of instrumentalists and listeners. "The notion of having complete control over one's composition, of being complete master of all you survey," remarked Babbitt, "seemed to be a practical solution, a musical solution, a conceptual solution, and it removed one from the inappropriate milieu of presenting it to people who were not prepared or not interested."

While Babbitt and Boulez were busy electronically systematising the variables of musical form, John Cage was becoming a Buddhist, learning to withdraw his hand from the musical situation and to let sounds be. For Cage's Zen sensibilities, this release of control was a spiritual and ethical, even a political, imperative; one that led him to abdicate the role of composer in order to become an improvisor and collaborator. "When you get right down to it," Cage said, "a composer is simply someone who tells other people what to do. I'd like our activities to be more social – and anarchically so."

Electronics played a vital role in Cage's programme to liberate sound from the composer's clutches. In 1939 he premiered his *Imaginary Landscape No 1*, the first electroacoustic composition. Nearly a decade before Pierre Schaeffer's concrète studies, and four decades before "The Adventures Of Grandmaster Flash On The Wheels Of Steel", the piece featured two turntables spinning studio test tones transformed into sirens and pops by a variety of turntablist tactics. Significantly, the piece was devised as live theatre music for Jean Cocteau's *Marriage At The Eiffel Tower*, an oddball play narrated by two actors costumed as phonographs. Indeed, for Cage and the generation he inspired, electronic music was all about the vicissitudes of live performance and the total audiovisual spectacle. It was precisely the unpredictability of simple electronic devices that attracted him, the unexpected events that could transpire when audio signals were let loose into space.

Cage's aesthetic disposition and his affirmation of live music, collaboration and multimedia spurred the activities of the live electronic collectives. But they found their musical tools in the technological practice of Cage's associate, David Tudor. A legendary vanguard pianist, Tudor had given the first performances of works by Boulez, Cage, Karlheinz Stockhausen, Sylvano Bussotti, La Monte Young and others. Tudor's astonishing ability to interpret indeterminate scores prompted the composer Roman Haubenstock-Ramati to remark that he "could play the raisins in a slice of fruitcake". But Tudor found his own voice with live electronics, and over the course of the 1960s, gradually ended his career as a pianist.

Collaborating with Cage during the 50s, Tudor turned to electronics as a way of realising pieces, such as Cage's *Variations* series, that were scored "for any sound-producing means". He took to the medium with the same obsessive attitude he had earlier brought to his piano interpretations. Attempting to bridge the ever-widening gap between the engineer and the musician, he taught himself electronics from the inside out, soldering his own circuits and housing them in makeshift containers. Compared with Babbitt's RCA Synthesizer, Tudor's 'lunch boxes' were rudimentary indeed. But they were modular, portable and could be easily altered as the occasion demanded – necessary requirements for Tudor's peculiar electronic art.

Along with Cage, Tudor had worked with The Merce Cunningham Dance Company since its inception in 1953; and much of his electronic music was composed for them. Specifying only a given piece's duration, Cunningham left all further musical decisions to his composers, maintaining that the musical side should not be mere accompaniment but its own parallel and independent activity. He insisted only that it be live and that it should contribute to the total theatrical situation.

Tudor never disappointed. As one critic noted, "Anyone who has ever... seen Cage and Tudor threading their way about a stage cluttered with cables, amplifiers, speakers and electrically wired instruments, can testify at least that the spectacle does not induce drowsiness." Tudor's magnum opus, 1968's *Rainforest*, was particularly memorable. As the Cunningham dancers glided among Andy Warhol's hovering mylar balloons, Tudor animated a jungle of resonant objects strung from the ceiling and fitted with contact microphones. Set into vibration with an oscillator, the objects' amplified tones were broadcast across the stage, fed back into Tudor's electronic filters and sent out again into the space, generating a recycling chorus of synthetic monkeys, parrots and insects.

ONCE BITTEN

Gordon Mumma had also written music for the Cunningham ensemble and assisted Tudor with the construction of *Rainforest*. An electronics geek who had spent time around broadcast engineers, Mumma's abilities as a bricoleur rivalled Tudor's; and his vast knowledge of transistors, capacitors, electrodes and the like was mined by associates such as David Behrman and Richard Teitelbaum. In 1958, at the age of 23, Mumma, along with Robert Ashley, set up the Cooperative Studio for Electronic Music, inaugurating a phenomenal period of experimental activity in Ann Arbor, a university town less than an hour outside of Detroit. A few years later, Mumma and Ashley hooked up with a network of film makers, artists, dancers, actors and architects to hold a multimedia blowout, which established itself as an annual event for the next seven years, oddly enough, seeing how it was called The ONCE Festival.

ONCE activities ranged from the sparest items of conceptual art – such as Mary Ashley's *Hole (A Sculpture)*, which consisted of the instruction: "Walk backwards all day Saturday" – to audiovisual extravaganzas of almost ridiculous magnitude, epitomised by Mumma's *Megaton For William Burroughs* (1963-64). In total darkness, the piece began with four minutes of a dense and deafening electronic drone. As the drone faded, stage lights slowly illuminated an electroacoustic sculpture surrounded by five performers. Communicating with one another via aircraft headsets, the performers drew from the sculpture an array of squeaks and squeals, while flashing projectiles sped by on overhead wires. Minutes later, all of this was drowned out by the taped sounds of an aircraft squadron and the voices of bomber crews carrying out a raid. A blast of heroic movie music and the tape ended, leaving the spotlight to fall on a lone drummer methodically riding a cymbal and snare.

SONIC ARTS AND SCIENCES

Such lavish and unwieldy productions could hardly be sustained on The ONCE Group's shoestring budget. Indeed, few managed more than a single performance. But the ingenuity and outrageousness of the Ann Arbor crew attracted worldwide attention, prompting visits by experimental artists from all over the USA, Europe and Japan. Among the festival's guests were Alvin Lucier and David Behrman, who struck up a friendship with Mumma and Ashley. Sharing similar interests in live electronics and theatre, the four began to work together and to develop a repertoire of modest, small scale pieces. Called The Sonic Arts Union on a 1966 concert programme, the quartet toured throughout the US and Europe.

"Our performances explored aspects of music and performance that were outside the bounds of what contemporary music generally accepted," remembers Behrman. "Partly that had to do with homemade electronics, partly with exploration of the nature of acoustics, partly with crossing the lines between theatre, visual arts, poetry and music." Lucier adds, "I think we did such different work that sometimes it just bypassed people's perceptions. Sometimes the audiences just couldn't process it as music."

In the hands of Lucier, a Sonic Arts performance could appear to be a bizarre medical procedure, or a high school science experiment gone awry. In *Music For Solo Performer* (1965), Lucier sat calmly while an assistant attached electrodes to his scalp with paste and gauze. After a period of meditation, his alpha brainwaves transmitted signals through amplifiers to resonate percussion instruments scattered about the room. Another favourite, *Vespers*, celebrated the sensory hierarchy of the common bat (Latin name Vespertilionidae). The piece required a dark room and a set of performers supplied with handheld echo-location devices emitting rapid clicking pulses. Wandering around the space, the performers attempted to orient themselves by monitoring the rate and timbre of sound as it bounced off surrounding objects.

Featuring his own homemade electronics, Behrman's pieces were no less odd or dramatic. *Runthrough* was for two performers operating battery powered wave generators and modulators, and two holding flashlights. Turning dials and flipping switches, one pair sent out eerie waves and twitches of synthetic sound while the other two modified the volume and direction of the signals by shining their flashlights on light-sensitive sound distributors. Manifesting his populist, hands-on aesthetic, Behrman commented: "No special skills or training are helpful in turning knobs or shining flashlights, so whatever music can emerge from the equipment is available to non-musicians as to musicians. Because there is neither a score nor directions, any sound which results... remains part of the 'piece'. (Whatever you do with a surfboard in the surf remains part of surfboarding.)... Things are going well when all the players have the sensation they are riding a sound they like in harmony together, and when each is appreciative of what the others are doing." It is telling that Behrman often used surfing analogies; his pieces were conceived not as attempts to control wanton natural forces but as a means of being carried along by them.

Indulging his enthusiasm for theatre, Robert Ashley often assumed the guise of a mysterious nightclub singer for performances of *The Wolfman*. In a lone spotlight, his hair slicked back and wearing dark glasses, Ashley stood silently, the taped sounds of nightclub chatter playing softly in the background. Mouth pressed against the microphone, he began to groan louder and louder until voice and feedback became indistinguishable and human utterance was transformed into an electronic monstrosity.

Mumma's slightly more high-tech productions also experimented with the electronic modification of acoustic phenomena. *Hornpipe* featured his 'cybersonic console', a box of circuits built to monitor the resonance of an instrument and offer electronic tones to match. With the console attached to his belt, Mumma introduced *Hornpipe* with a few minutes of virtuosic solo improvisation on French horn until the animated circuits spat out an electronic complement, turning the piece into a full-fledged duet between the horn and its uncanny electronic other.

POLITICS AND THE ELECTRONIC DOUBLE

While The Sonic Arts Union was fulfilling Cage's programme for the exploration and liberation of sound, a group of American expatriates in Rome calling themselves Musica Elettronica Viva (MEV) set out to realise his social and political vision. After studies at Harvard and Princeton, Frederic Rzewski travelled to Italy on a Fulbright fellowship in 1960, where he gained a reputation as a gifted avant garde pianist. Rzewski's concerts attracted an arty crowd; and a group of experimental musicians soon formed around him. "We were all Ivy League dropouts who were denied access to studios," recalls the outfit's synthesizer whiz Richard Teitelbaum. "We just decided we'd buy or build our own equipment and make electronic music."

Formed in 1966, MEV's original project was modest: to perform concerts of experimental music by the likes of Behrman, Lucier, Cage and Cornelius Cardew. But the following year the quartet began adding a session of collective improvisation to their shows. Soon, composition was entirely displaced by "music created directly in the moment of performance using electronic instruments". For these iconoclastic noisemakers, "electronic instruments" meant everything from amplified glass plates, steel springs and olive oil cans, to homemade oscillators and Moog synthesizers. Thus armed, the group produced a throbbing, clanging maelstrom that sounded like documentary recordings from a steel factory or construction site.

Sonically, the group seemed to be reanimating Marinetti and Russolo's Italian Futurism; but MEV's politics were closer to that of the Italian Marxist Antonio Gramsci. Indeed, in Rzewski's view, each MEV performance was to be a kind of political therapy. As he saw it, the collective membership was involved in the creation of a utopian zone, a 'created space' apart from the 'occupied space' of capitalist individualism that each of us unconsciously inherits. This meant freeing music from the idea of the composer and the score, as well as liberating performers from their own habits and preferences, helping them to overcome conflicts with others and their resistance to collective activity.

For Rzewski and Teitelbaum, electronic sound literally carries performers outside themselves. "The performer's entire body and his sense of identity are affected by such things as intermodulation and feedback," Rzewski noted, referring to the "harmony... created between the individual and his own 'double' – the electronically transformed signal issuing from the loudspeaker membrane." For Teitelbaum, this whole experience had a mystical significance and confirmed the kabbalistic dictum that, in the state of ecstasy, a man "suddenly sees the shape of his self before him talking to him and he forgets his self and it is disengaged from him". In such a state, Teitelbaum concluded, "we no longer know who we are or what we do; we are embraced by all without us. 'WITHIN US WITHOUT US.' WE ARE ALL ONE."

In 1969, this longing for unity led MEV to experiment with audience participation. "If the composer had become one with the player," announced Rzewski, "the player had to become one with the listener." Now a large collection of improvisors (including, at times, Steve Lacy and

Anthony Braxton), MEV took to the streets of Venice and Rome in the autumn of 1968, inviting the audience to bring instruments and join in. Away from power outlets, the group began leaving the synthesizers and photocell distributors at home, instead favouring more ordinary and portable instruments. Rzewski's position was becoming increasingly populist and romantic in its criticisms of the conceptual and technological elitism of music's avant garde. "Now that machines have become such a dominant part of our environment," he remarked in 1969, "we are beginning to become aware of the need for rediscovering our bodies, which have become atrophied by dependence on machines and from which machines have alienated us. Our music has to be a demonstration of something simple, physical, universal, and liberating. Machines, electronics, and fancy technology get in the way of this demonstration."

Rzewski's about-face was extreme; but his attitude was symptomatic of a general turning point. By the early 1970s the energy had been drained from the power sources of live electronic music. The ONCE Group had disbanded, The Sonic Arts Union was decreasingly active, and improvising collectives like MEV and AMM no longer found it de rigueur to perform with transistor radios, contact microphones or homemade synthesizers. Many of the individual composers continued to experiment and perform with electronics, but nearly all did so from positions of security as professors of music at colleges and universities scattered around the US. Commercial synthesizers and effects pedals with preset patches had become cheap and easy to use, drying up the market for old-style parts and do-it-yourself kits. The age of popular mechanics and the experimental collective appeared to be over.

But by the end of the century, the current was once again surging through the circuits of experimental music and live electronic improvisation. Scanner's on-the-spot channelling of voices from the ether updated Cage's live radio experiments. British improvisors John Butcher and Phil Durrant both cited Tudor as an important antecedent for their brand of real-time electronic manipulation with homemade gadgetry. Multitasking musician and Sonic Youth member Jim O'Rourke played a residency with The Merce Cunningham Dance Company, twiddling knobs beside his childhood heroes Behrman and Takehisa Kosugi (the Japanese violinist and former leader of Taj Mahal Travellers). And the acoustic/electronic pile-up created by Norway's Supersilent or the Swiss unit Steamboat Switzerland draws comparisons with MEV.

But the new live electronic music didn't just look backwards. If the sluggishness of hard drives and the rigidity of music software previously made live performance on computers a tortuous and tiresome affair, the hyperspeed and portability of laptop computers and the real-time fluidity of programs like MAX, LiSa and Super Collider put live electronics into the hands of Powerbook powerhouses such as Christian Fennesz and Peter 'Pita' Rehberg. In truth, there is little distance between electronic instrument-enhancers like Durrant and data crunchers like Rehberg. Indeed, the two joined forces in a spectacular live electronic orchestra, MIMEO (Music In Movement Orchestra), whose rare performances once included a 24 hour non-stop session. A fluid 12 piece 'led' by AMM's guitarist Keith Rowe, MIMEO brings together generations of electronic experimentalists to battle it out on radios, tapes, samplers, analogue synthesizers, Powerbooks and other electronic paraphernalia. Chalk it up to the mysterious and unpredictable life of the electronic signal, which, released from its source, will always reappear transformed in strange and beautiful new guises.

WORSHIP THE GLITCH

DIGITAL MUSIC, ELECTRONIC DISTURBANCE

BY ROB YOUNG

"We are in greate haste to construct a magnetic telegraph from Maine to Texas; but Maine and Texas, it may be, have nothing important to communicate." Thus wrote Henry David Thoreau in 1854, in *Walden*'s opening chapter. Thoreau's fear, expressed through the filter of what would now be seen as a mild elitism, was that the new, electronic communications technologies would only amplify the inarticulacy, gibberish and trivialities of everyday life. Even as he pottered around Walden Pond, plans were afoot to connect both sides of 'the Pond', America and Britain, by means of a transatlantic cable. "We are eager to tunnel under the Atlantic and bring the old world some weeks nearer the new;" he continues in the same passage, "but perchance the first news that will leak through into the broad, flapping American ear will be that the Princess Adelaide has the whooping cough."

Even Thoreau and his Transcendentalist mentor Ralph Waldo Emerson could not predict how far the telephone, and its eventual gushing into the delta of communication, recording and recombinant media available at the turn of the 21st century, would wrench human perceptions of time, space, distance, nationality and locality into unrecognisable shapes. Nor that, as those technologies proliferated, the inherent qualities of their mechanical or silicon based operating systems would thoroughly inscribe themselves into the content of what was being communicated.

But inscribe themselves they did, making it less surprising that certain sectors of contemporary music sound like a facsimile of the sort of ghost crackles that so religiously absorbed Watson, assistant to telephonic pioneer Alexander Graham Bell, when he jacked his ears into that subaquatic phone extension running under the Atlantic Ocean.

From beneath the frenetic, threshing rhythms of Jungle (touted in the mid-90s as quintessentially 'millennial' street music), a very different vibration has fermented, feeding off the technical errors and unplanned outcomes of electrified society – the world at the mercy of the glitch. Crackles, pops, pocks, combustions, gurgles, buzzes, amplitude tautenings, power spikes, voltage differentials, colliding pressure fronts, patterings, jump-splices, fax connections, silent interjections, hums, murmurs, switchbacks, clunks, granulations, fragmentations, splinterings, roars and rushes have overwhelmed the soundscape – as if the Ambient soundfields on the Cage-Eno axis have been zoomed in on until we are swimming amid the magnified atoms of sound. Characterised by colossal shifts in dynamics, tone and frequency, this is an urban environmental music – the cybernetics of everyday life – that reflects the depletion of 'natural' rhythms in the city experience, and in the striated plateaux of the virtual domain.

The glitch is only conceivable in a world where music has become partly or wholly mechanised. Recording converts sound into an object, and as an object it is vulnerable to breakage. At the same time, the object as capsule of sound (a measure of lived time scooped *out* of time, just as the photograph snatches a single instant out of visual, ontological reality) can accumulate power, potential energy. William S Burroughs recognised this when he experimented with cut-up speech recordings as sonic weaponry. In *The Job*, Burroughs describes a plot to put out of business a coffee bar which had treated him disrespectfully, with a tape recording of its ambience: "a deadly assassination technique" for annihilating a public authority or other offending establishment figures. By electronically trapping a fragment of time in a specified space, then re-injecting it into the building or playing it back to the subject, with various extraneous noises of disapproval bled into the mix, Burroughs believed its blood would be poisoned.

Burroughs's glitches in time – packages that can be torn open and the contents spilled – had the power to "discommodate or destroy" their intended targets. For Jacques Attali, the French economic theorist and prophetic author of *Noise: The Political Economy Of Music* (1978), the potential of music-as-interference – 'unmusical' music – was latently, inherently revolutionary. "Music announces that we are verging on no longer being a society of the spectacle," he wrote, and for the many individuals and collective labels currently utilising sonic detritus as the main ingredient of their music, this strikes a deeply resonant chord. For the 'glitch' electronics of the late 90s and early 21st century – equally audible in the rhythmic athletics of Autechre, the skipping playbacks of Oval, the delicate sampling compositions of John Wall, and the lunar song of Coil – have shifted the emphasis of 'spectacle' from the event we look *at* into the lens we look *through*: a society of the speculum, probing the deep internal/infernal percussion of the frequency spectrum.

The etymology of the word glitch is instructive. In mechanics, a glitch is a sudden irregularity or malfunction. It suggests simultaneously a slippage of gears or wheels – a failure to engage – and a scratch, a small nick in a smooth surface that recalls Gilles Deleuze's statement that the smoother the surface, the easier it is to deterritorialise. In German, the word 'glitschen' means to glide, slide or slip – a greasy or oily surface is glitschy. So there's this duality embedded in the word, of skidding and catching, which perfectly encompasses the Oval track "Do While", from the 1994 CD *94 Diskont*. Following the previous year's *Systemisch*, this record drew closer attention to the creative potential of malfunctioning or mistreated equipment. Damaged, scratched or otherwise harmed CDs are set running and jumping on standard issue players and the results sampled, then reorganised into kaleidoscopic patterns or caustic interludes.

Glitches abound on a double CD on the German Mille Plateaux label entitled *Clicks + Cuts*, which features many of the global electronic musicians who have followed in the wake of Oval, including snd, Crank, Stilluppsteypa, Pan Sonic, Pole, Dettinger, Kit Clayton and Kid606. Regular use of the word to describe a musical gesture originates around 1994, the year of Oval's seldom bettered *Systemisch* CD, as well as *Worship The Glitch*, credited to ELpH vs Coil. But one of the first decomposers must have been Pierre Schaeffer, whose *Symphony Pour Un Homme Seul* (1950), assembled in cooperation with Pierre Henry, still sounds like a turntablist's drum breakdown, with shouting voices and whistles that cut out before their own sounding has expired (condensed sonic ciphers not unlike the grunts and thuds triggered in a kickboxing arcade game). Heard half a century later, Schaeffer's pieces are irretrievable from their own tape decay – the crackling aesthetic which has translated into work by Christian Marclay, Philip Jeck, Pole, Pure (their *End Of Vinyl* mini-CD, issued by the Austrian Mego label, was totally composed of vinyl run-out groove recordings).

Previous locked-groove experiments in vinyl (beginning with Boyd Rice/Non's *Pagan Muzak* 7"album of 1978) brought out the infinity factor in the process – turning a disposable single format into a drone stretching from here to eternity. When the Fairlight sequencer emerged in recording studios around 1982, chart hits began skipping and stuttering in a strange foreshadowing of Oval's underground digitalia. Double Dee &

Steinski's "The Motorcade Sped On", Paul Hardcastle's "19", Duran Duran's "The Reflex", and the chorus of Black Box's "Ride On Time", all pockmarked the consciousness of anyone exposed to daytime radio during this period.

In underground digital music, where the glitch currently resides, it has released its grip on the vocal tic, and seized hold of pulses as they materialise out of silence. It could be the deep internal percussion of the bowel or of plumbing (Pan Sonic, Pita); random cracklings like a bicycle ridden over a path strewn with leaves (Bernhard Günter, Yasunao Tone); the rasp of a plastic shopping bag caught in a wind gust (Neina, Pole, Noto); interference from a mobile phone on an analogue line (Microstoria, shuttle253); tiny pops like sherbet exploding on the tongue (snd, Frank Bretschneider); painful cattleprod power surges (Ryoji Ikeda). When you let sound be itself, strip it of the imperative to represent human sentiments literally, you are not necessarily making something inhuman. At their best, these nicks and cracks are wounds – reminders of the frailty, mortality and imperfection of human endeavours.

At the end of 1998, the New Zealand guitarist Dean Roberts issued a CD called *All Cracked Medias*. Its three longform tracks of computer-processed acoustic/environmental sound foregrounded the notion of the 'crack' between layers in the music making process. The glitch is very often the product of so-called 'cracked' software – computer applications for either altering signals or structuring and laminating them in some way, which has been hijacked, bootlegged, altered or customised in order to evade copyright. Popular software for distorting and bending sound files include Super Collider, Audio Mulch, Metasynth (an audio-visual translator in which a picture file can be converted into sound digitally); GRM Tools (a morph-ware product from the Paris audio research centre founded by Pierre Schaeffer); Akira Rabelais's Argeiphöntes Lyre, Max and its shareware successor MaxPlay (included by Tokyo based Christophe Charles on his *Undirected* CD-ROM in 1995), ProTools and SoundHack. Bootleg software is known to be unpredictable: features can be missing; crashes are common, unexpected effects and clashes between computer operating systems all make the use of cracked material perilous. Early versions of Macintosh laptops running at 333 MHz were reported to run *too fast* for the existing version of Cubase, so the software's inbuilt metronome would veer and stutter erratically.

When the metronome does run like quartz, though, sequencers have assisted in bringing glitches to the post-Acid House dancefloor. The leading exponents of this 'Crack House' have included the US's Theo Parrish, The Martian and Kit Clayton; the UK's Surgeon and Cristian Vogel's Trash collective (not forgetting his vocal duo Super_Collider); Germany's Wolfgang and Reinhard Voigt, Thomas Brinkmann (who would incise cuts in his 12"s with a Stanley knife while they were spinning), Jürgen Paape, Bernd Friedmann, Farben and the Berlin Basic Channel/Chain Reaction faction. The snipping, scything backbeats of Jürgen Paape's "Triumph", released in late 98 on Kompakt, gouge the ears and force the feet into a hot tin roof dance – not so much beats as potholes sucked out of the ground you're treading on.

Structured around a 4/4 Tech-pulse, the skittering minimalism of the likes of Autechre, snd, Vladislav Delay, Arovane, Monolake and Frank Bretschneider slice Techno off the bone, building a twitchy, edgy microfunk around an absent centre – all that remains are the offbeats, syncopated clicks and imagined accents, accidental pulses that might have come from a blemish on a side of vinyl. Taking this concept even further is sound sculptor Kim Cascone, whose 'triptych' *blueCube* takes its structure from what Cascone calls "residualism" or "pulsar synthesis". In his words, this involves "the process of removing a signal until all that's left is its ghost-signal or the artifacts thrown off by the signal". The glitch is the residue, detritus, fading light, the dead skin of industrial standards.

Oval's Markus Popp states that most digital music is based on the reproduction and replication of industry standards. In other words, when musicians begin utilising software packages, modular synthesizers, effects units, computers and a combination of all these, they enmesh themselves in a creative environment over which they have little control. Popp's productions disobey instructions, discovering a sound quality and mode totally unplanned by the manufacturers. A jump or skip is no longer a problem or a fault, but a musical gesture in its own right.

Throughout the history of electronic music, pieces have been composed specifically for certain instruments – Morton Subotnick's *Silver Apples Of The Moon*, for instance, was practically a demonstration piece for the late 60s Buchla Modular Series 200 synthesizer, which was one of the first electronic keyboards to integrate the previously separated modular blocks of the Moog system into one compact dashboard. Now, synthesizer design has kept pace with the need to disrupt, transmute and distort: the analogue Wasp, favoured by Add N To (X), and the devilish red and black modules made by the Swedish company Nord, for example, seem calculated to appeal to glitchers, dirters, fluffers, splatterers – the inbuilt noises and filters on these expensive machines are inherently lo-res.

Granular synthesis, a blanket term for the bitmapping of sonic information in digital music, pulverises sound, returns music to dust. In the hard drive's gigabyte wilderness, grains can be scattered like seeds and the potential for genetic modification seems infinite. In 1994 a handful of artists dedicated to recycling this floating audio-litter emerged fully formed in Vienna. Pita, Rehberg & Bauer, Christian Fennesz and Farmers Manual became synonymous with state of the art glitch through releases on labels like Mego and Touch. Complemented by the sliced up digital graphics of Tina Frank (aka Skot), CD releases by Pita, General Magic, Fennesz and Farmers Manual cleave closely to the singularities of computerised sound. How do you announce the title of Pita's "~/" out loud, for example? It is a title – and by extension, a music – that can only be typed, not spoken, which explains why so many glitch tracks end up with names that use invented or hybrid words, or signifiers that look more like binary code. Filenames such as Autechre's "Acroyear2" and "Fold4,Wrap5" typify the 'working titles' Michael Fakesch of Funkstörung calls "Euro-English": a prototype form of the universalised technoid Newspeak that's likely to become standard across the continent ("Surfaise", "Diesehle", "Sega").

    Farmers Manual specialise in invented words and apparent nonsense, and an early version of their Website provided a subroutine to pick an (un)word at random. Their own Web-posted statement of intent reads as follows: "During the performance we seek to shift the local atmosphere from dissolution and clumsiness through manual change and ecstatic fiddling into an imaginative state of complex monotony, structured calm and chill, or endless associative babbling, so that towards the end the authors become the audience and the audience can be confronted with a stage populated by machines only, which can't get out of infinitely rendering a stream of slight semantic madness. The set-up then is what is normally considered a sort of installation. All this with the help of extreme freqencies and distorted, flickering images." Quoting among their influences Marcel Duchamp and radical graphix artist David Carson (whose most infamous tricks, as art director of *Raygun* magazine, included converting an entire Bryan Ferry profile into Zapf Dingbats font, that is a page of unreadable icons, and running a Survival Research Laboratories feature in a font which only reproduced capital letters, leaving only a light dusting of the alphabet), the Farmers experience is a profoundly disorienting, psychedelic anti-art ordeal that one report of a live show described as "luring the mind along some previously uncharted perceptual interface".

Farmers Manual tend to either delight or infuriate live audiences with their static Powerbook performances. Aural outcomes refuse to tally with what you actually see the individuals doing on stage – there is a perceptual displacement that leaves you feeling there's something wrong with where you are. Not leaving the listener any room for interpreting via language, or by supplying linguistic clues to the 'meaning' of tracks, you are thrown back on the spikes of the music itself – its raw aural power. It's significant that Pita, Fennesz and their recent collaborator Jim O'Rourke increasingly find their Powerbook operations welcomed among free improvising caucuses. Like the 'moment to moment' deep listening of groups such as AMM and Morphogenesis, and 'microvisors' like Radu Malfatti, Thomas Lehn, Phil Durrant, John Butcher and Mats Gustafsson, their real-time patchworks enact Attali's phrase about "doing solely for the sake of doing, without trying artificially to recreate the old codes, in order to reinsert communication into them". In other words, improvisation's substitution of textures and intuition for tempered scales, the geometry of the stave, and the internal logic of the sonata or symphonic form, arrives at a new definition of composing. In Attali's words, the self-sufficient composer "takes pleasure in the instruments, the tools of communication"; whereas previously composers manipulated limited harmonic means to enact narratives already ingrained in history and myth (as in opera). The glitch is the condensed essence of this new fundamental shift: an effluenza virus.

At the same time as pulverising sound, though, granular synthesis also makes it into a pliable material that can be subjected to laws of gravity – or even have unearthly forces applied to it in the computer environment.

The most celebrated operation in IDM circles is the 'Bucephalus's Bouncing Ball' effect – an algorithm used by the likes of Autechre (check "Drane2", the final track on *LP5*) and Aphex Twin (who titled one track after the equation) that speeds up a pulse as if it was an object bouncing on a table, subject to the force of gravity. You can imagine a future software containing algorithms that can be tweaked to apply laws of gravity stronger or weaker than that of Earth, acting on different substances, accelerating or decelerating them, squashing or compacting them. In the glitching, serrated burr-beats of Aphex, Squarepusher, Autechre, Nonplace Urban Field, Funkstörung, Mouse On Mars, et al, a multitude of clicks are crunched together, tamped down into an illusory single pulse. These ripped, zipped beats provided a tentative bridgehead between the glitch and 'street' musics like Jungle and drum 'n' bass. Earlier, on *Grayfolded*, Canadian John Oswald used similar techniques to pack hundreds of hours of Grateful Dead live recordings into a single audio meatloaf. Common time (use time, exchange time, leisure time) locks you into the tyranny of sequential time; the earthbound temporality that mystics and hermits meditated their way out of.

In Francis Bacon's 1627 Utopian tract *New Atlantis*, which describes an imaginary world in which European travellers step into a kind of Pacific future-parallel universe, the scientific society of Bensalem is found to contain "sound-houses, where we practise and demonstrate all sounds, and their generation", according to the travellers' host. "We represent small sounds as great and deep; likewise great sounds extenuate and sharp; we make divers tremblings and warblings of sounds." Such an approach to sound was the diametric opposite to the course of music in the ensuing centuries, which saw the growth of the symphony and the lionisation of the compositional ego – a sector which has created a classical music industry in which music is praised or criticised solely in terms of (a) its faithfulness to or departure from a score; and (b) its recorded clarity.

But the call of *New Atlantis* finds its response down the centuries in

Jacques Attali's *Noise*. Attali's discussion of new modes of production, written in full knowledge of avant garde and electronic music practices, anticipates the play of textures and grains with uncanny accuracy. "The only possible challenge to repetitive power takes the route of a breach in social repetition and the control of noisemaking," he writes, his version of repetitive power equating to authoritarian and socially repressive tactics. In place of rigorously controlled cultural production, Attali imagines a more improvisatory, on-the-fly method of productivity, but he already envisages a mode in which harmony has been shattered, with a musician working with the nuts and bolts of sound rather than their fine tuned, well tempered scales – the checks and balances that civilise untrammelled noise. "The musician, once outside the rules of harmony," he writes, "tries to understand and master the laws of acoustics in order to make them the mode of production of a new sound matter. Liberated from the constraints of the old codes, his discourse becomes non-localisable. Pulveriser of the past, he displays all of the characteristics of the technocracy." In other words, digital freedom comes with a price attached: confusion gets disseminated from the fringes as much as from power centres. It therefore becomes the task of acoustic engineers to make a humanised noise, to wrestle the new tools into a language usable and accessible by the listener.

The apparition of the glitch displays the desire for an art that wrinkles time. On its own, a glitch does not amount to much. It accumulates power by insertion, by its irruption in a flow of events. It is the random factor, the spark that ignites the primordial soup, the flash that illuminates the status of music as phantasmagoric time, not a utilitarian timekeeper.

German composer Bernhard Günter, celebrated for his Zen-like microscopic flakes of sound, which he describes as attempts to pass into a post-linguistic state of meditation, prefaced his 1999 recording *Slow Gestures* with notes towards a new valuation of time. Subjective time elapsing while listening to music, reading or studying an artwork, contends Günter, passes differently from regular clock-time. "In my work as a composer," he says, "I have often found that listeners believed a shorter piece to last longer than an actually longer one, and that their estimates of the duration of a work were often quite far from the actual chronometrical one. These considerations together with the interest I have taken in neurological research into our perception of time have led me to devise a new time unit for measuring the duration of my musical works... Research has found that our perception of 'present', 'now', 'the present moment' is a time window of about three seconds; everything else is memory or anticipation." *Slow Gestures* is 464.3 dim in length, the dim being the name he gives the new unit (from the French 'durée; ici, maintenant', or 'duration; here, now').

The background crackling that suffuses Coil's *Musick To Play In The Dark Vol 1* silverpoints John Balance's vocal invocations, communions with dead family spirits, vegetable meditations and misanthropic critique. The record is a transmission of intimate thoughts, nocturnal secrets, worldly advice – curious digital outlaw songs, spun round a wilderness blaze. "Drew [McDowall] gave us a great source of very deeply tweaked granular synthesis material," Balance wrote on the Coil Website at the time of its release in late 1999. "The clicks are meant to represent the digital equivalent of the fire crackling... This Is Moon Musick. Coil are creating lunar consciousness musick for the foreseeable future. It goes against previous magickal currents we have invoked. We are letting things in we shut out before. The feminine. The tidal. The cyclical." Who better than the original glitch worshippers to embark on the task of pulling the glitch away from its Techno-utilitarian origins, charging it up with the urgency of myth, and stitching it into a narrative of cyclical time?

PART TWO

OCCULTISM

THE ETERNAL DRONE

GOOD VIBRATIONS, ANCIENT TO FUTURE

BY MARCUS BOON

Boredom is the dream bird that hatches the egg of experience. A rustling in the leaves drives him away
Walter Benjamin

Once upon a time there were enormous halls, which could be found in many cities, where it was possible to hear the raw blast of Just Intonation tuned drone music under a cascade of multi-coloured lights. It was said by those who had visited these halls that this was the loudest sound in the world, and people crowded into these halls week after week, to be saturated in drones and light, and have ecstatic experiences. I am not talking about the lofts of downtown Manhattan, where in the early 1960s, La Monte Young, John Cale, Tony Conrad and friends created the colossal drones of The Theater Of Eternal Music, from which The Velvet Underground, My Bloody Valentine and indeed most of what was best in late 20th century Western culture issued forth. Nor am I talking about the communes and basements of West Germany and Switzerland in the 1970s, where Can, Amon Düül, Ash Ra Tempel and company took keyboard driven raga rock into interstellar overdrive. I am not even talking about the legendary drum 'n' bass, Techno and Trance clubs and outdoor raves that sprung up all over the world in the 1990s, wherever you could find a power socket or a generator, where synthesizer-created drones provided a trance-inducing bedrock for a Dionysian festival of percussive and pharmacological experiment.

There was no electricity in the cathedrals of medieval Europe, such as Nôtre Dame in Paris, where enormous pedal organs tuned to specific, harmonically related pitches accompanied drone or sustained tone based vocal recitations written by composers such as Leonin and Perotin, or the anonymous Gregorian chant masters. Operated pneumatically using a bellows, the organs were vast, and the cathedral functioned as a resonant chamber that amplified the organ so that the space was saturated with rich overtones, as strange psychedelic colour effects created by the stained glass windows illuminated the walls and the faces of the congregation. An English monk, Wulstan, described the newly built Winchester Cathedral organ in 960 AD: "Twice six bellows are ranged in a row, and 14 lie below... worked by 70 strong men... the music of the pipes is heard throughout the town, and the flying fame thereof is gone out over the whole country." "No one," it was said, "was able to draw near and hear the sound, but that he had to stop with his hands his gaping ears."

Such experiences were not 'marginal' or 'esoteric'. They occurred at the very centre of European culture. But with the growing use of the keyboard in the 14th century, and the gradual adoption of standardised tuning systems, such as the equal tempered scale which has dominated Western music from the 18th century until this day, the drone disappeared from view. Because the equal tempered scale is slightly out of tune from the point of view of the natural harmonics of sound (it 'equalises' the differences in pitch between notes on a keyboard to simplify and standardise tuning), the matrix of harmonies that makes the drone so pleasing when a Just Intonation tuning system (ie one using natural harmonics, and the acoustic laws that determine which pitches are in tune with each other) is used, is lost. And so the word drone became an insult, an indication of boredom, repetitiveness, lack of differentiation.

It's true: drones remain boring, irritating even, to many people. When Lou Reed issued his dronework homage to avant garde composers La Monte Young and Iannis Xenakis, *Metal Machine Music*, in 1975, it was reviled by most of the unsuspecting fans who bought it expecting a repeat of the glam rock of *Transformer*. If by drones we mean music that is built around a sustained tone or tones, there is something about a sound that does not shift, something about the experience of a sound heard for an extended duration that nags at consciousness. Drones interrupt the pleasure the brain takes in compositions built on an infinite variety of notes, combinations and changes, or pull it towards something more fundamental. Which is more important: that which changes, or that which stays the same? It need not be a question of either/or. In fact, it cannot be. But at least when it comes to artificially created sounds – to music – there is no such thing as a music that remains the same for an infinite duration. Even La Monte Young's extended tone pieces, such as his sinewave tone pieces from the 1960s like *Drift Studies*, or the installation scheduled to continue running for eight years in a New York loft, *Dream House: Sound And Light*, started once, and will end – although Young has made the silences at the beginning and end of some of his compositions part of the piece, which can therefore be said to extend into eternity. Meanwhile, human sensory perceptions shift and alter, and bodies decay and die, even when the music does not.

Beneath all that changes, is there a constant sound that is to be heard? In India, one way of saying drone is "Nada Brahma" – "God is sound", or "sound is God". What we call music is ahata nad – "the struck sound". But inside this sound is anahata nad – "the unstruck sound": the sound of silence. The relationship between the struck and the unstruck sound can be modelled in different ways. Indeed, at the moment when the drone re-emerged after World War Two in America, with La Monte Young's *Trio For Strings* (1958), we can see divergent but complementary models very clearly in John Cage and Young's attitudes to sound. As Kyle Gann has written: "In Cage's aesthetic, individual musical works are metaphorically excerpts from the cacophonous roar of all sounds heard or imagined. Young's archetype, equally fundamental, attempts to make audible the opposite pole: the basic tone from which all possible sounds emanate as overtones. If Cage stood for Zen, multiplicity, and becoming, Young stands for yoga, singularity and being."

Cage's *4'33"* (1952), with its 'silent' non-performance, forces the listener to become aware of the omnipresence of sounds within silence and vice versa, both inside the listener and in the environment of the performance space. Young's *Composition No 7 (1960)*, which consists of a notated B and F# together with the instruction, "To be held for a long time", provides a single constant sound that changes as what Young has called "listening in the present tense" develops. Freed, at least temporarily, from the distraction of change and time, the listener enters the stream of the sound itself and discovers that what seemed to be a single drone shifts and changes as the listener scans and focuses on different parts of it, opening up into a universe of overtones, microtones and combination tones. Of course, this experience is entirely dependent on correct tuning. B and F# on a conventionally tuned piano won't sound that amazing – nor will a drone that's tuned this way. Young's interest in sustained tones and Just Intonation, which he grew increasingly fascinated by in the early 1960s, support each other, because Just Intonation brings out the full spectrum of overtones which makes drones so satisfying to the ear. This music may be 'minimalist', but the resulting sound, as Terry Riley has quipped, is actually 'maximal' – or, to use a word Young says he once preferred, it's 'meta-music'.

Why has the drone become such a key element in contemporary music, from Keiji Haino's hurdy gurdy and effects-laden guitars to the Gregorian chant driven club music of Enigma, the ecstatic jazz of Alice Coltrane or composed works like Ligeti's *Lux Aeterna*, popularised on the film soundtrack to Kubrick's *2001: A Space Odyssey*? Marshall McLuhan defined the electronic universe that opened up after World War Two as being one of participation, immersion and acoustics, in contrast to the predominantly visual culture that dominated the West for the previous 500 years since the early European Renaissance, which was a culture of spectators, distance and the written word. Drones, embodying and manifesting universal principles of sound and vibration, in a fundamental sense belong to nobody, and invite a sense of shared participation, collective endeavour and experience that is very attractive.

Just as the drone can cause powerful shifts in individual consciousness, so it also reorganises traditional hierarchies of music production and consumption. Drones are ill-suited to commercial recording formats such as the CD, due to their length, the way they rely on the acoustics of the room in which they are produced, and their paradoxically intimate relationship with visual culture. The CD of Alvin Lucier's *Music On A Long Thin Wire*, with its warm, resonant humming tone, is gorgeous, but it hardly captures the original sound installation from which the sound recording was made – just as no sound recording of La Monte Young's work can capture Marian Zazeela's accompanying, integral light sculptures, and no movie soundtrack recording can supply the experience of actually seeing the film it comes from.

The battle between Young, Zazeela, John Cale and Tony Conrad[1] over who 'owns' recordings of The Theater Of Eternal Music's rehearsals and

---

[1] In 2000, The American Table Of The Elements label released a CD credited to John Cale, Tony Conrad, Angus MacLise, La Monte Young and Marian Zazeela, entitled *Inside The Dream Syndicate Volume 1: "Day Of Niagara" 1965*. Young and Zazeela disputed the legalilty of the CD with Cale, Conrad and Table Of The Elements – who endorsed the release – claiming that they had not given permission for it to appear. Young's statement about the CD appears on his Website (www.lamonteyoung.com).

performances embodies basic contradictions contained in the rediscovery of the drone in Western culture. Young discovered sustained tones in a sense that could be covered by traditional notions of authorship and copyright, but, as he himself once asked, how do you copyright a relationship between two pitches? Or, for that matter, the mathematical principles governing Just Intonation pitch relationships which Tony Conrad pointed out to Young in the early 60s?[2] From the point of view of the performers, the creation of drones, even according to someone else's instructions, feels like an intense collective experience and endeavour. More recently, groups like Vibracathedral Orchestra, or Bardo Pond, or The Boredoms have returned to the tribal spirit of drone creation, in which drones are collectively improvised. Meanwhile, the profusion of electronic drone based musics, of 'microsound', 'lower case', minimalist House, Ambient, etc, on labels like Brooklyn's 12k, Mille Plateaux or Raster-Noton extends this idea of community in a different way, as the line between producer and consumer is blurred by limited edition CDs and CD-Rs, which are mostly bought or exchanged by those who are part of the scene, themselves making drone based music.

La Monte Young speaks of tuning tamburas to a pitch of 60Hz, which is the speed at which electricity is supplied in the USA (in Europe it's 50Hz). As a series of dogmatic but useful books such as Joachim-Ernst Berendt's *Nada Brahma: The World Is Sound* and Peter Michael Hamel's *Through Music To The Self* have documented, from the point of view of physics, everything vibrates and therefore can be said to exist *as* sound, rather than merely "having a sound".

The word 'vibration' has come to stand in for all that people find loathsome about hippy, New Age, California spiritual vagueness, but it entered 60s culture through Sufism, and in particular through the work of an Indian musician and philosopher Sufi Hazrat Inayat Khan, who

---

[2] In *Halana* magazine (issue 1, winter 1996, p31), La Monte Young says: "Well, I think that my first really big interest in numbers started in the early 60s when Tony Conrad was working in my group, and he had come out of a mathematical background. He pointed out to me that it was with the integers that you could really define the whole system of Just Intonation... Once Tony pointed out to me the significance of the integers, I found my way immediately into the system of Just Intonation in a way that I had never found before..."

travelled to New York for the first time in 1910. In his classic book, *The Mysticism Of Music, Sound And Word*, Khan sets out a doctrine in which sound, movement and form emerge out of silence: "Every motion that springs forth from this silent life is a vibration and a creator of vibrations." According to Khan, matter and solid objects are manifestations of the power of vibration and sound, and not vice versa. Sound comes first, not matter. So, the universe is sound, and the drone, which sustains a particular set of vibrations and sound frequencies in time, has a very close relationship to what we are, to our environment, and to the unseen world around us. Khan: "With the music of the Absolute the bass, the undertone, is going on continuously; but on the surface beneath the various keys of all the instruments of nature's music, the undertone is hidden and subdued. Every being with life comes to the surface hidden and subdued. Every being with life comes to the surface and again returns whence it came, as each note has its return to the ocean of sound. The undertone of this existence is the loudest and the softest, the highest and the lowest; it overwhelms all instruments of soft or loud, high or low tone, until all gradually merge in it; this undertone always is, and always will be." The traditional name given to this never-ending undertone, which has been repeated in hte modern era by musicians from John Coltrane and Can to Stockhausen and Sheila Chandra is OM, and by saying OM, the monk or the musician tunes into perfect sound forever.

Drones can embody the vastness of the ocean of sound, but they also provide a grid, or thread, through which it can be navigated. La Monte Young has talked about using his sustained tone pieces as a way of sustaining or producing a particular mood by stimulating the nervous system continually with a specific set of sound vibrations – thus providing a constant from which the mind can move, back and forth. In a recent interview, one of Pandit Pran Nath's disciples, Indian devotional singer Sri Karunamayee, pointed out that the tambura, the four stringed drone instrument that accompanies most Indian classical music performances, "gives you a feeling of groundedness, so you do not get lost as in Western music. It is said that even Saraswati, goddess of wisdom and learning and music, when she enters the Nada Brahma, the ocean of sound, feels that it is so impenetrable, so profound, and is concerned lest she, the goddess of music may be lost, inundated by it. So she places two gourds around her, in the form of Veena, and then she is guided by them into it." Indian singers love to say that to be between two tamburas is heaven. They mean it literally, for the correctly tuned and amplified tambura contains a world of infinite pitch relationships. And to be perfectly in tune with universal vibration means to be one with God.

Although the drone has often been used as a sacred technology, there is nothing that says it has to be so. Indeed, like all former sacred technologies in the modern era, including drugs, dance and ritual, erotic play or asceticism, musicians have appropriated and reconfigured the drone's power in many ways that question traditional notions of the sacred. The Theater Of Eternal Music were famous for their use of hashish and other substances, which allowed for extended periods of concentration and sensitivity to micro-intervals. The Velvet Underground made this link explicit, with John Cale's droning viola underpinning Lou Reed's vocal on "Heroin". More recently, Coil, in their *Time Machines*, have produced a series of long drone pieces, each named after one of the psychedelics. Conversely, writers like René Daumal who have described their drug experiences have reported the effects of synaesthesia, where sounds become embodied before their eyes, or have experienced their own identities as sustained tones.

In fact, the drone is a perfect vehicle for expressing alienation from conventional notions of the sacred – either existentially, through a cultivation of 'darkness', as Japanese avant garde musician Keiji Haino, dressed in black, with his hurdy gurdy and effects pedals, has done; or through a music that emphasises mechanism and dissonance in imitation of the drone of the machinery of industrial society (hence 'Industrial music' and Throbbing Gristle's 1970s utterances in alienated sound). In his essay on Reed's *Metal Machine Music*, Lester Bangs dwelled on the "utterly inhuman" quality of Reed's drone, and what he saw as Reed's deliberate attempt at negating the human for "metal" and "machines", and of the masochistic pleasure that he and other noise lovers took in the experience of depersonalisation and subjugation to the sounds of machinery. Both of these kinds of alienation are present in the dark, negative, profane spirituality that we find in various recent mutant drone subgenres: dronecore, Dark Ambient, 'Isolationist'...

From the modern viewpoint, drones are effective because of their relationship to the void that existentialists believe surrounds human activity. In 1927 Georges Bataille spoke of the universe as "formless", and of all "official" human culture being an attempt to resist this fundamental fact, which reduced the cosmos to nothing more than "a spider or a gob of spit". There is something of this quality of formlessness at work in 'dark' drones, with their dissonant tones, the endless decay, distortion and degradation of pure tones, in the name of entropic noise. This formlessness, which blurs and loosens the boundaries of individual identity, could be the source of the ecstatic, 'high' quality often stimulated by drone music. If we take away Bataille's existential pessimism, we can see how the formlessness of the drone leads us to use words like 'abstract' or 'Ambient' to describe it. Indeed, the word 'drone' itself is used by critics and musicians alike to stand in for a whole realm of musical activity that is difficult to describe using words, because drones lack the series of contrasts and shifts that give music form or definition. But does that mean that drones are truly formless, or do they embody deeper aspects of musical form?

It would be easy to say that the sacred, spiritual qualities of the drone were connected with harmony, and the consonance of different pitches – g the saccharine sweetness of New Age music – and that the profane, modern drone is connected with dissonance, with the exploration and equalization of 'forbidden' pitch relationships. But the Just Intonation system actually moves beyond such crude distinctions. To begin with, it should be pointed out that the equal tempered scale is itself slightly out of tune, ie dissonant, while certain pitch combinations that are in fact in tune according to the physics of sound will sound dissonant or 'flat' at first to ears that have heard nothing but music in equal temperament. As with distinctions between 'black' and 'white' magic, so there are harmonious combinations of pitches that create a wide range of moods. Think of the diversity of ragas, all of which are tuned according to Just Intonation scales, from the serenity of a dawn raga like *Lalit* to a dark, moody raga like *Malkauns*. There are dark harmonies as well as light ones.

In fact, the electric feedback which is so key to alt.rock's embrace of the drone (My Bloody Valentine's "You Made Me Realise" or The Jesus And Mary Chain's "Upside Down", for example), based as it is on the amplification of the resonant frequencies from a sound source, is by definition in harmony – the feedback being composed of naturally occurring overtones within a sound. What we call noise is often merely a different kind of harmony, and the celebration of it in post-Velvets guitar culture is a celebration of harmony. That's why it feels so good: it's the raw power of vibrations. Keiji Haino has talked of his desire, when he plays "covers" of pop songs in his Aihiyo project, to "destroy things that already existed" and to liberate sound from the "constraint" of the song. But his noise pieces can never truly destroy song, for the pleasures of song and noise enjoy secret common ground. Haino may replace banal, cliched sound relationships with powerful, fundamental ones – but these are already actually contained inside many pop songs, waiting to be liberated by amplification, by being sustained over time. When it's at its most satisfying, noise, like pop, embodies the laws of harmony and universal sound.

Depersonalization, alienation, spiritual kitsch, immersive sacred sound: how do we reconcile the different uses to which drones can be put? I don't believe, as Hamel and Berendt do, that anything good can come from lecturing people that they're bad boys and girls who should eat their spiritual spinach. I don't believe that theory should control practice and bully it with claims of expertise either. It was Cage and the minimalists (or Louis Armstrong maybe) that finally dispatched that notion after centuries of the composer's hegemony. We know very well by now that expertise in music is a matter of coming up with the goods. Indeed, drones have always been as much a part of folk music as sacred or 'classical' music – think of the bagpipes or the many indigenous instruments that have a drone string. But in this respect, the lack of understanding of what sound is that informs much of the contemporary drone scene is revealing. A new piece of software is developed, a new synth, a new trick with a distortion pedal, which sounds great for a few months, is quickly passed around and imitated, and then exhausted. Nothing is learnt, just the iteration of possible combinations surrounding happy accidents, and momentary pulses of novelty. In contrast, the drone school surrounding La Monte Young, which is notable for Young's emphasis on setting the highest possible motivation and goals, and for the depth of its scientific and musicological research, has been endlessly productive, both in the case of Young himself, and those who have studied with or around him (alumni including Terry Riley, Tony Conrad, John Cale, Jon Hassell, Rhys Chatham, Arnold Dreyblatt, Michael Harrison, Henry Flynt, Catherine Christer Hennix) – precisely because it does not rely on happy accidents, but upon a knowledge of the powers of sound.

In his notes to Young-protégée Catherine Christer Hennix's Just Intonation drone masterpiece, *The Electric Harpsichord*, Henry Flynt writes: "The thrust of modern technology was to transfer the human act to the machine, to eliminate the human in favor of the machine, to study phenomena contrived to be independent of how humans perceived them. In contrast, the culture of tuning which Young transmitted by example to his acolytes let conscious discernment of an external process define the phenomenon. The next step is to seek the laws of conscious discernment or recognition of the process. And the next step is to invent a system driven by improvisation monitored by conscious apperception of the process." In other words: don't just let the machines run. And don't hide behind Cage's culture of the accident, of chance. Become conscious of what music can be, dive deeper into that vast field of sonic relationships that, at least in the West, remains almost totally unexplored.

The drone, like drugs or eroticism, cannot be easily assimilated to one side of the divide by which modernism or the avant garde has tried to separate itself from history or tradition. Like psychedelics, the drone, rising out of the very heart of the modern, and the domain of machines, mathematics, chemistry and so on, beckons us neither forward nor backward, but sideways, into an open field of activity that is always in dialogue with 'archaic' or traditional cultures. This is an open field of shared goals and a multiplicity of experimental techniques, rather than the assumed superiority of the musicologist or the naive poaching of the sampler posse. How vast is this field? I once asked Hennix what the ratio of the known to the unknown is, when it comes to exploring the musical worlds contained in different Just Intonation based tuning systems. She laughed and said, "Oh, it's about one to infinity!"

SLAPPING PYTHAGORAS

THE BATTLE FOR THE MUSIC OF THE SPHERES

BY ROB YOUNG

"From the sounds of a monochord, the Pythagoreans deduced a universe." With these words, scientific historian Thomas Levenson encapsulated one of the biggest leaps of faith ever taken in the history of Western civilisation. In the sixth century BC, a reclusive cult from the Greek island of Samos, supposedly led by a fanatical maths genius, devised a musical tuning system that affirmed its belief in the hermetic doctrine that what happened above must also occur below. Since the planets, sun and moon are so vast in size, they reasoned, they must make an almighty racket while floating on their allotted orbits through space, and the regularity of their motion suggested that the noise would add up to a celestial symphony, a Music of the Spheres, that amplified the voice of God and provide an aural pathway signifying the order of the cosmos. A system of harmonic proportions, derived from experimental acoustic physics, provided the incontrovertible arithmetical truth of their faith. The solar system was effectively mapped through music and the heavenly music ineffably reverberated around their cosmos.

When musicians played in the ancient world, therefore, the notion that they were expressing *themselves* was utterly alien. The musician or singer was an anonymous servant of God, the sounds he or she produced were not a representation of cosmic Truth, but literally rang with that Truth.

Rabid celebrity may have acted as the benchmark of art appreciation during the last century, but Pythagoras's monochord (more of which later) has continued to send shivers down the spine of modern music, latching on to the shift in sonic investigations from substance/content to texture/form. Music of the Spheres is ultimately reducible to a metaphor for all musics that originate outside the self, and there have been plenty of those in the last 100 years: serialism; vastly expanded tuning scales; and, latterly, attempts to set up self-organising or chaotic musical systems.

Greeting the arrival and increased employment of musical automata in 1926, Arnold Schoenberg wrote: "Ensuring the production of sounds and their correct relationship to each other, freeing them from the hazards of a primitive, unreliable and unwilling sound producer – to that degree the use of all mechanical musical instruments could be of the greatest advantage." In Schoenberg's serialist compositions, and those of his

Second Viennese School associates Alban Berg and Anton Webern, music unhooked itself from the emotionalism and intuitive structures that had brought it to its opulent and overripe state in late Romanticism. Schoenberg hastened the move to atonality – meaning the lack of any defined key – as speedily as his contemporaries Picasso and Braque accelerated the destruction of Renaissance perspective on the canvas.

Schoenberg converted music into pure data: groups of 12 notes were used as amelodic cells throughout any given composition. Capable of being inverted, intermixed or run into palindromes, their relationship to each other was as abstracted, isolated notes, not linked to a previously chosen dominant key. Fixed keys give a sense of progress in a composition by pegging music to a tonic resolution. Schoenberg tried to inscribe a new, secret, inaudible system as the modus operandi in his music, but at some point he lost his nerve in the shadow of several hundred years of classical tradition: "One uses the series and then one composes as before," he once wrote. But his operas *Die Jakobsleiter* (*Jacob's Ladder,* 1917-22) and *Moses Und Aron* (1932) both remained unfinished when he died. It was as if he balked when finding that the ladder he was trying to construct was fatally complexified by numbers: as if in acknowledgment, his *Pierrot Lunaire* is a poem of the lost soul – fractured, confused, alienated.

For better or worse, serialism has come to represent all that is popularly loathed about 'modern' music: the sonic equivalent of 'bricks in the Tate'. Most significant modern composers have utilised the system to a greater or lesser extent, from Messiaen and Stravinsky to Boulez, Milton Babbitt and Stockhausen. But as an audible expression of mathematical arrangements, its structures remain a hidden presence within the music. In order to hear the palindromes, reversals of pattern, fold upon fold (*Pli Selon Pli*, in one of Pierre Boulez's titles) of the manipulated note-row, you have to be an initiate. In fighting for atonality, Schoenberg engendered a complexity that shut out the people.

When music imagines itself as a scientific gauge, a capsule of cosmic truths, then the discourse of the imagery of the Music of the Spheres is never far away. In ancient history, Pythagoras and his cronies arrived just as Greece was flushed with enthusiasm for democracy – perhaps the first in an era of tyranny. But the geometers of Samos had other ideas – this cacophony of newly liberated voices needed tuning up, and Pythagoras was the one to beat out the conductor's rap.

What, exactly, did Pythagoras discover? The story of his chance encounter with metal beaters in a smithy (celebrated in Händel's keyboard work *The Harmonious Blacksmith*) is often retold; how he experienced a eureka moment on hearing the noises produced by hammers of different weights bashing metal anvils. A hammer of a certain weight would produce a frequency twice as long as a hammer half the mass of the first – or in acoustic terms, it would sound one octave lower. Further experiments showed, according to the medieval music theorist Boethius, that the ratios between the musical notes produced in the experiments corresponded precisely; by systematising the fundamental musical intervals that are still in use today, Pythagoras brought into the open the deep connection between mathematics, numbers and sound. In Harry Partch's rerouting of the Pythagorean musical theorem to take account of much more ancient tuning systems (cf the history of intonation in his exhaustive book *Genesis Of A Music*), the hobo composer sources the discoveries attributed to Pythagoras way back in older Babylonian, Egyptian and Chinese civilisations. As in so many other areas of knowledge, the Greeks had ripped off other cultures wholesale.

The definitive image of the divine monochord, tuned by the hand of God and encircled by a weblike filigree of arcs and connected nodes describing significant tonal regions and harmonic proportions, has become a familiar image from modern record sleeves and book jackets. The monochord's solitary string – mounted on a single body, divided into two lengths by a movable bridge – allowed the division of sound into the magic proportions sought by the Pythagoreans. With the bridge dividing the string exactly halfway in a ratio of 1:2, it sounds a perfect octave. Move the bridge three-fifths down the string in a ratio of 3:2, and the two segments will sound together in a perfect fifth, and so on; the arithmetic holds good for the entire length of the instrument.

In his sleevenotes to an album called *Slapping Pythagoras* (1994), the American composer and researcher Tony Conrad sounds an exasperated note that propels his own musical investigations of the frequencies that reside far off the ancient Greeks' tonal highway: "Yessir, Pythagoras, I do have to see you as a paradigmatically European guy: you travelled abroad, imperialistically raped the East of its 'Exotic' knowledge, and returned with a plan to straitjacket your own people. But we're going to start changing all of that, beginning *now*."

Retuning the debate around musical truth to a specifically American frequency, Conrad's conception of Radical Democracy is set against the Platonic Republic(an) World Order. Democracy, in this case, is represented by the breadth of timbre, in all the harmonic variations between the traditional octave, and divergences from what Conrad refers to as "The Three Chords" – dominant, subdominant and tonic – which have kept a stranglehold on Western music from the sonata through to the three minute pop song. With *Slapping Pythagoras*, Conrad spurs his followers to slip between the tones and pitches established by Western tuning systems, and to "crack apart the voices [Pythagoras] forced to blend as 'One'".

This voice crack – the untrammelled chaos of heterophony, and deregulated human expression – is most vividly documented across the 12 sides of Harry Smith's original *Anthology Of American Folk Music*. Robert Fludd's Pythagorean monochord sits squarely on the box cover; but while Smith was fascinated by the encodings of ancient, sometimes arcane information, and mapping the forgotten migrations of tribal cultures through an archaeology of folk song, the monochord's presence has an ironic undertow. Smith colour-coded the three slipcases holding the six records: red (fire), green (water) and blue (air). Earth is the missing element, but it must have seemed as if the records themselves were pressed from hardened loam. The grit and physicality of the sounds and voices inscribed within the grooves crackle and shout as the needle grinds along its allotted spiral path. This heterophony of voice and grain splits off the main theme in a similar fashion to the micro-splittings of tones that are foregrounded in Conrad's violin drones.

The main bone of contention for Conrad and other campaigners for more varied tunings is that equal temperament – the modern system of tuning – is a keyboard-centric fudge. Before the 18th century, there was no fixed system dictating the proper intervals between notes in the scale. Equal temperament, as modern ears know it, only became enshrined when JS Bach compiled the keyboard exercises that have come to be known as *Das Wohltemperte Klavier* (*The Well-Tempered*

Clavier). A sequence of 48 progressively more difficult preludes and fugues, *The Well-Tempered Clavier* was created between 1722-42, for piano pupils at the court of Cöthen in Germany, where Bach was director of music. The system equalises the harmonic distance between each of the 12 notes in the scale (the eight whole notes of the octave, plus the sharps and flats in between). The effect is to sweeten the scale, making it more palatable to the drawing room. These exercises would become an integral component of the daily practice regimen of later composers at the heart of the classical tradition: Mozart, Beethoven, Schumann. A tuning system designed for the children of a ruling European elite has become the fundament of all Western music: it was only a matter of time before such a system would come under intense scrutiny by those seeking to revolutionise and democratise the harmonic air we breathe.

The 12 arbitrary divisions of the octave mean that certain sustained pitches beat and buzz against each other, creating an effect that musicologist Kyle Gann has called "aural caffeine", and leading Terry Riley to state that "Western music is fast because it's not in tune". Riley is one of a growing number of musicians who have tried to bypass this effect with a system called Just Intonation (JI), or pure tuning. Beginning with Harry Partch, who split the octave into 43 pitches, American New Music has often equated music that unhooks itself from the equal tempered scale with the quest for freedom.

Californian composer Lou Harrison followed with his tunings for orchestra taken from studying Indonesian gamelan orchestras; and composers including La Monte Young, Pauline Oliveros, James Tenney, Glenn Branca and Ben Neill have at various times adopted those ideas. In Just Intonation, intervals between notes are assigned values in cents: the exchange rate is 100 cents per half-tone. Given equipment sensitive enough to be tuned cent by cent, the number of possible ratios suddenly start to spiral into the thousands. There are two unfortunate side effects. First, JI has rapidly turned into an arcane mathematics of its own, the subject of digit-riddled theses in music departments the world over. Second, because JI tunings aim to cut out dissonance, its apologists tend to privilege the somatic, calming and meditational qualities of music. It's no accident that JI also surfaces at the borders of New Age, or in 'serious' Ambient types such as Robert Rich and Larry

Polansky. It's not long before we're back in the realm of Pythagoras, for whom one of music's prime functions was as a healing agent.

The Music of the Spheres is being fought for in other theatres of war as well, not just in the shadowy byways of tuning theory. Sometimes you have to be wary of the Romantic wolf wearing a white coat. Karlheinz Stockhausen's version of cosmic music, for example, is something of a red herring. In Stockhausen's pronouncements, musical magnetic waves are always discussed in terms of how they affect his individual being. "There's a music of the spheres all the time," he has been quoted as saying, "but these sounds would make the worst pollution you can imagine, it would be too loud." Not in my back yard, in other words – it might drown out his own masterpieces. *Licht*, the gargantuan opera that Stockhausen has had in development for nearly three decades, is a cosmic conceit too far for most observers. Through *Donnerstag Aus Licht*'s astronaut-angel Michael, Stockhausen enacts the interlocking of musical laws with the human sphere. He's less interested in what happens when music penetrates the social domain than in how it affects his quasi-mystical reading of the body.

The clockwork regularity of the Newtonian universe has ceded to 'weirdness', as particle physicists term it, which finds its musical counterpart in xenharmony – strange harmony. The atomic age imports 'strangeness' into the scientific – and by extension, musical – equation. More and more music unfolds according to its own internal logic, or is constituted of elements far removed from notions of personal expression. 30 years on from Charles Dodge's *Earth's Magnetic Field* – 'composed' by mapping geophysical statistics into musical data – there is renewed interest in sucking the noise of solar emissions or national power grids out of the atmosphere, or in using computer software to transmute raw data into corresponding sound (the latest being the program that converts image data into a sonic equivalent). Process/pulse musics, such as that of Terry Riley, or the type of Techno whose building blocks are pure frequencies, such as the tracks on pretty much any record by Plastikman, leave you searching for metaphors in gene mutations, orbital eccentricities, shifting gravitational masses. Sonic art is put to work as a filter for feeding deep structures back into the human ear.

The synthesizer's tone generators created a new facility of pitch constructions, and computer synthesis allows you to compose graphically with the sinewaves themselves – the physical stuff of sound that the microtonalists' numbers represent.

Pythagoreans built up a mathematical world view based on specific points, not admitting that the lines can be infinitely divisible. At the beginning of the 21st century, points of musical information, like most other information, have multiplied even as they have become more closely spaced. Digital data is granulated; the granules are infinitely rearrangeable, paralleling the fine chopping of the harmonic scale. "We are all Pythagoreans," Iannis Xenakis once said. Even though he neglected to define the 'we' in that equation, his prophecy resonates anew in the world of consumer electronics, where compositional processes once laboured over for days are now instantly accessible via cheap synthesizers, composition programs and mobile phone ringtones. Xenakis's abstruse mathematics are put at the service of the replication of 'natural' forms. He engineers events among groups of instruments that replicate the opening of fans or sweeping brushes, with composition structures called "arborescences" – tentacles or bushes of sounds stemming from a common root. Software allows the manipulation of the position, rotation and textural appearance of the forms created in this way. These arboreal works superceded Xenakis's earlier stochastic experiments, which were determined purely by arithmetic logic. "In determinism the same cause always has the same effect," he told interviewer Bálint András Varga, describing his quest to unlock the chaotic value of numbers. "There's no deviation, no exception. The opposite of this is that the effect is always different, the chain never repeats itself. In this way we reach absolute chance – that is, indeterminism."

In the 20th century, the human ear had to adapt to more crowded and information rich environments. Part of that evolution has conditioned it to desire and detect more noise – that is, the sound and textural detail that falls between the mathematical divisions laid down by Pythagoras. The amplified, detuned sounds of warfare, decomposition and decay characterise much post-war art music. In the new millennium, the monochord is not long enough to express all that has changed in the form of music. "If one 3:2 was good," said Harry Partch, referring to the Pythagoreans' leader, "12 were 12 times good, and after 2500 years we are still trying to correct the excesses of his judgment."

THE RAGGED TROUSERED ANTHOLOGIST

THE SECRET WORLDS OF HARRY SMITH

BY PETER SHAPIRO (I) & PHILIP SMITH (II)

|

If God were a DJ, he'd be Harry Smith.
Peter Stampfel

America, 1952: Senator Joseph McCarthy was still running rampant; Richard Nixon saved his political ass from accusations of benefitting from a slush fund by invoking the family dog "named by his six year old daughter" in his infamous "Checkers" speech; it was the age of the relentless uniformity and homogeneity of Levittown and Ozzie And Harriet; the grey flannel suit or, if you were really pushing the boat out, blue serge; pert homemakers who understood that Daddy in a cardie knew best; McDonald's; Jimmy Boyd's "I Saw Mommy Kissing Santa Claus" and Vera Lynn's "Auf Wiederseh'n Sweetheart"; when "what [was] good for General Motors [was] good for the country"; atomic safety videos telling school children to "run, duck and cover" when the Russkies dropped the big one.

Five years after Dalton Trumbo and Hanns Eisler were run out of Hollywood and two years after the McCarran Act set up concentration camps for leftists, 1952 wasn't just the year of blandness, it was the year of silence. For those who managed to make art in such a climate, however, it was also the year silence, and once-silent voices, roared. 1952 saw the first performance of John Cage's *4'33"* and the publication of Ralph Ellison's *Invisible Man*. It was also the year Moses Asch's Folkways label released Harry Smith's *Anthology Of American Folk Music*, a three volume, 84 song distillation of Smith's prodigious collection of 78s that marked the first time Appalachian breakdowns, Acadian one-steps, coalmining ballads, Delta blues, Piedmont blues, Texas blues and baptist spirituals became readily available to the wider public.

While Norman Vincent Peale was rewriting Christianity as proof of the power of positive thinking, Smith reanimated Blind Lemon Jefferson begging for his grave to be kept clean, as well as Bascom Lamar Lunsford singing, *"If I was a mole in the ground, I'd root that mountain down"*, and *"Dry bones in that valley got up and took a little walk"*. While Gene Kelly was singin' and dancin' in the rain, Nelstone's Hawaiians sang of a boy playing in the rain who got stabbed by a gypsy. Elsewhere, a frog marries a mouse, railroad men turn into vampires, a coo-coo bird hollers only on the fourth of July, a wife tries to convince her husband that the guy in her bed is really a head of cabbage, and a woman meets the devil and *"picks up a hatchet and splits out his brains"*. Even weirder than the stories these songs related, though, were the voices that told them. The singers were what the stuff of rural myth must have sounded like: snake oil salesmen, Miles Standish, Jesse James, witches being led to the gallows in Salem, Paul Bunyan and Nellie Bly. Some sounded like dying roosters, others like plucky Civil War veterans, and still others like Cotton Mather delivering a sermon. Dock Boggs, as Greil Marcus memorably described him, "sounded as if his bones were coming through his skin every time he opened his mouth".

The *Anthology* was the sound of a history coming home to roost that people were deliberately trying to ignore or desperately trying to forget. In a time of rampant racism, anti-Semitism, anti-Catholicism and anti-intellectualism, the *Anthology* didn't tell you who was black or white. Featuring crackers singing archetypal African-American songs, while seguing immediately from the most severe high-collar primness to the most physical, raspy Pentecostal shouting, it was the embodiment of the democracy that the GIs had fought so hard to preserve. With America entering its second most prosperous era, TV, suburbanisation and highway construction were leading the country headlong into a new kind of modernity that threatened to lay waste to everything in its path. The *Anthology* stood in direct defiance: it not only sounded like it came from a different century, but the songs spoke of the human cost of new technology and chastised the hubris that caused train and boat crashes. It wasn't just coincidence that Smith included two John Henry songs (plus another two on *Volume 4*, which went undiscovered for half a century).

In the late 90s, America entered its most prosperous period, largely on the back of the growth of a new technology that was again threatening to lay waste to everything in its path. Although the *Anthology* had always been available through the Smithsonian Institute, who have acted as custodians of the Folkways catalogue since 1987, the six CD box set reissue in 1997 was nothing short of an event, moving crazy units and attracting attention from the unlikeliest of quarters. In the years following capitalism's ultimate triumph over communism, at the 'end of history', as Francis Fukuyama had it, the relentless conformity might have been without an obvious, frightening, overarching political component, but the climate wasn't all that dissimilar from 1952: the Cold War had ended only a decade before; there was a stultifying political consensus; America was enjoying unprecedented economic growth on the back of Europe being unable to respond to technological developments; Bill Clinton saved his political hide by stretching the truth and by making solemn speeches; it was the age of the combat trouser, or if you were really pushing the boat out, the cargo trouser; McDonald's; Hitler youth boy bands; when what was good for Microsoft was good for the country.

Yet here was that dead thing, history, rearing its proudly ugly head, proving that the digital prophets' victory over materiality and dirt and grit and impurity wasn't as complete as they pretended. The reissue of the *Anthology* was only the tip of the iceberg. In the mid-90s, Rounder began reissuing the entire collection of recordings made by folklorist Alan Lomax; Yazoo Records released *Anthology*-style collections like *The Secret Museum Of Mankind*, *The Cornshucker's Frolic* and *My Rough And Rowdy Ways*; Revenant cornered the market on 'American primitive music'; the French Frémeaux & Associés label issued collections of folk, Country, gospel, jazz, Western swing and proto-rock 'n' roll records from the 20s; and the Austrian Document label busily attempted to fulfil its mandate of reissuing every extant pre-World War Two 'race' recording.

The reasons for the resurgence of interest in 'primitive' music are numerous and obvious: an 'underground' consisting of nothing but well-scrubbed media careerists in 90s snowboarding wear; the absence of a really interesting, engaging rock record in a good seven or eight years; HipHop being run by bloated megalomaniacs who, believing their own raps, were destined to become tax exiles holding pool parties with members of Deep Purple; Country music being about as Country as a Japanese tourist in a ten-gallon Stetson and snakeskin boots; ten-plus years of digital perfection. Where the 'glitch' movement is about making music out of the stuff digital technology leaves behind, the resurgence in 'primitive' music tries to apprehend the qualities totally absent in digital technology. Listen to something like Andrew and Jim Baxter's "Georgia Stomp" from *Volume 2* of the *Anthology* and it sounds like an old wind-up car, chugging and wheezing, spitting out fumes, barely making it to the top of the hill before collapsing in exhaustion, hubcaps rolling this way and that. Of course, it's not just sequencers and synthesizers that lack this quality. While such *Anthology* stars as Bascom Lamar Lunsford and Buell Kazee (both gentrified scholars of folksong) were undeniably self-conscious in their performances, in an age dominated by media-savvy, hyper-self-aware urban smartasses, the unadulterated power of Blind Willie Johnson, the unashamed artlessness of The Bently Boys and the 'life sucks and then you die' crankiness of The Carter Family are about the most beautiful sounds imaginable.

The reissue of the *Anthology* did more than preserve these archaic voices in chrome disc vitrines. Since the 60s, the *Anthology* had been cloaked in the iconography of the folk revival movement, both literally and figuratively. For more than 30 years, the cover of the *Anthology* was a Ben Shahn photo of an itinerant farmer in perfect Works Progress Administration (WPA) house style: shabby denim overalls, hollow eyes, a face battered by weather, the stylised romance of poverty of American socialist realism versus the heroic peasant of Stalinist socialist realism. The CD reissue reinstated the cover that Smith had originally designed: an engraving of the 'celestial monochord' being tuned by the hand of God, which Smith had found in a book on mysticism by the Elizabethan intellectual Robert Fludd. Perhaps this was crucial in the reissue's success: gone was the link to the naive, singleminded, namby-pamby if well-intentioned protest of the late 50s/early 60s folk movement; the quirkiness and mystery of Smith's original work had been restored.

The monochord was supposedly invented by Pythagoras, and in its simplicity (it's just a string attached to a resonating box) it represented the harmony of the universe, imagery which connected to Smith's interest in the music of the spheres. When asked about the cover by New Lost City Rambler John Cohen in 1968, Smith replied, "The type of thinking that I applied to records, I still apply to other things, like Seminole patchwork or to Ukrainian Easter eggs. The whole purpose is to have some kind of a series of things. Information as drawing and graphic designs can be located more quickly than it can be in books... It's like flipping quickly through. It's a way of programming the mind, like a punchcard of a sort. Being as it goes through the vision, it is more immediately assimilated than if you listen to a two minute record."

Even stranger than the cover, though, was the accompanying booklet. Resembling a handbill from the 1800s, it was a collage of old record catalogue reproductions, stock images from ancient printing presses, newspaper headline summaries of the songs, text that looked like it came off of a tickertape newswire. In the notes, there is no mention of the artist or performance whatsoever; his only interest is the patterns and the similarities to other music. As Greil Marcus says of the original booklet, "Visually it was dominated by a queer schema: heavy, black, oversized numbers, marking each of the 84 selections as if their placement altogether superseded their content."

Indeed, as Smith told Cohen, "Being as my essential interest in music was the patterning that occurred in it – intuition or taste only being a guide to directions where this patterning might occur – it was just as well to collect some other object. I'm sure that if you collect sufficient patchwork quilts from the same people who made the records, like Uncle Dave Macon or Sara Carter's houses, you could figure out just about anything you can from the music. Everything could be figured out regarding their judgment in relation to certain intellectual processes. Like certain things sound good to a person in music, certain things look good to the eye. And at some level those two things are interconnected."

On the surface, Smith's obsession with patterns has a resemblance to the empirical approach of the gestalt psychiatrists. However, with his connections to Aleister Crowley, use of imagery from Robert Fludd (as Erik Davis notes, Fludd was a mystic who attempted to unite with divinity through the art of memory), the "programming the mind" metaphor, setting one of his films in Zürich and his collections of tarot cards, Smith was more reminiscent of a rather different form of psychoanalysis – that of Carl Jung. As a student of the Kabbala, Smith certainly attached a special significance to the act of listening. Since anthropomorphism and 'graven images' of God were strictly forbidden in the Torah, it is only the word (the voice) of God that reveals itself. Thus, hearing becomes the most holy of perceptions. Nevertheless, visual imagery is unavoidable when trying to apprehend the ineffable. Instead of the old cliche of a 'photograph in sound', Smith approached these records almost as 'mandalas in sound'. Sanskrit for 'circle', a mandala for Jung was a geometrical diagram filled with shapes and symbols that represented a picture of the whole self "in conditions of psychic dissociation or disorientation". Crucial to the symbology of the mandala is the squaring of the circle. "The quaternity of the One", as Jung called it, had numerous resonances for a Kabbalist and alchemist like Smith, recalling both the Tetragrammaton (the four letter word that represents the totality of the world and God, which is so powerful that Jews are not allowed to write it down) and the quadratura circuli (the alchemical representation of the four elements).

The *Anthology* was divided into three colour-coded sets which represented three elements: air, fire and water. *Volume 4*, which was first issued by the Revenant label in 2000, represents the missing element, earth. *Volume 3* (air) ends with Henry Thomas's "Fishing Blues", a song of deceptively simple joy, ostensibly about a man sitting on the banks of a river, with his trouser legs rolled up, dipping his toes in the water and losing himself by dipping his rod in the water. It may be an erotic image, but the song is devoid of the sexual charge blues of this type usually have (Jimi Hendrix's "Catfish Blues", for example). Instead, the imagery is similar to the way Walt Whitman or Mark Twain imbued acts of simple pleasure with mythical potency. Also, "Fishing Blues" becomes Smith's vision of America in miniature through its almost epic figurative language (*"Went up the hill at 12 o'clock"*), quotations of minstrelsy like "Shortnin' Bread" and the antique, but timeless, sound of the quills (panpipes made of sugar cane). *Volume 4* begins with The Memphis Jug Band's "Memphis Shakedown", an instrumental that, with its hokey jug bassline and spoken interjection, continues the archaic yet timeless quality of the panpipes in "Fishing Blues". But, as blues archivist Dick Spottswood has pointed out, "Memphis Shakedown" is also a version of a ragtime composition, a reflection of a jazz recording, not dissimilar from the Western swing records that were beginning to gain prominence at the time of the recording (1934), and a blending of hillbilly fiddle breakdowns with rhythms from the Shake, an African-American dance craze of the time.

The big mystery of *Volume 4* is why this microcosm of defiantly American music is followed immediately by Bradley Kincaid's genial reading of "Dog And Gun (An Old English Ballad)". The song may tell the tale of a squire and a lady, but the story and action is pure American frontier. After becoming smitten with a lowly dairy farmer, the wealthy lady jilts the squire and goes hunting in the woods with "Dog And Gun" to meet the farmer. Recalling such Wild West characters as Shotgun Annie and Belle Star, the lady is far too assertive to have been a chaste victim so typical of British folk balladry. Instead, she is more like John Henry's wife who takes over when that great American archetype is killed by his hammer and *"drives steel like a man"*. Likewise, the social mobility the song speaks of was an impossibility in 'Old English' society.

The key phrase of "Dog And Gun" is the penultimate line, *"Now that I have him so close in my snare"*, which sets us up for the tales of entrapment, betrayal, humiliation, loneliness and punishment which follow. However, the songs on *Volume 4* are nowhere near as ghostly as those on the first three volumes. The vast majority of songs on *Volume 4* were recorded during the Depression, a fact which gives that collection a different dimension. *Volume 4* is less about history and continuity, and more about finding mechanisms to cope with the brutal present. JE Mainer's Mountaineers treat the John Henry myth as a hoedown: 'this happened to John Henry, but it ain't gonna happen to me'. This is only emphasised by Wade Mainer's salacious aside about John Henry's wife Polly Ann after seeing her driving steel like a man: *"Some woman, boy."* (Contrast this with The Williamson Brothers & Curry's "John Henry" on *Volume 1*, which treats Henry as a hero, and Mississippi John Hurt's "Spike Driver Blues" on *Volume 3*, in which the narrator unconvincingly claims that the hammer won't kill him.) Similarly, The Monroe Brothers' "Nine Pound Hammer Is Too Heavy" is all about escapism, as the song's narrator goes into the hills to *"see [his] darlin'"* and he ain't comin' back. Meanwhile, Jesse James's version of the Casey Jones saga is simultaneously barrelhouse rowdiness, WC Fields comic cynicism and hard-bitten anger.

Although a surprising number of the songs on a volume supposedly linked with 'earth' concern heaven, the performances keep them firmly rooted on terra firma. As writer David Keenan intimated in a review of *Volume 4*, on "Hello Stranger" and "No Depression In Heaven", The Carter Family sounds like a choir of George Romero zombies. Starker than the grimmest Dark Ages woodcarving, these songs present a vision of release from this mortal coil so unappealing that it gives atheism a good name. (Smith claims that the first time he took peyote was outside Sara Carter's trailer park – on this evidence, an act of masochism I can only to compare to an acquaintance of mine who dropped acid and went to see the Pope at the Pontiac Silverdome.) Roosevelt Graves & Brother sound more joyous about meeting their maker on "I'll Be Rested (When The Roll Is Called)", but the recording, with its tambourine that sounds like the chains of a work gang rattling and Graves's primordial frog moan, is the most alluvial track here.

Sister Clara Hudmon (better known as The Georgia Peach) was probably the first singer to move away from the old hymns to the new gospel style embodied by the compositions of Thomas Dorsey and Charles Tindley. Her "Stand By Me" is marked by her scarred but studied delivery, jazzy arrangement and the city slicker interjections by the choir which inaugurated a new era for African-American religious music. Unlike the wretched fatalism of the spirituals and hymns which sound so archaic as to be otherworldly, "Stand By Me" could only have been more earthly if it was accompanied by the Cotton Club dancers. The introduction to the original *Anthology* said that *Volumes 4, 5* and *6* would examine the rhythmic changes of music from 1890-1950. Seen in that light, the inclusion of "Stand By Me" and the Cajun bust-ups that recall Western swing makes perfect sense. Smith also understood that more than just the rhythm was changing during this period. Coming right after the religious material, Memphis Minnie's tribute to Joe Louis, "He's In The Ring (Doing The Same Old Thing)", and Minnie Wallace's "The Cockeyed World" (a song about Mussolini invading Ethiopia) reveal Smith's grasp of the shift taking place in black culture. Linking them with songs about redemption and deliverance, Smith attempted to reveal the huge importance of these symbolic struggles to African-Americans.

While there are still plenty of stylistic similarities between black and white performers, there's no longer a sense of unity, of everything belonging together. The imagery in Memphis Minnie's and Minnie Wallace's songs suggests a growing black consciousness that would soon manifest itself more clearly in the music. As John Fahey says in his sleevenotes: "Alienation. That is what *Volume 4* of *The Harry Smith Anthology* is all about." Despite many appearances to the contrary,

Volume 4 is where Smith attempted to cast a magickal spell on Joe McCarthy and his cronies, and get all alchemical by trying to turn ancient, ignored music into social upheaval, by trying to "see the world change by music".

II

It is hard to imagine, after 50 years of frenzied social transformation, what must have been a typical reaction to the Harry Smith *Anthology* upon its initial release in 1952. Every bit as disorientating as the sound of that collection's unearthly music would have been its presentation: the cover label of each of the set's three original volumes (each containing two LPs) incorporated an antique engraving of a single-stringed instrument being tuned by a hand reaching down from the heavens, with an indistinct caption in Latin. Similarly, the weirdly arranged accompanying booklet included cryptic quotations from persons named Rudolf Steiner, Robert Fludd and Aleister Crowley.

Aside from the relative handful of persons who were interested in folk music and well versed in occult history, it is unlikely that this image or these names would have been familiar to Americans of that era; and it is probably a reflection of the *Anthology*'s lack of precedent – as well as of Folkways Records founder Moses Asch's instinctive respect for its compiler's peculiar genius – that such an eccentric presentation was permitted. As Smith himself observed in 1968, "The whole *Anthology* was a collage. I thought of it as an art object... I felt social changes would result from it."

And so they did. Although the *Anthology* may not have lived up to the dizzying expectations of its creator, who had aimed for an entire transmutation of society, it did plant the seeds of much of what was to follow, including you. The cover image, an allegorical diagram illustrating the hierarchical relation of form to matter by analogy to the harmonic intervals along a fretboard, was taken from the first volume of the *History Of The Macrocosm And The Microcosm* by Robert Fludd (1574-1637), the most influential populariser of Neoplatonic and Rosicrucian ideas in Renaissance England. This picture of the 'divine monochord' embodied the *Anthology* in a musically apt and visually attractive image, and suggested something of the project's larger aims to the thoughtful observer; nonetheless, in 1966, against Smith's wishes, the *Anthology*'s cover was altered to display a grim photograph of a Depression-era farmer, this being presumably more acceptable as a comprehensible – if ultimately trite and shortsighted – emblem of the social context and aims of 'folk music'. This switch should be seen in the bitter context of Bob Dylan's concurrent move away from the agenda of politically manipulative topical folksong into realms of the individual spirit, a schism that presaged the disagreements between psychedelic anarcho-decadents, such as the Diggers and Yippies, and more conventional political and social activists, which came to an unproductive head in 1968. In retrospect, the failure of the social revolution of 1964-68 can be seen in part as a reflection of the impossibility of translating individual illumination into the sort of didactic commercial context that passes for benevolence in some quarters.

Only with the lavishly packaged reissue of the *Anthology* on CD by Smithsonian Folkways in 1997 was Smith's original conception accorded the publicity it warrants, a process that continued with Revenant's version of the long-rumoured *Volume 4*. It is one of the characteristic ironies of cultural history that Smith's cosmic-minded idealism today seems a good deal more convincing as a strategy for bettering the world than do the leaden cliches of his adversaries; and a more widespread understanding of the esoteric underpinnings of Smith's work may likewise serve a deeper purpose than simple promotion of yet another recording.

Occult pursuits seem to have run in Smith's family: his paternal great-grandfather, John Corson Smith, was a highly prominent Freemason in Illinois. Both of Smith's parents were reportedly interested in Theosophy, that turbid blend of balderdash and erudition that sprang from the brow of Helena P Blavatsky (1831-91), one of the most learned women of the 19th century. Smith's birth in 1923 and upbringing in the then-remote Pacific Northwest region of the United States gave him a fortunate vantage on the cultural traditions of the area's aboriginal inhabitants, which led to a natural interest in anthropology, a field then dominated in the United States by the work of Franz Boas (1858-1942), a German-Jewish emigré who is credited with having overthrown the overtly racialist regimen of earlier writers in the field. Indeed, a Boasian profession of the equality – or even the equivalence – of all races and cultures, and a firm resistance to ethnocentric standards of comparison, are distinctive tendencies throughout Smith's career. He had the intellectual scope and taste to study and appreciate every conceivable human culture, and to respect them as they were.

By all accounts the 'record' component of what Smith was to term his 'book and record mania' began while he was an anthropology undergraduate at the University of Washington during World War Two. Supplementing his income by mounting guns in the nosecones of Boeing aircraft (a task for which he was unhappily suited by a rickets-induced childhood curvature of the spine), Smith availed himself of the centralised collection of records for wartime shellac recycling to amass the beginnings of his wide-ranging collection of the world's music.

The collecting behaviour continued and "became like a problem" when Smith relocated to Berkeley after the war. It was here that his film making began in earnest, with hand-painted films that manifested the shifts in consciousness he experienced with various drugs. At this time Smith was exposed to the experimental cinema of the day through the Art In Cinema series of screenings curated by Frank and Jack Stauffacher. Smith experienced the 'non-objective' animations of film maker Oskar Fischinger (1900-67), whose mystical aesthetic derived from the same tradition as that of Alexander Scriabin or Nicholas Roerich.

It is difficult to conceive of Smith's early esoteric career without reference to the works of Manly P Hall (1901-90), an astonishingly prolific populariser of the occult whose magnum opus, *An Encyclopedic Outline Of Masonic, Hermetic, Qabbalistic, And Rosicrucian Symbolical Philosophy* (aka *The Secret Teachings Of All Ages*) was first published in 1928 in a plywood-slipcased folio deluxe edition designed by Hearst choreboy John Henry Nash that took the nascent California flake scene, as well as the fancier Masonic lodges nationwide, by storm. Hall's gigolo-like appearance and oratorical facility, which earned him the fealty of legions of widows raised in the afterglow of the great spiritualist and theosophical outcroppings of the 19th century, have tended to camouflage a mind that was truly adept at synthesizing the most disparate and abstruse crannies of lore into an occasionally bland but monumental whole.

The Secret Teachings – which remains in print as the most comprehensive survey of its kind ever attempted – includes a large volume of curious and quaint colour plates by artist J Augustus Knapp, who had earlier illustrated the proto-psychedelic allegory *Etidorhpa* (1897) by Masonic pharmacist John Uri Lloyd (a work that includes perhaps the earliest description of psychedelic mushroom use by a European, as well as depictions of a being that looks disturbingly like images of alien 'greys' drawn 60 years later). According to film maker and fellow cannabis enthusiast Jordan Belson, the young Harry Smith was profoundly tickled by the oddly naive depictions of demons, elementals and various other nonhuman entities in Hall's work, and had even conceptualised an animated film set in the various allegorical worlds Knapp visualised. Sadly, this project never received the funding it so richly deserved, and remains a tantalising Might Have Been beside the groaning accumulation of stultifying abstract expressionist works subsidised by many a departed Maecenas.

Another crucial influence – who was to approach at times the status of an obsession for Smith – was Aleister Crowley (1875-1947), the notorious British occultist who managed to combine one of the most penetrating and eloquent intellects of his age with a flair for scandal and ambience of demonality, thereby effectively relegating himself to the lunatic fringe for decades (while Crowley's posthumous reputation has steadily improved, his works remain well off the academic map, and those of his successors such as the fascinating CF Russell (1897-1987) are almost entirely unknown). Exactly when Smith's obsession with Crowley began remains a point of contention – he occasionally claimed to be Crowley's love child – but it unquestionably happened at a time when the notoriety of the self-styled 'Beast 666' had taken a post-mortem dip, and when most of his works were only available to those few who sought them out in their lavish original editions or as study materials distributed by groups of Crowley acolytes.

Crowley's work was in some areas an extension of the career of SL MacGregor Mathers (1854-1918), the leading figure of the Hermetic Order of the Golden Dawn, the most extensively scrutinised occult organisation of modern times, whose distinguished membership included William Butler Yeats (described by Crowley as "a lank dishevelled demonologist who might have taken more pains with his personal appearance without incurring the reproach of dandyism"). Mathers used his powerful intellect to combine elements of many esoteric traditions; the Golden Dawn, along with the Theosophical Society, set the pattern for all subsequent Western occult groups.

Smith moved to New York City around 1951: immediately upon his arrival, he put on a pair of shoes "that were supposed to have come from the head of the Rosicrucians of Belgium". These had been supplied by his friend George Andrews, author of the long-suppressed *Drugs And Magic*. Thus shod, Smith ambled directly to the apartment of Lionel Ziprin, a legendary poet, artist, occultist and eccentric, beside whose intricately tangled biography Smith's own pursuits appear practically Apollonian. Ziprin encouraged Smith's interest in Aleister Crowley and the then-exotic doctrines and visual culture of Tibetan Buddhism, as expounded in the somewhat sentimentalised presentations of early populariser WA Evans-Wentz (as the late Art Kleps observed: "Evans-Wentz could not think, a failing which seems almost sublime in a person of such scholarly attainment and mental industry"). Ziprin also shared with Smith a fearless commitment to the direct experience of mind-altering drugs, and, most importantly, functioned as his guide into the traditions of the Hebrew Kabbala.

Of all the esoteric traditions, the Kabbala seems both the most historically suggestive and the most resistant to historical modes of scrutiny; it may indeed be the most paradoxical and treacherous domain of the occult. Though it has left indelible traces as the source of much or most of what we think of as 'magic' – especially in the realm of theurgy, or the practice of summoning and dealing with discarnate entities – it continues to elude empirical study, being above all an experiential science.

Ziprin facilitated Smith's direct participation in the Kabbala by introducing him to his grandfather, the Rabbi Naftali Zvi Margolies Abulafia. Although linguistic difficulties prevented Smith and Rabbi Abulafia from engaging in direct conversation, they had enough of a personal affinity that Smith was inspired to spend several years recording the rabbi performing a massive body of unaccompanied vocal songs and recitations of a Kabbalistic nature. (These recordings were eventually assembled around 1955 into a mindblowing 15-record set that was pressed in a run of 1000 copies. For years the discs, never distributed, languished in the basement of a Bronx housing project from which they eventually vanished. A rare surviving set in Ziprin's possession awaits remastering and release.)

The mid-50s also saw Smith's development of the distinctive style of collage animation for which he is best known. This allowed for the combination of occult themes from existing visual and aural traditions into esoterically synaesthetic, frequently perverse combinations (the film maker summarised one as "An exposition of Buddhism and the Kabbala in the form of a collage"). The principal visual and thematic preoccupation of this period was alchemy, especially as depicted in the great illustrated works of the early 17th century, such as Michael Maier's *Atalanta Fugiens* (1618), which combines artfully bizarre engravings, emblematic verse and musical compositions in what may be the first 'multimedia' book. Another major inspiration in this field was John Dee (1527-1608), the Elizabethan astrologer and scientist whose whacked-out communications with discarnate beings emblematise the still untapped potential of paranormal investigations when pursued by those at the frontiers of human knowledge.

Smith's only equal as an occultist film maker was Kenneth Anger, whose surviving films, collected to form the *Magick Lantern Cycle*, manifest the Magian counterpart to Smith's Faustian schtick. Well known as an acolyte of Aleister Crowley and as an occult mentor of Mick Jagger, Jimmy Page and Manson Family associate Bobby Beausoleil (whose offing of a nebbish mescaline dealer inadvertently inaugurated the Family's 1969 spree of butchery), Anger fused an over-the-top visual lushness redolent of the most decadent aspects of the silver screen's golden age with an over-the-top ritual elaborateness redolent of the most decadent aspects of the occult tradition, to create an over-the-top cinema redolent of decadence. He also wrote that notorious compendium of celebrity malfeasance, *Hollywood Babylon*, which was first published in France in 1959 and only officially permitted to be published in English in 1975. Anger's best known film, *Scorpio Rising* (1963), expresses a uniquely personal and creative version of the pop art sensibility of the times, and also enjoys the dubious distinction of being the ur-text of music video.

Both Smith and Anger have characterised their film work as an extension of magical practices (experimental film maker Stan Brakhage has described how Smith kept a beaker of his own semen in the projection booth for some occult purpose), and both have interestingly spoken of motion pictures as an unfortunate influence upon mankind. Smith in particular manifested a violent conflict between creative and destructive impulses, and not infrequently destroyed his own work as well as rare and valuable books and artefacts in fits of uncontrollable rage. Certainly the contrast between Smith's pacific ideals and his often notoriously obnoxious behaviour raises questions about the soundness of his convictions, though like a very select company of contemporary artists (Philip K Dick comes to mind), Smith seems to extend beyond the range of classification.

Smith's collage technique reached its pinnacle in *Film No 13 (Oz)* (c 1962), a 35mm widescreen transformation of L Frank Baum's story *The Wonderful Wizard Of Oz* (as visualised by its brilliant original illustrator, WW Denslow) into a fantastical landscape that included elements from Tibetan art, the work of Hieronymus Bosch and the schematic natural-science prints of Ernst Haeckel. This film, whose substantial financial backing fell apart midway through production, survives only in the form of camera tests and one sample sequence; like its less lavish predecessors, it masterfully combines elements of widely divergent cultural traditions into a visionary fusion unencumbered by banality.

The *Oz* debacle was followed by an even greater tragedy when an unpaid landlord discarded the contents of Smith's apartment – including the majority of his artwork – while the artist was away. This reportedly led Smith to develop an increased esteem for the effects of alcohol, which would be one of the defining characteristics of his subsequent life. This lifestyle choice was extensively explored during a 1964 residency among the Kiowa Native American people around Anadarko, Oklahoma, whom Smith recorded for the Ethnic Folkways LP set *The Kiowa Peyote Meeting*, which was not released until 1973.

After his return from Oklahoma, Smith began a long term residency at the notorious Chelsea Hotel in New York. As a mentor to younger artists, including Patti Smith and Robert Mapplethorpe, Smith became well known in New York's bohemian circles as "the Paracelsus of the Chelsea Hotel". Although there is some anecdotal evidence that the freewheeling ethos of the time limited his artistic output (when not endangering his existence outright), Smith's later film work – including his self-proclaimed magnum opus, *Film No 18 (Mahagonny)* (c 1968-80), a four-screen epic that has been exhibited in a pricey restoration of questionable accuracy at sterile, plutocratic museums of the sort Smith rightfully loathed – combined animation with live-action sequences according to a complex quasi-palindromic shot arrangement. A number of interviews conducted during this era (roughly 1965-83) reveal a brilliant intellect in varying states of amphetamine-driven adumbration.

Smith lived until the end of 1991, saved from street-dwelling dereliction only through the concern of poet Allen Ginsberg and a few wealthy patrons. Although he received an honorary Grammy Award in 1991 for his pioneering assembly of the *Anthology*, it was only after his death that the widespread rediscovery of his work began, assisted by the tireless efforts of a few devoted enthusiasts such as Paola Igliori, who was alone with Smith when he died and whose freewheeling book and film *American Magus* vividly evoke his balls-out freakishness.

Today Smith's material and intellectual legacy is more secure than could have been imagined at the time of his passing, though the very widespread appeal of much of his work has made it easy prey for that dire vacancy of spirit to which 'intellectual property' is a more meaningful concept than 'intellectual exchange'. Fortunately, Smith's work comes from and speaks to a deeper level of experience, before which such hungry ghosts evaporate as at the rising of the sun, and to which any well-meaning attempt at 'contextualisation' can only gesture with the forefinger of one hand, the other pressed to the lips in a token of eternal silence.

THE SOLAR MYTH APPROACH

THE LIVE SPACE RITUAL: SUN RA, STOCKHAUSEN, P-FUNK, HAWKWIND

BY KEN HOLLINGS

'Reality' is always plural and mutable.
Robert Anton Wilson

SCIENCE UNLIMITED

"Welcome, traveller!" A hearty masculine voice offers greetings from
long ago. "Direct from the Seattle World's Fair comes Art Mineo with the
sounds of man in space; an exciting, truly out-of-this-world tour that
takes you across vast frontiers, straight into the heart of the future."
Welcome to Science Unlimited, circa 1962. Arriving from downtown
Seattle on the first urban monorail system, you head for the 'World Of
Tomorrow' pavilion, where a globe-shaped, transparent 'Bubbleator' will
take you and 149 fellow passengers on a 20 minute journey into the
next century. A guide wearing a silver jumpsuit sits at the centre of the
huge plastic ball, giving you the technical lowdown on things to come.
"Your final destination," the booming voice explains, "is the Boeing
Spacearium, where you'll thrill to a simulated flight through outer space.
See Mars, Jupiter and Venus flash by in glowing colour! Travel through
amazing three-dimensional galaxies!" Kennedy is alive and in the White
House, US hardware is now orbiting the Earth just as effectively as its
Soviet counterpart, and UFO sightings among the American public have
hit an all-time low. But, damn, this music sure is gloomy.

Originally written in 1951 but not recorded until 1959, Attilio 'Art'
Mineo's *Man In Space With Sounds* is a strange mix of orchestral
sounds and electroacoustic effects that conjures up images of menacing
Martian invaders rather than fun-filled lunar vacations. Strongly
reminiscent of the low-budget textures and tones to be found in the work
of Ronald Stein and Albert Glasser, who both scored dozens of science
fiction and horror flicks for American International, *Man In Space With
Sounds* indicates the extent to which projects such as the Seattle State
World's Fair required a densely-coloured soundtrack precisely because
they had become movies. The emphasis placed upon speed, mobility
and spectacle required that visitors be transported to a drive-in future
capable of defining itself in the most sensational terms.

Progress, as Nietszche observed in *The Anti-Christ*, is a modern
concept and therefore false. In 1962, the future meant outer space,

which was still inhabited by the monstrous, brooding terrors of the 1950s. However, for two of the most advanced musical minds on the planet – Sun Ra and Karlheinz Stockhausen – it had become a complex, living, glittering entity. By 1944, Sun Ra was already lecturing his musicians on space travel, rocketry and the possibilities of electrically produced sounds, while Stockhausen was describing compositions as "star music" as early as 1952. At the start of the 1960s, both were using electronics to connect their audiences with the future, in other words, with space – which is also the past, when measured in light-years. Elements of Wernher von Braun's three-stage Saturn V rocket, which took American astronauts to the Moon, were also found inscribed in an ancient Egyptian stone carving depicting the god Osiris's 'Ladder to Heaven'. It was from Huntsville, Alabama, where von Braun had been building rockets for the United States government since 1950, that Sun Ra experienced his first "transmolecularization" to the planet Saturn. That was back in 1936, way before the US space programme began linking gods, planets and rockets together.

Stockhausen once defined intuition as "everything that's transferred from the intelligence of the universe to the human spirit". The past and future are linked spiritually. Consider the vast distances covered in the titles which Sun Ra chose for his compositions: "Starships And Solar Boats", "Atlantis", "Friendly Galaxy", "Pyramids" and "As Spaceships Approach". Or Stockhausen's use in 1955 of a child's voice to declaim an Old Testament text, taken from the Book Of Daniel, as part of *Gesang Der Jünglinge*, the first electronic piece to explore the possibilities of five-channel stereophonic playback, projecting sounds out into space and setting them in motion. Set against the panorama of such possibilities, the World's Fair offers only the briefest moment of summation. Stereophony, like the arrangement and design of concert halls, exhibition centres or movie screens, is a small historical event. Something more in the nature of ritual is required to access the creative, organising principle behind Stockhausen's notion of intuition.

Live and immediate, space rituals were not only intended to add a cosmic dimension to humanity, but also present the cosmos on a human scale. Sun Ra and his Galactic Research Arkestra created elaborate "cosmo dramas" involving music, dance, costumes and poetry.

Stockhausen has spoken of his ambitious, unfinished opera cycle *Licht* as "the first example of a theatre that goes beyond the thinkable". But be warned: questions of proportion, taste and perception become meaningless at this point. The minute certainties of modern science quickly disappear on the journey from outer to inner space. Are we wandering through a living universe, charged with deep significance and profound meaning, or simply the gaudy interior of some cheap and cheerful fun house located in the seedy confines of a tattered amusement park? The choice, as always, is yours.

THE MYTH SCIENCE APPROACH

Brightly coloured waves of dyed silks undulate among the percussionists and musicians, while a procession of paintings showing monsters and scenes from life in Ancient Egypt is taking place. The baritone sax player wants to tell the audience about his home planet: Saturn. On stage there are performers dressed as pharaohs and space explorers, or richly attired in the antique futuristic styles favoured by the *Buck Rogers* and *Flash Gordon* movie serials of the 1930s. From the far reaches of time to the furthest interstellar depths, Sun Ra created a complex stage ritual enacted by living hieroglyphs. Although the contents would change and evolve over the years, the broad mythological sweep remained constant: there are other worlds they have not told you about. You may not even be from around here anyway.

Enlightenment alters your relationship with the past. In 1969, American astronaut Buzz Aldrin carried a Masonic flag with him on his journey to the Moon. The names, places and dates involved in the assassination of President Kennedy have been reconfigured by conspiracy theorists to conjure up an audacious sacrificial rite performed by high-ranking Masons in preparation for that first landing. History, as always, is whatever you can get away with. In 1966, somewhere between those two huge events, Sun Ra and The Arkestra supplied the live music accompaniment to *A Black Mass*, Amiri Baraka's mordantly poetic account of how the white race came into being.

Based on the teachings of the Honorable Elijah Muhammad, founder of the Nation of Islam, *A Black Mass* presents the black magician

Jacoub, consumed by aesthetic and intellectual pride, dreamily turning loose his pale and leprous creation, the white monkey beast, to wreak havoc upon the world. The play, in which actors and musicians were brought together in painful ceremony, gave public expression to a black hermetic tradition that has existed in America since the Revolution and founding of the first Black Masonic Lodges. From the creation of the Shriners (the quasi-Masonic spiritual movement known for its charitable work) in 1877 to Noble Drew Ali's Moorish Science Temple in the early years of the 20th century, an awareness of the ancient mysteries has been the keystone to acquiring a future identity. Knowledge transforms reality. Names have secret powers. For Sun Ra and Elijah Muhammad, they conferred both a history and a destiny.

Appearing on Alan Burke's brutal CBS TV talk show in 1967, Sun Ra was clear about his message: "Try and understand about the ancient Egyptians." At around the same time, occultist and underground film maker Harry Smith was circulating an English translation of *The Pale Fox*, an account written by two eminent French anthropologists, Marcel Griaule and Germaine Dieterlen, about their experiences with the Dogon tribe in sub-Saharan Africa. Originally published in France in 1965, it offered the first complete guide to the Dogon cosmology, which comprises unusually detailed knowledge of not only our own solar system but also the Sirius star system 8.7 light-years away. The Dogon priests first revealed their secrets to Griaule and Dieterlen in the form of sacred diagrams and myths, giving information on the orbit of Sirius B, a dwarf star which was only detected by powerful Western telescopes at the end of the 19th century. Harry Smith claimed a blood connection with the founder of a branch of American Freemasonry based upon the Knights Templar and had declared himself the illegitimate offspring of Aleister Crowley, Outer Head of the OTO, or Ordo Templi Orientis, in whose rites and practices Sirius plays an important part.

The translation was passed on, in manuscript form, to Robert KG Temple, Fellow of the Royal Astronomical Society, from whom it was later stolen by an unidentified American "associated with the CIA". Another more recent translation is now available. In 1976, Temple published *The Sirius Mystery*, in which he argued that Dogon sacred traditions recorded the arrival on Earth of aliens from the Sirius system 6500 years ago.

Furthermore, this advanced race of amphibious creatures passed their knowledge on to the inhabitants of predynastic Egypt, Sumeria, Mesopotamia and Babylon. Claiming its descent from the stars and the fertile prima materia of the Nile Delta, Sun Ra's cosmo-drama has been up and running ever since.

THE DESIRED EFFECT

Once upon a time called right now, the deep-space concept of specially designed Afronauts "capable of funkatizing galaxies" was first laid upon mankind via the expanded consciousness of Detroit composer, producer and arranger George Clinton. A sacred and forbidden knowledge, it had been secreted aeons ago among the secrets of the pyramids, where kings and pharaohs lay like sleeping beauties, awaiting the kiss that would release them to multiply in the images of the Chosen One: Dr Funkenstein. Clinton had spent his early years growing up in Washington amid Cold War atomic bomb scares and massive searchlights raking the night sky. "And in the daytime," he recalled, "you couldn't see the sky for rows and rows and rows of planes. I mean it literally had a top on it, all day every day." Clinton combined mad movie science and myth science into a dancefloor cosmology that made an open display of its secret codes and esoteric rites: an encrypted Black Mass acted out in plain sight for the Television Age.

Putting Whitey on the Moon had been a massive publicity triumph for the buzz-cut squares and Ivy Leaguers of Cape Kennedy: those who weren't afraid, as William Burroughs dryly noted, to say a little prayer during lift-off. The political and cultural revolutionaries of the 1960s couldn't even get close. Jack Parsons, a Cal Tech rocket scientist who was also a deeply committed member of the Agape Lodge of the OTO, corresponding extensively with Crowley and experimenting with drugs and sex magick, had blown himself to bloody chunks in a mysterious accident back in 1954. Wernher von Braun, on the other hand, a former colonel in the Waffen SS, knew the value of wearing a clean shirt and doing TV science shows for Walt Disney. If the future was space, then for people like George Clinton the sky still had a lid on it.

However, with Aleister Crowley appearing in the same row as

Stockhausen on the cover of The Beatles' psychedelic landmark, *Sgt Pepper's Lonely Hearts Club Band*, it was clear that sex, drugs and magic were to play an important part in the Aquarian Age. Crowley himself had presented a live ritual involving dancing, music and poetry, *The Rites Of Eleusis*, at the Caxton Hall, Westminster in 1910. The time had now come to crank up the amps. By the late 1960s, Clinton had hooked up with high-voltage Detroit rockers The MC5, The Amboy Dukes and The Stooges, incorporating into his main outfits, Parliament and Funkadelic, the group dynamics of a heavy rock act. It gave Clinton's sly cartoon universe an aggressive ritual edge. Early footage of Funkadelic in New York shows a member of the group near naked and painted up as Jacoub's white monkey beast, while Parliament's tales of extraterrestrial brothers declaring they had "returned to claim the pyramids" revealed that the main difference between Jacoub and Dr Funkenstein was one of attitude. "This boy was definitely out to lunch," George Clinton once remarked of Sun Ra, who shared a bill with The MC5 in 1969, "the same place I eat at."

Lifting a term first coined by veteran flying saucer contactée George Adamski, Parliament's groundbreaking 1975 release, *Mothership Connection*, "put niggers in places that you don't usually see 'em", as Clinton explained it. "And nobody had seen 'em on no spaceships! Once you seen 'em sittin' on a spaceship like it was a Cadillac, then it was funny, cool." The Mothership Connection was a space-age urban myth designed to navigate the street corner and the back alley as well the far-flung reaches of the galaxy. Clinton's Afronauts came with a definite gangster lean, just as he would later present Funkadelic as Cuban revolutionaries on rollerskates and Black Panthers toting Bop Guns. The flamboyant futurism of the Parliament/Funkadelic project was expressed through wild costumes that blended aliens with disco divas, pimps and pushers: fabulous creations of leopardskin, Mylar, velvet and Lurex. Taking such concepts to the stage, however, meant hardwiring into the surging mass mind let loose at rock concerts, what Motörhead mainman Lemmy had described during his early 70s Hawkwind days as "the growth of a collective consciousness". Hawkwind's Space Ritual had been an attempt to involve their audiences at this level through the integrated use of mime, dancing, lights, film and chemical smoke.

The desired effect is what you get. When Clinton used the proceeds from Parliament's US smash hit "Give Up The Funk (Tear The Roof Off The Sucker)", taken from the *Mothership Connection* LP, to finance their P-Funk Earth Tour in 1977, it would feature dazzling costumes, elaborate stage machinery including a working model of the Mothership, and a monster sound system supplied by Aerosmith.

SEVEN DAYS OF LIGHT

When Karlheinz Stockhausen read the manuscript of Temple's *Sirius Mystery*, which had still not yet been published, he was already hard at work on the multiple time-layers of his own composition, *Sirius*, which would later inform the super-formula for *Licht*, in which every detail of the music, libretto, action and gesture were to be fixed and notated. Stockhausen's statement that he had visited the star Sirius and trained as a musician there while composing *Sirius* has caused some confusion over the years, helping to obscure the far more interesting fact that both he and Temple were actively involved with the same star system over exactly the same period. "So there," Stockhausen has remarked of this strange phenomenon. "Find an answer."

Stockhausen had been sent the Temple manuscript by author Jill Purce, whose book *The Mystic Spiral* had already influenced the creation of his *Spiral* for soloist and shortwave radio back in 1968. At that time, human beings had yet to walk on the Moon, and Stockhausen was talking of a "space age music" in which familiar forms become isolated and subsequently transformed when set against the infinite expanse of the universe. "That space I have described," he observed, "is the space of a direct physical experience, and by going through this experience, we arrive at a new inner space." Stockhausen had heard at least one recording of Dogon music in 1969, after the realisation of his electronic works *Telemusik* and *Hymnen*, but without discovering any connection with Sirius. By 1981, however, he was listing the esoteric rites of the Dogon priests alongside the Catholic Mass, the Ramayana and Japanese Noh drama as rituals from which a new concept of live performance could be derived.

Sirius itself had been preceded by a series of clarinet pieces, such as

Der Kleine Harlekin (*The Little Harlequin*), in which movement, expression and costume are all determined and regulated by the final score. Shortly after completing *Hymnen*, Stockhausen wrote that "music in the post-war period was not an expression of human feeling, but a re-creation of cosmic order". The use of bright, almost fluorescent colours, arcane symbols and exaggerated mime in *Der Kleine Harlekin* can be interpreted as an extension of that principle into live performance, adding a strong mythic dimension to what occurs on stage. This reaches its apotheosis in the symbolic rituals contained within the super-formula for *Licht*, through which each of the characters not only has their own melodic figure, but they can also be represented simultaneously by a singer, an instrumentalist or a mime, allowing symbolic connections to be made between each specific element. *Licht*'s cyclic nature, together with its main division into the seven days of the week, reflects Stockhausen's observation that "periodicity and control is the principle of the universe on a large scale and free play is the principle of the universe on a smaller scale". These two levels, however, must remain inextricably linked.

In his revised edition of *The Sirius Mystery*, Robert Temple proposed that a close statistical comparison between Sirius B and our own Sun would reveal a correlation "so extraordinary and precise that it suggests whole avenues of research and offers the hope of absolute numerical expressions in the cosmos where none had been suspected". The universe, according to Temple, is capable of spontaneously ordering itself along specific mathematical constants and harmonic principles. "Superior beings," Sun Ra once observed, "definitely speak in other harmonic ways than the Earth way because they're talking something different, and you have chord against chord, melody against melody, and rhythm against rhythm; if you've got that, you're expressing something else."

DOREMI FASOL LATIDO

"The basic principle for the star-ship and the Space Ritual is based on the Pythagorean concept of sound," reveals the manual accompanying Hawkwind's live 'multimedia' Space Ritual performances, which they toured with in 1972-73. "Briefly, it conceived the Universe to be an immense monochord, with its single string stretched between absolute spirit and at its lowest end absolute matter. Along the string were positioned the planets of our solar system. Each of these spheres as it rushed through space was believed to sound a certain tone caused by its continuous displacement of the ether." Presented to coincide with the release of their 1972 *Doremi Fasol Latido* album, and preserved on the following year's live *Space Ritual* LP, the ritual had been designed to have specific effects upon its audience. The group members were to be positioned according to certain "planetary seals" marked out on the stage floor to invoke "spheres of influence", while the speakers and amplifiers, painted to represent the planets, were carefully located to initiate specific sound patterns.

The theme of the event concerned the dreams or fantasies of seven space explorers who, like Clinton's sleeping Afronauts, are in suspended animation. In contrast with Parliament's "Chocolate Milky Way", Hawkwind inhabited a much harsher experiential universe. "Space is a remorseless, senseless, impersonal fact," the manual affirms. "Space is the absence of time and matter." Poems by Bob Calvert and science fantasy novelist Michael Moorcock used in the Ritual, such as "The Awakening" and "The Black Corridor", emphasised the horrors unleashed upon a human consciousness confronted with the phenomenological vastness of space. There would be no friendly galaxies, no shared sense of humanity which had once inspired Lemmy to observe that audiences at Hawkwind performances "don't say 'me', they shout 'us'".

Outer space was violently transformed into the isolated and terrifying loneliness of inner space, squeezed up against the back of the skull after too many nights spent wired on bad speed. Crowley's strange Dionysian rites had worked too well. The space/time continuum had become dislocated, the senses sharply pulled out of focus. Calvert's lyrics for "Master Of The Universe", part of both the Space Ritual and *Doremi*, celebrate the frenetic supremacy of the isolated ego; celestial mechanics apprehended entirely in the first person. The harmonious arrangement of people and sounds to which the Space Ritual aspired was based upon a discrepancy: the relationships between each musical interval on the monochord and the planet it designates "do not", their manual points out, "coincide with the reality of their actual positions."

During the 1970s, the cosmos relocated itself to a Ladbroke Grove squat, its outer limits lying somewhere within the confines of the Camden Roundhouse, where the electronic oscillations of Dik Mik's audio generators plunged and rose and echoed over Hawkwind's urgent, repeated riffs. Moorcock's text for "Sonic Attack" calls for all bodies to be brought to immediate orgasm in the event of "imminent sonic destruction", while the lightshow, overlaying smoke, slides and film clips, recreates the blurring of consensual experience projected directly into the eyeball. Even Miss Stacia's dancing couldn't completely distract attention from the delirious jaw-grinding comedown of "Silver Machine", reputedly written by Lemmy and Dik Mik at the end of a four day drug binge. "The bigger the headache, the bigger the pill," as Parliament would later remark. Space, like a body in orgasm, had become a state of perpetual, euphoric crisis.

Meanwhile, during Parliament's own stage shows, the Mothership – upon whose wiring Philip Glass is rumoured to have worked – was brought roaring down to Earth via a bass-heavy vamp of "Swing Low, Sweet Chariot", like a Baptist pageant swimming in dry ice and stage lights. Drawing upon a tradition of celestial rapture embodied in such spirituals as "Ezek'el Saw The Wheel" and "This World Is Not My Home", from which Sun Ra had also derived chants for his cosmo dramas, the climax to Parliament's P-Funk Earth Tour pointed towards a space that remained deep, liberating and ecstatic. *"If you ain't gonna get it on,"* their audiences were encouraged to chant, *"take your dead ass home."* As Hawkwind went on to reveal, it is the business of the future to be dangerous.

LUCIFER'S DREAM

Events and people have the power to harmonize themselves into coincidences: a form of instantaneous communication by which connections are established across time and space. There is, for example, Stockhausen's *Helicopter String Quartet*, from *Mittwoch*, the fifth opera in the *Licht* series. An ambitious presentation in which a conventional string quartet is transported through the sky, high above the concert hall, by four helicopters, it's possible that this piece carries within it a hidden acknowledgement of one Arthur M Young of Philadelphia. It was Young, the author of *The Reflexive Universe* and *The Geometry Of Meaning*, who first drew Temple's attention to the Sirius mystery, sending him a copy of *The Pale Fox* in the same English translation then being passed around by Harry Smith. Young had another claim to fame. He was also responsible for inventing the Bell helicopter, the first ever to receive a commercial licence, back in 1947.

By such means does the local universe communicate with itself. In 1950, as the skies over America filled with rocket ships and flying saucers, the Urantia Foundation was set up in Chicago to distribute *The Urantia Book*, a vast 2097-page cosmic reinterpretation of the Bible, comprising 196 'papers' revealing the future history in store for the inhabitants of Urantia, more commonly known as planet Earth. The first 31 alone "depict the nature of Deity, the reality of Paradise, the organization and working of the central and superuniverses, the personalities of the grand universe, and the high destiny of evolutionary mortals". This particular series of revelations dates back to 1934, when it was "put into English by a commission of 24 spiritual administrators acting in accordance with a mandate issued by high deity authorities (the Ancients of Days), directing that they do this on Urantia". At the time, Stockhausen was still learning to play the piano in Altenberg, West Germany, while Sun Ra was on the road with Fess Watley's group, accompanied by a tapdancer and a male singer.

Explorations of other worlds, awaiting Sun Ra just a few months away in Huntsville, Alabama, began for both composers with the mathematical illusion known to the West as the well-tempered keyboard. The Music of the Spheres had been industry standard since the 17th century, capable of running through the entire spectrum of all 24 major and minor keys, but only because the Pythagorean purity of its original intervals had, with the exception of the octave, been sacrificed. Robert Temple has described the numerical expression of the difference between the mathematics of the octave and that of the fifth in harmonic theory, the decimal 0.0136, as representing the "minute discrepancy between the ideal and the real" in the perceived universe.

By 1950, however, classical notions of structure and harmony in music had been shattered, while the possibilities of sound being electronically manipulated in time and space offered composers the chance to create new forms and enter previously uncharted sonic regions. And were there two more enthusiastic cartographers of this new cosmos than Sun Ra and Karlheinz Stockhausen? The complex unities of interstellar space had replaced the historically calibrated interval in music as a means of expressing the divine spiritual order. The future was out there. As the title of a 1950s Sun Ra recording put it: "Rocket Number Nine Take Off For The Planet Venus".

Published only a few years in advance of the electronic age, the huge interlocking, multilayered universe described in *The Urantia Book*, with its mythic personalities, arcane vocabulary and cosmological perspectives, presented a fascinating corrective to the prevailing Copernican system of ellipses and rotations. Contact was simply a matter of time. In 1971, at the end of a performance of *Hymnen* at the Lincoln Center in New York, Stockhausen was approached by a stranger, carrying a copy of *The Urantia Book*, who asked the composer to become a world representative responsible for preserving this planet's sounds in the event of its inevitable destruction.

The following year, while filming *Space Is The Place* – the movie in which Sun Ra, dressed in futuristic ancient Egyptian clothes, lands on Earth in a spaceship to "plan for the salvation of the black race" – Sonny was daily seen reading *The Urantia Book*. The Arkestra was in Oakland, California, during this period, staying at a house owned by the Black Panthers and under constant FBI surveillance as a result. The film, which includes sequences filmed at the Rosicrucian Building in Los Angeles, ends with the FBI, in unholy alliance with NASA, forcing Sun Ra to terminate his mission here and return to outer space. "Only a very few artists in each epoch have had this power," Stockhausen had said of the ancient Greek augurs. "Today the artist is obliged to take this role, and take it much more seriously than ever, because what is coming will be unbelievable for most human beings."

LIGHTS ON A SATELLITE

Sun Ra once had a dream in which Christ and Lucifer were friends. He claimed that he saw the two of them together at some kind of union call-up, waiting to be given their next allotted tasks. The street kids who learned close harmony from Sun Ra in Chicago knew him simply as 'Lucifer'. Developing ideas from *The Urantia Book*, Stockhausen's *Licht* cycle is based upon the conflicts and interactions between Michael, master of our local universe, "also known on this world as Jesus of Nazareth", Master Lucifer, Prince of Satania, and the spirit of Eve. *Samstag*, the second opera in the cycle, is Lucifer's day, and his name is given to all four of the main scenes, including "Luzifers Traum", from which *Klavierstück XIII*, which involves the pianist launching space rockets across the stage, is derived. Later, in "Luzifers Requiem", for flute and percussion, six percussionists, representing the human senses, process into Lucifer's tomb after his apparent death. "If possible," Stockhausen has stipulated, "this work should be performed at the place where someone has died for 49 days after physical death. The music is composed in such a way that these études, or exercises, might protect the departing spirit from being caught by other spirits which hover round this planet so that the leaving spirit can reach the White Light." And which is the sixth sense? "Thinking is a medium of perception, you see, like the other senses."

Sun Ra often had his Arkestra conclude each cosmo drama by marching out through the audience at the show's finale, still chanting and playing their instruments. "My musicians leaving the stage at the end," he explained, "symbolize leaving the planet while alive, rather than dead. You hear the voices leaving." A procession is also a potent rite through which the participants advance towards initiation. As a representation of the passage from birth to death and back again, it possesses an apocalyptic, revelatory power, which both composers have drawn upon to heighten awareness and alter consciousness. *"It's after the end of the world,"* runs one of the Arkestra's most famous chants. *"Don't you know that yet?"* Sometimes, it's necessary to remind people that they're dead. *"Someone say, 'Is there funk after death?'"*, George Clinton remarks on *Mothership Connection*. *"I say 'Seven Up'"*. How else will you ever get them to move on? Hawkwind included the urgent repeated instruction "Time We Left This World Today" from *Doremi Fasol Latido* in the latter half of their Space Ritual.

"We have to go through these crises at the end of the century and during the next," Stockhausen once said. "There is no other way." Such moments of crisis require belief. Part cryptic ceremony and part floorshow entertainment, any ritual requires the common assumption of a shared reality with its audience, however temporary, for it to work. In the early 1950s, Stockhausen worked as an accompanist for a touring magician, making up tunes on the piano to distract the audience at crucial moments. 50 years later, consensual reality may be undergoing its most radical transformation in the casinos and hotels of Las Vegas. Set against the vast ridges and plains of the Nevada Desert, Vegas is a city of hallucinations and distractions, from the animatronic destruction of Atlantis to the simulated exploration of the galaxies. That replica of the Great Pyramid you see over there, flanked by a Sphinx and a carved obelisk, is actually the Luxor Casino. At night it projects a beam of light into the sky so powerful that it can be seen from outside the Earth's atmosphere. In the basement, tourists watch as the ancient remains of extraterrestrial beings are removed from the Pyramid's foundations, while at the nearby McCarran air terminal, another unmarked Janet Airlines Boeing 737 takes off for Area 51, the top-secret military installation where alien spaceships are rumoured to be kept.

With private capital and corporate business getting ready to expand into outer space, it's entirely possible that Vegas will become the new centre of our local universe. Designers and architects eager to create similar leisure complexes on the Moon are now studying such vast artificial environments as the Luxor. Imagine a hotel lobby in which it would be possible for visitors to walk directly upon the lunar surface. Such activity might have unforeseen consequences, however. Robert Temple believes the creatures that visited the Earth from Sirius may not have completed the long return journey. Instead, they could still be out in the solar system somewhere, probably in suspended animation, waiting for signs that humanity has reached the next stage in its cosmic evolutionary development. According to Dogon tradition, they could well have relocated to Phoebe, a small, eccentric satellite which serenely orbits Saturn every 523 days and 15.6 hours. Backwards.

PART THREE

MECHANISM

HUMANS, ARE THEY REALLY NECESSARY?

SOUND ART, AUTOMATA AND MUSICAL SCULPTURE

BY DAVID TOOP

The men of the Middle Ages were so mechanically minded they could believe that angels were in charge of the mechanisms of the universe: a 14th century Provençal manuscript depicts two winged angels operating the revolving machine of the sky.
Jean Gimpel, *The Medieval Machine*

In 1650, the Jesuit polymath Athanasius Kircher published 1500 copies of a treatise on music and acoustics called *Musurgia Universalis*. Taking over the role of the angels, Kircher had invented an eccentric collection of mechanical devices that generated, amplified and ordered sound. Floating in a late Renaissance netherworld of science and mysticism, Kircher's designs for sound machines included solar powered singing statues, Aeolian harps powered by the wind, a hydraulic organ that seemed to sound through automata representing the gods Pan and Echo, and spiral tubes that projected sound out of the mouths of statues or eavesdropped on conversations in adjacent rooms. He also built an elementary computer, described by Joscelyn Godwin, researcher in esoteric sound, as "a 'musarithmetic ark' or box of sliders on which the patterns are written, that serves as a composing machine".

The ventriloquism of speaking statues and articulated masks, used by the priesthood to conjure spirit voices on demand, was a formative stage in the history of automata. In their turn, automata were the forerunners of robots, replicants and recording. In 18th century Japan, where an optimistic belief in the robotic future of classic sci-fi still survives, Dutchmen were entertained by karakuri performances staged by live musicians and mechanical dolls. An illustration from a guide to Osaka published in 1798 shows the Takeda theatre, where a Kabuki style percussion ensemble accompanied a mechanical cockerel banging a large drum.

These mechanical inventions played an important role in technological evolution. "Just as the European automata of men like Vaucanson anticipated the machines of the Industrial Revolution," wrote Mary Hillier in *Automata And Mechanical Toys*, "the Japanese performance of karakuri was an awakening of automation." According to Hillier, this example of human-machine interfacing led to improvements in the making of medicines and sugar with the use of treadmill machines.

Similarly, the development of Virtual Reality has been traced to another mechanical musical instrument, the player-piano. In *Virtual Worlds*, Benjamin Woolley's exploration of VR simulation, a genealogy is mapped: notions of computer simulated reality, formulated in the late 1960s by computer graphics pioneer Ivan Sutherland, were inspired by the Link Trainer flight simulator. In turn, the source of inspiration for the Link Trainer was the Pianola. Having been born into a family business of mechanical musical instruments, Edwin Link used the pneumatic mechanism of player-pianos as a basis for his invention of the first flight trainer in 1930.

A technology that allowed music to be perfectly and repeatedly reproduced until the mechanism broke, mechanical music also anticipated the phonograph. Extraordinary creations such as Alexandre Theroude's violin-playing monkey, designed in 1862, became refined and miniaturised for public consumption. A brisk luxury trade in musical boxes, clocks adorned with mechanical singing birds, even musical pictures enhanced by chiming bells, only declined with World War One as other forms of recorded sound became more widely available. This evolutionary obsolescence inevitably becomes a sign of mutated history within the work of composers and performers who create with machines, whether Conlon Nancarrow's or James Tenney's compositions for player-pianos, Stockhausen's *Zodiac* piece for music boxes, or the post-John Cage, post-Grandmaster Flash turntablism of Philip Jeck, Project Dark, Christian Marclay or DJ Disk.

Life sized musical automata of the 19th century were shrouded in an air of exoticism, occultism and horror that matched the contemporary fictional obsessions of Edgar Allan Poe and HP Lovecraft, or the profoundly influential modern creation myth of Mary Shelley's *Frankenstein*. Films as diverse as *Dead Of Night*, *Blade Runner*, *Toy Story* and *Bride Of Chucky* have exploited the ambiguously disturbing yet comic implications of toys coming to life, existing on the threshold of consciousness, taking revenge on their lords and masters.

Rooted in magic, machines that can play music independently of humans also invoke the most modern of fears. Like the HAL computer in *2001: A Space Odyssey*, they ask a chilling question: "Humans, are they really necessary?" Futurist theorist, poet and activist Filippo Marinetti posed a similar threat in an essay called "Multiplied Man And The Reign Of The Machine". "We look for the creation of a nonhuman type," he wrote, "in whom moral suffering, goodness of heart, affection and love, those sole corrosive poisons of inexhaustible vital energy, sole interruptors of our powerful bodily electricity, will be abolished... This nonhuman and mechanical being, constructed for an omnipresent velocity, will be naturally cruel, omniscient and combative."

Full up with modern vigour and primitive energy, the Futurist Marinetti encouraged Luigi Russolo to give performances of his intonarumori noise machines in Modena, Milan, Genoa, Paris, Prague and London. "I have the impression of having introduced cows and bulls to their first locomotive," wrote Marinetti, contemptuous of the public derision that this performance of Russolo's Art of Noise faced. Inspired by the noises of the world, natural, industrial and martial, Russolo bubbled with infectious enthusiasm about the possibilities of the new century. "This lyrical and artistic coordination of the chaos of noise in life," he wrote, "constitutes our new acoustical pleasure, capable of truly stirring our nerves, of deeply moving our soul, and of multiplying a hundred-fold the rhythm of our life."

The supposed barbarism of Russolo's machines was overshadowed in 1914 by the barbarity of total war. A tour was cancelled, the noise instruments were lost and Russolo enlisted in the Italian army, "lucky enough", in his words, "to fight in the midst of the marvellous and grand and tragic symphony of modern war". Wounded in battle, he was discharged from the army and resumed his public displays of noise in 1921. By 1928, there were hopes that his Noise Harmonium might go into production as the perfect accompaniment for silent movies. Then the talkies took over and all of Russolo's potential financial backers faded away; for the second time, Russolo was a victim of the progress he celebrated. Now ghosts at the millennial feast, the intonarumori stand mute, an intangible beginning for the 20th century's fascination with noise, industry and the operations of nonhuman mechanical beings.

He liked the happy-looking row of electrical meters and the fact that they ticked off in 3/2 time, claves time, that the multiple row of pipes with their valves whistled, water whirring through them. He liked the crunching noises when faucets were turned on, the conga-drum pounding of the washroom dryer: the thunder of the coal-bin walls.
Oscar Hijuelos, *The Mambo Kings Play Songs Of Love*

Russolo's machines were created in a climate of political upheaval and scientific discovery. "This branch of physics has received renewed attention from research workers during the past decade," wrote EG Richardson in the 1927 preface to *Sound: A Physical Text Book*, "stimulated no doubt in part by the European War and by the development of broadcasting." Musical instruments such as the piano – embodiments of the aesthetic values of European art music – were beginning to be challenged by the electrical world of the radio, the phonograph or the theremin. Erik Satie, equally inspired by the noise of typewriters and the sound of jazz groups, was one of the earliest composers to become alert to these changes and reflect them in music.

EG Richardson's textbook updated the work of late 19th century physicists such as Hermann Helmholtz and John Tyndall and predecessors such as Chladni, scientists whose researches have been echoed in the music of Edgard Varèse, Harry Partch and Alvin Lucier. Tyndall, for example, summarised many experiments in *Sound*, first published in 1898: bowing long monochords; optical illustration of acoustical beat frequencies; the action of fog, hail and snow on sound; echoes from flames; vibrations in metal plates; an analysis of sirens and the "clang of piano wires".

Although they were conducted with scientific rigour, the aetherial nature of sound imbued these experiments with an air of mystery. Smelling faintly of the alchemist's laboratory, they were less bizarre versions of Raymond Roussel's literary creations. Staged for one week at the Parisian Théâtre Fémina in 1911, Roussel's *Impressions D'Afrique* featured among its scenes the trained earthworm whose undulations in a mica trough dripped mercurial water onto the strings of a zither to produce complex melodies. Roussel's fantastic inventions lay in an interzone between vaudeville, anthropological Surrealism and future audio art. A fictive art that was improbable yet tantalisingly possible, the living sound sculptures of *Impressions D'Afrique* touch sensitive areas of cruelty, dream, perverted science, alien systems and an atavistic social subversion.

Buried in the interstices of science and Surrealism were the elements that demanded new tools for creating sound, new systems for organising it, new spaces in which to hear it. Born in Oakland, California in 1901, Harry Partch began to abandon the traditional scale, instruments and musical forms in 1923 after finding a copy of Hermann Helmholtz's *On The Sensations Of Tone* in a library. Like Antonin Artaud, Partch was driven by a vision of total theatre that would inspire audiences with unheard sounds produced on previously unseen instruments. Unlike Artaud, he set about constructing the machinery to create it. Partch's monumental book *Genesis Of A Music*, completed in 1947, was a manifesto for his Corporeal music. "The impulse to the growth and evolution of music," he wrote, "is generated by the human ear, not by the piano keyboard, without which the harmony classes of this day and age would be inoperative. And the missing element which the human ear wants and needs most is a musical instrument capable of expressing an infinite range of ideas and of infinite mutability, so that ideas can first be tested, then proved or corrected."

Partch's instruments – remarkable constructions such as Chromelodeons, Kitharas and Cloud-Chamber Bowls, designed to play a 43 tone scale and dominate the staging of his integrated theatre works – are as striking in their look and their materials as any sculpture or furniture design of the mid-20th century. Partch also questioned the formality of concert venues, suggesting that a bar might be a better place to enjoy music. Sound sculptures and audio installations challenged many of the precepts of 20th century concertgoing by working towards a deconstruction of the triangulated relationship of composer, performer and audience.

The sculptures of François and Bernard Baschet from France were artefacts of the space age, all silvered surfaces, steel flowers and translucent manta ray wing forms, yet they signalled a reaction against the omniscient control wielded by composers of electronic music. Like many sound sculptures, the Baschet brothers' constructions were acoustic, and they could be sounded by visitors to their exhibitions. What was implied (later to be demanded in the anti-elitist spirit of the late 1960s and early 1970s, a period of stage invasions, jam sessions and free festivals) was a democratisation of music making. Ironically, this easy accessibility has consigned the Baschet instruments to near-oblivion; their eerie, resonant tones suggested a kind of freedom, yet suffered from the same intractability that Varèse had criticised in Russolo's intonarumori.

The paradox of freedom created by machines was explored in isolation by Percy Grainger, one of the least classifiable, confoundingly contradictory composers of the 20th century. In 1924, a year in which his arrangement of "Country Gardens" had sold 27,000 copies in the US and Canada alone, Grainger gave a series of lecture-recitals in Australia that broached the subject of machines that could play 'beatless music'. "It seems to me absurd," he wrote in a 1938 essay called "Free Music", "to live in an age of flying and yet not be able to execute tonal glides and curves... Machines (if properly constructed and properly written for) are capable of niceties of emotional expression impossible to a human performer."

Ten years later, Grainger built his first Free Music Machine. He had been producing piano rolls since 1915 and the machines he constructed in later life were Heath Robinson extensions of the player-piano, mixing milk bottles, bamboo, ping-pong balls, children's toy records, brown paper and string with harmonium reeds, oscillators and a vacuum cleaner. Given names such as The Cross-Grainger Double-decker Kangaroo-pouch Flying Disc Paper Graph Model for Synchronising and Playing 8 Oscillators, the machines were recorded during the mid-50s by Grainger's collaborator, Burnett Cross. "Had Grainger lived longer," wrote biographer John Bird in 1976, "and been able to continue his experiments with more sophisticated equipment he would not be very far removed today from some of the electronic extravaganzas of such groups as Pink Floyd."

A gasoline-driven generator in the entrance hall was soon pounding away, its power plugged into the mains. Even this small step immediately brought the building alive... However, in the tape-recorders, stereo systems and telephone answering machines, Halloway at last found the noise he needed to break the silence of the city.
JG Ballard, *The Ultimate City*

"What interests me is sound moving from its source out into space," Alvin Lucier told Michael Parsons in *Resonance* magazine, "in other words what the three-dimensional quality is. Because sound waves, once they're actually produced, they have to go somewhere, and what they do as they're going interests me a lot." The articulation of space through sound has been a potent agent for decomposition in 20th century music making, either by dissolving the frame, dispersing the sound-source or absenting the composer/performer. In his 1974 book *Experimental Music*, Michael Nyman listed Ives, Debussy, Russolo, Varèse, Schaeffer and Cage as composers who have "pioneered the use of 'music' to make us conscious of the life and sounds outside the accepted musical-social environment".

But Cage's *4'33"*, despite its huge importance, had limitations. "Cage's piece is 'hindered' by being set in a concert hall," wrote Nyman, "by containing no specific directive for the audience, and by leaving what is heard completely to chance. [Max] Neuhaus 'remedies' this. An audience expecting a conventional concert or lecture is put on a bus, their palms are stamped with the word listen and they are taken to and around an underground railway system." Other Neuhaus pieces of the late 1960s used the telephone system, radio transmitters, swimming pools, power stations and subway entrances to create what are now called site-specific installations and events.

As art forms have merged, many individual works have tended to be categorised according to their prime element. Alvin Lucier's score for *Music On A Long Thin Wire*, a piece for audio oscillator and electronic monochord, concludes with the instruction: "Light the wire so that the modes of vibration are visible to viewers." In a sense, this locates Lucier's piece as kinetic audio-visual art, rather than music, though the sound is available on CD.

Artists such as Len Lye, Tsai Wen-Ying, Jean Dupuy, Takis, Pol Bury, Jean Tinguely and Harry Bertoia incorporated sound into their kinetic sculpture, either as the activating element of a cybernetic system or as the by-product of motion. "Sound interested me enormously," Tinguely told Calvin Tomkins, author of *Ahead Of The Game: Four Versions Of Avant-Garde*, "it is another kind of material to me." Tinguely's *Homage To New York*, gigantic, fallible and typically anarchic, was staged in the garden of MoMA, New York in 1960, self-destructing in front of an audience that feared for its safety. The spectacle included a radio that turned itself on yet nobody could hear it, an Addressograph machine that clattered into life and then fell over and stopped after one minute, an erratically mobile klaxon, and a piano that had been doused in petrol, then set alight. "All the unforeseen accidents and failures delighted Tinguely," wrote Tomkins. "The fact that only three notes of the piano worked moved him deeply."

As resonant or amplified solids move and interact, activated by unpredictable systems, the patterns of sound they create take on the drama of natural emergent phenomena. The effect can be compared with the optical illusions of Op Art, yet the experience of seeing and hearing sounding sculpture could be immersive, more prolonged and emotionally deeper. For the late Harry Bertoia, successful as a sculptor from the 1950s to the mid-1970s, sound extended sculpture's articulation of space to fill the air and permeate walls. "It all started in the 1970s," wrote Chris Rice in *Halana* magazine, "when Harry purchased a bunch of Navy surplus beryllium-copper wires for use in his sculpting. In the process of working with these rods, a few happened to knock against one another, producing a remarkably resonant and long lasting sound." Many of the sound sculptures that Bertoia made were kept in his studio, a renovated barn in Barto, Pennsylvania. Instead of selling them, Bertoia made recordings of the sounds, activated by himself and his brother Oreste, then sold the records in a series he called Sonambient.

The sound of Bertoia's sculpture was architectural – an articulation of a specific space – yet also oceanic – the articulation of infinite space. Like many other forms of music of the period, sound sculpture challenged conventional notions of performance: no composer, no performer, no beginning, no end, no narrative, no critical language of evaluation, some might say no point. Sound sculpture simply was and is: existing as a process that described space and shaped time.

John Cage's writings had implanted (at least) two important ideas: music grows out of silence and paradoxically, there is no silence, since the sounds of the world are invasive.

The UK artist Max Eastley began making sound sculptures in 1971, inspired by the wind and water-powered instruments of Athanasius Kircher and Robert Fludd, by Oriental whistling arrows and wind bells, by the military tactic of a Chinese general who in AD 34 placed bronze kettledrums under a waterfall to scare enemy forces with their noise, and closer to home and the present, by kinetic art, Marcel Duchamp, John Cage and the American minimalists. Stringed instruments were sounded by wind or water, flutes were voiced by wind, water dripped into boxes, and metal plates and strings were struck by hammers driven by electric motors.

As Eastley's work became more focused during the 1970s, his interest in complex natural rhythms, microscopic sounds and long durations deepened. La Monte Young and AMM had described their music as a continuum, a stream of sound that flowed without pause, only becoming audible and evident to the public when it was performed with listeners present other than the musicians. The metaphor was influential, though Eastley's work implied that metaphor might become actual, his instruments sounding for as long as the wind blew or the motors (and the electrical power that drove them) survived. The music of sound sculptures could become landscapes or oceans of sound: continuous, diffuse, immersive, a conglomerate of inner rhythms that was endlessly engaging, an enactment of a process that seemed to hover on the threshold of nature and culture.

Although they are not a performance in the strict sense of the word, the best sound sculptures are theatrical. Argentinian composer Mauricio Kagel used adapted, unusual, specially constructed and ethnic instruments in a number of his pieces, either to heighten theatricality or to challenge received notions of virtuosity and compositional form. *Staatstheater*, premiered in 1971 at the Hamburg State Opera, was a music theatre work of consecutive actions, many of them featuring strange 'instruments': mouth drumming using a plastic disc and wooden beater; a steel spiral whirled above the operator's head, then lowered to strangle him or her; a board of nails stroked with two double bass bows; a 'drum man' covered in tambourines; amplified wire netting; a perspex water drum that dripped onto suspended cymbals.

Kagel's *Acustica*, produced in Cologne in 1969, used many strange soundmakers – bullroarers, balloons, a gas blowlamp, a cross-blower to modulate the timbre of a book's pages, clapper sandals, a miniature window used for radio plays, a gramophone record played by a knife attached to a large paper cone, photocells and an audio generator. In Kagel's words, a "self-evident supplement to currently existent sound-makers", these arcane instrumental sounds were lined up as a cabinet of curiosities, their dry scrapings and whirrings, disembodied bangs, gurgles and tortured squeaks, recalling Raymond Roussel, the physics of Chladni and Tyndall, the monstrous vacuum and pressure system music boxes of Stephan Von Huene or the self-made instruments used in improvisation by Evan Parker, Paul Lytton, Hugh Davies, Jamie Muir and Paul Burwell.

Conceptual art, land art, ecology and the aftermath of Fluxus performance were pervasive influences on sound works during the 1970s, many of which seemed to be spiritual heirs of both Athanasius Kircher and Yoko Ono. Annea Lockwood's *Piano Transplant – Pacific Ocean Number 5*, composed in 1972, gave the following instructions: "Materials: a concert grand piano, a heavy ship's anchor chain. Bolt the chain to the piano's back leg with strong bolts. Set the piano in the surf at the low tide line at Sunset Beach near Santa Cruz, California. Chain the anchor to the piano leg. Open the piano lid. Leave the piano there until it vanishes."

Frustrated with the confines of the concert hall and the educated expectations of New Music's small audience, sound art aspired to a closer engagement with the environment and the listener. Either directly or tangentially, the results were a critique of musical behaviour that was tired, even within the so-called avant garde. So Laurie Anderson performed on her Viophonograph, a turntable mounted on a violin and played by a needle in a bow, or played violin while standing on a melting block of ice; Bill Fontana proposed a project that amplified the singing tones produced by traffic crossing the Brooklyn Bridge, then sent a mixed version via satellite to other parts of the world; and Alan Lamb recorded the Aeolian humming of telegraph wires in Australia.

From 1974, when she gave up flute playing for installations, Berlin based artist Christina Kubisch has used sound art to explore relationships of natural to technological, visible to invisible, and visual to acoustic, articulating symbolic space in specific sites with intangible sculptures of sound and light. Her *Clocktower Project*, for example, reactivated the bells of a clocktower at Massachusetts Museum of Contemporary Art. Kubisch encircled the tower windows with a band of black reflective solar panels. These registered the intensity and position of the sun, transmitting this information to a computer that assembled and played mini-compositions of bell sounds, sampled from the original 19th century clocktower bells.

Many of the original parameters of sound art are still being explored, given a new spin by the post-Techno installations and actions of younger artists such as Pan Sonic, Ryoji Ikeda, Disinformation and Scanner, or by the determinedly non-musical sound processes of Minoru Sato and Atsushi Tominaga in Japan, documenting the peripheral bug noise and fugitive crackle of loudspeakers saturated by steam or disconnecting electrodes planted in vibrating window frames. "When we reflect on the condition that most sound works have been requisitioned by music," Minoru Sato wrote in his catalogue essay for the 1996 Sonic Perception exhibition in Kawasaki City Museum, "we are forced to think that the perception/consciousness of the aspect of sound as a phenomenon has not been valued."

A new generation of artists has also turned to sound as a major component in installation work. They range from Angela Bulloch's *Sound Clash Benches*, featuring a film by Jimi Tenor, and her *Superstructure With Satellites* beanbags transmitting low frequency theremin sounds; to Heri Dono's speaking and buzzing satires on power in Indonesia; and Mariko Mori's video installations, particularly her *Miko No Inori* performance in Osaka's Kansai airport, Mori playing a cyborg shamaness performing crystal magic in one of the trance 'n' transit spaces of our disengaged present.

Appropriately for the age of Manga, robotsushi waiters, *Star Wars* droids and global positioning satellites, robotics has reappeared in sound sculpture, including Felix Hess's sound-pressure sensitive robots, the automata of Pierre Bastien and Maxime De La Rochefoucauld, and Chico MacMurtrie's distressed, chaotic and skeletal androids, playing drums like entertainers at a post-nuclear blast party. Perhaps they symbolise the post-human, post-musical condition. The club aesthetic, the laptop computer and downloadable plug-ins are the most recent strands in a 20th century musical trajectory that throws conventional performance routines into question. If there are answers to the question of how music will be performed, enacted or experienced in the 21st century, then some of them will be discovered in the past and future of sound art.

AUTOMATING THE BEAT

THE ROBOTICS OF RHYTHM

BY PETER SHAPIRO

The adaptation to machine music implies a renunciation of one's own human feelings.
Theodor Adorno, 1941

We have grown used to connecting machines and funkiness.
Andrew Goodwin, 1988

The pioneers of mechanical music either saw it as a vehicle for superhuman efficiency (Thomas Edison's phonograph) or as a way of transcending the weakness of the flesh and achieving the purity of function of the machine (Luigi Russolo's intonarumori). But the ultimate triumph of machine music has been achieved in genres concerned with shaking butts and moving booty. Dance musics like rock 'n' roll and funk are almost always discussed in terms of their 'primitive' and 'natural' characteristics; but this ignores the machine-like qualities of the element that purportedly embodies this naturalism: the rhythm. Although he is now routinely trashed in cultural studies programmes the world over, the German critic and philosopher Theodor Adorno was one of the few commentators who actually got it right. In the 1950s, while America's moral guardians were fretting over the effects of 'jungle music' on their under-sexed children, Adorno was warning that "the standardised meter of dance music... suggests the coordinated battalions of mechanical collectivity", and that "obedience to this rhythm" leads people to "conceive of themselves as agglutinised with the untold millions of the meek who must be similarly overcome. Thus, do the obedient inherit the earth". Even if he did see fascism everywhere he looked, Adorno raises a salient point: why have we entrusted to machines that which makes us most human – moving in time to sound? Perhaps it is the logical outcome of music's often expressed desire for the perfect beat, which is rooted in the drum's historical role as an instrument of war.

Modern popular music was born at the dawn of the 20th century in Congo Square, New Orleans, where marching brass bands comprised of freed slaves and immigrants from Haiti and Cuba would congregate on Sundays. One reason for the popularity of the marching band sound was that a large number of decommissioned soldiers ended up in the city after the Civil and Spanish-American Wars, making brass instruments readily available – a fact which served as a constant reminder that the marching band was originally developed as the motor force of the military's killing machine, disciplining and regimenting the troops with metronome beats. If the same beat discipline is at the root of dance music's proximity to mechanisation, the New Orleans bands customised the military's march steps to satisfy their very different needs.

Not as well trained as the mixed-race Creole groups who enjoyed white patronage, the black bands developed a style of playing that was 'hotter' and more rhythmically charged than the European brass band orientations of the Creoles. The gatherings in Congo Square represented the first 'cutting sessions' and the group who played the 'hottest' would take the 'second line' with them as they marched in victory (the second line being the crowd that marched behind the group and clapped, stomped and shouted along with the music). As it became an established pattern, the second line, musically speaking, was a combination of John Phillip Sousa with Latin American clavé patterns. This syncopation is at the root of not only jazz but just about every form of African-American music.

Even in the hands of New Orleans's funkiest musicians, the second line pattern couldn't escape its mechanical roots. Thanks to his transposition of the local marching band style to the drum kit, Earl Palmer is the father of funk, yet whenever he played, regimentation and swing existed in tense communion. His drumming on Dave Bartholomew's "Messy Bessy", which was recorded in 1949 but only released in 1991, sounds like the fount of modern rhythm. Palmer's controlled torrent of triplets and snare rolls anticipated rock 'n' roll, surf music and the funk of James Brown and The Meters. At the same time, his rhythms sounded as though they could be transposed back to a fife and drum band leading the Minutemen against the Redcoats at the Battle of Concord in 1775.

The ground zero of dance music's militarist metaphor is represented by Palmer's performance on Jesse James's "Red Hot Rockin' Blues" from 1958. On this track and Eddie Cochran's "Somethin' Else" (1959) Palmer's punishing percussive volleys were so overwhelming that they browbeat Phil Spector into recruiting him for the 'wrecking crew' that helped create Spector's wall of sound. Here is the proof that the drill-sergeant precision of Palmer's drumming was primarily responsible for the creation of rock 'n' roll's monolithic backbeat.

Long before Miami and New York had Hispanic populations to speak of, Latin rhythms took hold in New Orleans's cosmopolitan melting pot. At the turn of the century the city contained significant numbers of Caribbean immigrants, and the practices of voudou and Santería were widespread. Inevitably the clavé, the basic 3/2 pattern driving the ceremonial cross-rhythms used to summon voudou's loa and orisha spirits, spread outside the shrines and were integrated into the brass bands. Elsewhere, however, people couldn't afford tubas or drums, so they created basslines by blowing into empty moonshine jugs and made beats by thrashing cheap guitars. The rhythm of life in most of America was created by the railroad, and pre-war blues and Country records were often little more than imitations of the locomotive using jugs and guitars: listen to The Memphis Jug Band's "KC Moan" from 1929; Darby & Tarlton's "Freight Train Ramble", also from 1929; or Bill Monroe's 1941 "Orange Blossom Special".

As the funkafied marching band sound advanced up the Mississippi from New Orleans, it was smelted together with the new piston-pumping train rhythms, and the Bo Diddley beat was born. With its chugging momentum, Diddley's first single, 1955's "Bo Diddley", established his trademark rhythm. Everything, including the guitar, which imitated the sound of steel wheels on a track and a steam engine going through a tunnel, was at the service of the beat. "Bo Diddley" may have sounded a bit like the "Little Engine That Could", but by 1956's "Who Do You Love?" and 1957's "Hey Bo Diddley", the Bo Diddley beat had all the forward motion of a Japanese bullet train.

The link between the noise of industry and 'the backbeat you just can't lose' was emphasised at the tail end of the 60s by The Stooges. Motown may have appropriated the car industry's production line techniques, but The Stooges harnessed its sound. With their Detroit homebase just down the road apiece from the enormous River Rouge car plant, The Stooges banged metal against metal, emitted enough noxious feedback fumes to set a river on fire and suggested links between machines, sex, animal debasement and technological alienation. Along with The Beach Boys, The Stooges were Kraftwerk's favourite rock group. Indeed, The Stooges' industrial clangour and motor rhythms are at the heart of the German power plant's greatest record, "Trans-Europe Express". Like Bo Diddley, Kraftwerk created popular music's most· enduring rhythms by mimicking trains and, later, computers. Where Diddley's guitar was a steam engine moving off in the distance, Kraftwerk's synth lick was the Doppler effect trail left by a French TGV. Sounding more locomotive than any of its competitors, "Trans-Europe Express" is the greatest train song of them all, the final link in the man-machine interface.

Significantly, when they produced "Planet Rock", Arthur Baker, John Robie and Afrika Bambaataa lifted the most futuristic, un-locomotive element in "Trans-Europe Express" – its melody line. Even though HipHop kids were busy bombing the A Train with their graffiti tags, their imaginations and fantasies were being spurred by video games and computers, just as their parents had been by trains and automobiles. HipHop was the first music to realise that travel wasn't necessarily about physical motion anymore, but a virtual journey inside your own headspace. Thus, for the bottom end of "Planet Rock", Baker, Bambaataa and Robie borrowed the beginning of Kraftwerk's "Numbers", from their *Computer World* album, which sounded like the transfer of information between two microchips.

The Kraftwerk fetishism of "Planet Rock" meshed human and machine like no record before it. Its influence rapidly transmitted down Highway I-95 to Florida, where the ultimate fusion of flesh and metal was born in the back rooms of the Orange State's strip clubs. Even though it came out of Fort Lauderdale, MC ADE's 1985 single, "Bass Rock Express", was one of the founding moments of Miami Bass. As its title suggests, the track reimagines "Trans-Europe Express" as a neon-lit nightride through south Florida's strip malls, complete with additional claves from a Roland TR-808 drum machine, scratching, a vocoded voice listing the equipment used to make the record, a snippet from the theme of the US sitcom *Green Acres*, and an overmodulated synth bassline. Within a couple of years, however, Bass music had become firmly fixated on the female posterior, and while its union of ass and steel may be perilously close to Freud's infamous equation of shit and gold, Bass music is the ultimate victory of mechanical regimentation over human feelings. For all Bass music's claims to innovation, however, its march to victory was marked out decades earlier by the cyborg timekeepers of funk.

According to its self-image, funk is supposed to be greasy, dirty, stinking of sex – the epitome of human earthiness, in other words. But funk is as rigid as any current 4/4 House track – and Earl Palmer laid down its ground rules once again with his metronomic precision. However, the finest exponent of the New Orleans swing that eventually mutated into funk was Charles 'Hungry' Williams. As the drummer behind Huey 'Piano' Smith & His Clowns on records like "High Blood Pressure", "Little Liza Jane", "Everybody's Whalin'" and "Rockin' Pneumonia And The Boogie Woogie Flu", Hungry took the marching band's gumbo flavour into more polyrhythmic directions. Hungry swung like crazy, but however far out he went, he never forgot 'the one'. 'Everything on the one' is funk's only commandment, and those who break it have their own circle in Hell, where they are condemned to an eternity in a dentist's waiting room with Perry Como on tap.

Hungry taught the New Orleans mandate to Clayton Fillyau, drummer on James Brown's *Live At The Apollo*, and in Fillyau's hands the James Brown beat was born. On Brown's 1962 single "I've Got Money", perhaps the most intense and electric record of his entire career, Fillyau's rapid, syncopated chatter-notes behind the main beat set the new standard for modern funk drumming: a kind of live Junglist percussion 30 years before the fact. Fillyau, and every drummer who followed him, hit 'the one' with digital accuracy – back in the 60s and 70s they used to get fined if they missed it. From the immaculate stage outfits to the precision-tooled beats, every one of Brown's groups was a well-oiled machine. With Brown policing the hard and fast rules governing the rhythm like a Stasi enforcer, you didn't really need The Gang Of Four to spell out the connection between funk and control.

What Fillyau started, The Meters' Joseph 'Zigaboo' Modeliste raised and refined to hitherto unimagined levels of dexterity by combining New Orleans martial rhythms with the JB beat. Modeliste may sound like an octopus behind the kit, but the reason he's such a badass is that he keeps time like Swiss quartz – it's not for nothing that the group is called The Meters. Modeliste played on Labelle's *Nightbirds* album (1974), the record that truly subsumed funk into disco. On its two best tracks, "What Can I Do For You?" and "Lady Marmalade", the drums are flat and angular; the N'worlins swing only implied.

Given funk and soul's marching band roots, the kind of severe regimentation advanced by disco was inevitable. The hit factory output at Motown was already close to assembly line interchangeability when the label released the first two disco records into the world. Eddie Kendricks's 1972 single, "Girl You Need A Change Of Mind", was disco's prototype even though its main beat, which sounded like a snare rather than a kick, was a bit too human (the drummer is noticeably late a couple of times during the track). But no such flaws marred The Temptations' "Law Of The Land", released a year later, in which producer Norman Whitfield made his apocalyptic funk even more dystopian with a strict 4/4 beat that embodied the inevitability of human nature described in the song.

Sceptical of the 'certainties' of the material world, disco once and for all banished the naturalism ascribed to dance music. Academic Walter Hughes has called the music "a form of discipline" in which, along with body building and safe sex, gay men turned the practices of regulation into acts imbued with eroticism. "Disco," wrote Hughes, "takes the regular tattoo of the military march and puts it to the sensual purposes of dance music." Of course, this had been happening all along; but with its own self-awareness, and an insistence on the metronomic 4/4 beat, which was aided and abetted by the development of the synthesizer and the drum machine, disco made discipline its main attraction. Disco's greatest moment was Donna Summer's "I Feel Love". Dumping on the concept of biology from a great height, producer/arrangers Giorgio Moroder and Pete Bellotte cast Summer as a Teutonic ice queen with a machine heart and surrounded her with the most synthetic textures ever heard on a pop record. Through the music of Summer, and artist/producers such as Sylvester and Cerrone, disco fostered an identification with the machine. By strongly identifying with this increasingly mechanical music, gay culture took to it as a release from the tyranny of the natural which dismisses homosexuality as an aberration, a freak of nature.

Although disco was a world populated by the utterly fabulous, one of its strangest phenomena was Hamilton Bohannon, a straight-laced session musician who used to drum in the Motown touring ensemble. No one has taken 'groove' as literally as Bohannon – there are no peaks, no builds, no intensity anywhere in the records he made for Brunswick between 1974-76. Working for the Motown hit factory had left its mark, for Bohannon made dance music like an assembly line worker – his hypnotrance rhythms were so monotonous you could get RSI just listening to them.

Bohannon's numbing regularity was taken up by 'the human metronome', Chic's Tony Thompson, whose unwavering timekeeping, synthetic sound and hi-hat hypnotism might have provided the model for Roland when they developed their first drum machines in the late 1970s.

In 1979, a year before Roland's TR-808 came on the market, Candido's version of Olatunji's "Jingo" would set the pattern for the most novel use of the rhythm box. Remixed by Shep Pettibone into a fierce soundclash between dub effects and percussion pandemonium, "Jingo" turned the clavé bionic. With the advent of the 808, US producers like The Latin Rascals and Chris Barbosa combined disco and "Planet Rock" to create an android descarga called Latin Freestyle. With its angular rhythm tics and woodblock percussion, Latin Freestyle sounded like a cross between Gary Numan and Tito Puente.

Perhaps the most startling example of the meeting of futurism and roots music, however, was Madame X's 1987 obscurity, "Just That Type Of Girl". Madame X were a trio of LA vocalists who wanted to be Prince girls. The real star of the show was producer Bernadette Cooper, who was the drummer for the all-female funk troupe Klymaxx. Even more than Freestyle's robotic rhumba, Cooper's drum programming is suggestive of cyborgs playing mbiras, balafons, cowbells and congas in a Kingston dancehall designed by George Lucas.

Unlike "Just That Type Of Girl", which probably owed its existence to the kind of serendipity that occurs when a producer is looking for a new sound to get a leg up on the competition, A Guy Called Gerald tried to make explicit the connection between machines and ancestry. With its atomised beats and gravity-defying Nyabinghi drumming, his 1995 *Black Secret Technology* album expanded on his idea that the sampler was a time-machine by explicitly linking ancient African rhythms and more modern funk beats with futuristic breakbeat science to produce, in his words, "trance-like rhythms [which] reflect my frustration to know the truth about my ancestors who talked with drums". As Gerald understood, music organises time with its rhythm, and dancing to it is one of the few ways we have to suspend and stretch time. Even more than solar and lunar cycles, rhythm machines are presently the arbiters of time.

THE AUTOBAHN GOES ON FOREVER

KINGS OF THE ROAD: THE MOTORIK PULSE OF KRAFTWERK AND NEU!

BY BIBA KOPF

The story of rock is the glory of speed, and the speedometer is its one reliable measure. The Ramones said it all when they remarked: "Our sets used to be 37 minutes long. Now they're 31 minutes long. We're getting faster all the time." Leaving all other aesthetic measures gaping open-mouthed at the starting line, speed logic wins every time. Rock is white line fever or it is nothing. Any music that doesn't strain furiously to reach the city limits before daybreak, burning up traffic cops and crashing the old traffic regulations, has no place in the history of rock rewritten as a chronicle of speed.

If such a chronicle begins on the North American continent, with Chuck Berry's backseat equations of rock 'n' roll and fast sex, it will not linger there for long. From Berry through Canned Heat's "On The Road Again" to Steppenwolf's "Born To Be Wild" and The Byrds' title ballad for the Dennis Hopper/Peter Fonda film *Easy Rider*, American road mythology is rooted in a quest for its lost frontiers. These frontiers were already lost when film director John Ford composed his late elegiac Westerns mourning their disappearance, after devoting much of his film making life to eulogising the trailblazing frontiersmen who cleared the wilderness of 'savages' for the railroad builders and settlers. Ford changed track after being struck by the same blinding illumination that disarmed his heroes as they neared the end of the trail: like all utopias, the untamed West vaporised at the very moment its frontier was breached. Yet when America's reigning grease monkey laureate Bruce Springsteen souped up Berry's hotrod rock 'n' roll on his third album *Born To Run* (1975), he lit out for the Old West in search of Ford's disappeared routes. In the process he renewed American optimism by superimposing dream images of an earlier, more innocent age onto the scarred landscape passing by. But like the movies, his illusory America only held good in the blur of speed on which it was screened. And speed has no time for nostalgia. Easy Riding Peter Fonda's Hell's Angel admitted as much in Roger Corman's 1966 biker picture, *The Wild Angels*, when he sighed, "There's no place to run." Such sentiments only made the younger Springsteen go faster, as though he was trying to outrace fate.

Even as American road mythology is ultimately founded in the heroic failures of the preceding century, it came across as the epitome of modernity and mobility to many young Europeans. Though they were seduced by its promise of speed and fast sex, they were much slower to emulate it. Indeed, only one European country has formulated a challenge to America's road supremacy. That country certainly isn't Britain – far too small an island to generate sufficient speed. Besides, the word 'motorway' carries zero poetic charge, and British auto design is hardly the stuff of dreams.

The one country to successfully challenge American road mythology is pre-unification West Germany, where the Autobahn has superceded Route 66 in the roadmap of rock history. German motorik still burns up Springsteen's souped-up barroom boogie; and for a short while in the late 1980s, some US rap stars found Volkswagen and Mercedes insignia sexier than Cadillac fins.

If the Bundesrepublik's speed-addicted musicians, film makers and trailblazers – its Dromomaniacs – have not come up with anything as fast as The Ramones, they can always take them over the distance. The quick burst is all very well, but the conquest of speed itself is accomplished through pacing. Road mythology is as much about endurance – how can anyone keep on trucking at Ramones speed? Where Americans burn out within the timespan of two Beach Boys songs, it's the German Dromomaniacs who keep on keeping on until they crash song and city limits. Coded with America's failed frontier myths and gridlocked with broken heroes, the highway ultimately goes nowhere. The Autobahn, meanwhile, goes on forever.

The Autobahn goes on forever? Not an easy thing for Germans to say without raising the memory of Hitler uniting the Reich with a network of arterial routes designed to shrink time and space and speed up military mobilisation. By 1939, he had built 3000 kilometres of road and dreamt of extending the run from Berlin to Paris, to Moscow and the Urals, from Trondheim in northern Norway to the Crimea in southern Ukraine. Wollt Ihr die totale Mobilmachung? Do you want total mobilisation? If it means an end to unemployment and economic depression, then perhaps. 1.5 million workers, a good many of them forced, helped to construct the Autobahn network. Rapid road expansion contributed to the success story of the German motor industry, even if the majority who invested in the Nazi ideal of 'to each family a Volkswagen' didn't get to own one before the outbreak of war.

Yet despite Hitler's grand designs, he played a neglible role in getting Germany's future road mythology 'Unterwegs' (literally 'on the way', and which coincidentally is the German title of Jack Kerouac's *On The Road*). Of course, his spectre haunts Edgar Reitz's epic 1980s film serial *Heimat*. How could it be otherwise, when the central love affair of the saga's binding mother figure, Maria, involved a Todt regiment engineer engaged in the construction of the Autobahn that wrestles her sleepy Hunsrucker village out of the 19th century and flings it into the 20th? Elsewhere, Der Alte/The Old Man in Wim Wenders's 1975 Unterwegs movie *Wrong Movement* is drugged by perpetual motion into revealing his guilty concentration camp secrets to road companion Wilhelm Meister.

That Hitler and his architects of speed, those road builders, the constructors of paths to his monumental glory, failed to permanently landlock Unterwegs culture within his Autobahn network is down to the singular contribution of Kraftwerk. Like the other important German Dromomaniacs (Neu!, La Düsseldorf, Harmonia), Kraftwerk members were born circa Year Zero (1945). They grew up in the culturally sterile years of the economic miracle, a monotonous landscape overshadowed by the immediate past and the American presence. With "Autobahn" (1974) – which at 22 and a half minutes does seem to go on forever – they freed a new generation's imagination from both, at a single stroke. Abroad, the song cleared the word 'Autobahn' of its Nazi connotations, while planting it in that select German vocabulary understood internationally.

"Autobahn is a word the Americans know as well as sauerkraut or kindergarten," Kraftwerk told German *Sounds* writer Ingeborg Schober in 1978, describing the piece as "the European rejoinder to American 'keep on trucking' songs". After "Autobahn", German roads are once again fit for transports of business and pleasure.

There has never been another Unterwegs hit quite like "Autobahn". Simple, witty, supremely corny in conception and flawless in execution, its transparent transcription of the driving experience matches school primer lyrics to onomatopoeic noises simulating the sound of wheels on asphalt, the whoosh of passing traffic, lights full on.

As empty as the open road stretching out before it, its most remarkable characteristic is its blankness, its neutrality. The piece is as functional as the Autobahns it describes; as accurate a summary of the joys of driving there is. The territory traversed becomes a blur, a land of velocity crisscrossed with the communications network connecting its distant points. Distilling a universal experience from the group's own roadwork, "Autobahn" lays down the blank *"grey strip/white stripes"* into which others can inscribe their own restless dreams. "The film [to Kraftwerk's soundtrack] happens in the heads of the people," Ralf Hütter told Ingeborg Schober. "There's not one Autobahn service stop in Germany that we don't know, and there we often had the dream of hearing our music on the radio one day. At that time we were never played on the radio. That was our dream, anyway, and suddenly, with "Autobahn", it became reality. When we were touring America we suddenly heard ourselves."

The song might go: *"Now we turn the radio on/Out of the speaker comes the song/We're driving, driving, driving on the Autobahn..."* However, it is in America, source of all the blasted century's road myths, where the song actually comes true. The image of Kraftwerk, cruising the land of The Beach Boys and catching themselves on rock radio, supplants T-Bird dreams: Wir fahr'n fahr'n fahr'n until daddy takes our VW away...

The test of a new milestone in culture is the distance put between itself and the last one. Kraftwerk's "Autobahn" might well leave all other comers standing. But as road users go, they come across as Old World courteous. It took two brasher and less polite crews, Neu! and La Düsseldorf, whose members briefly served as Kraftwerk's co-drivers, to force American myths off European roads during the early to mid-70s.

A third group, Harmonia, consisting of Neu! guitarist Michael Rother and Cluster's Dieter Moebius and Hans-Joachim Roedelius, worked the same territory, releasing two LPs during Neu!'s layoff between 1973-75. Unsurprisingly, given the characteristically tranquil, pastoral electronics Cluster had distilled from the earlier Kluster's noisier, more abrasive output, Harmonia were a pitstop on the Autobahn route, representing a curious reconciliation of a need for stillness and contemplation with motorik's incurable itch.

Together, this quartet of groups, plus Rother solo, shared the common factor of a Kraftwerk connection. Their output of Unterwegs records constitutes the complete overhaul of road music. But of them all, Neu! endure best. Two years before Kraftwerk's "Autobahn" breakthrough, Michael Rother and Klaus Dinger's partnership was forged in the shortlived Kraftwerk trio line-up with Florian Schneider (Ralf Hütter had temporarily quit the group he had co-founded) that toured their first album, *Kraftwerk*. The future musics that the Neu! pair and the reunited parent group went on to produce separately were both sparked from that album's circuit board manipulations. But Neu!'s work stayed truer to the bared electricity of the Kraftwerk live trio's improvisations.

Neu!'s Unterwegs music is remarkable for the urgency of its desire to keep moving. It is not so much a matter of musical composition – it's a competition of velocities. Powered by a rhythm tic clawing the asphalt – the basis of all motorik disko to follow – yearning, yawning guitar noises race against each other, some accelerating ahead, others receding in the distance. And every now and again, a menacingly low bass rumble hurtles past in the outside lane.

Neu!'s is a driving music constructed by Dromomaniacs driven to greater and greater excesses of speed in a frantic effort to escape the strictures of civic training. It has no discernible goal except to get lost in speed. It's a white line fever, an amphetamine madness pushing itself and its listeners towards oblivion. Pushing harder and harder, this music-as-vehicle inevitably disintegrates before it finishes, catapulting you into the ecstasy of the ultimate escape. At the other end, you either feel cheated to have survived or exalted to be alive. In the latter case you can share those moments of lucidity which Neu! log elsewhere – at the side of the road, perhaps, or at some Baltic shore where Germany runs out of road – as dawn breaks, the speed finally wearing off, giving speed-blurred horizons the chance to take shape against the gradually whitening sky.

Neu!'s concentration of absolutes – from zero to infinity in x seconds – is the warp factor through which they travel freely in time. Unlike Springsteen's nostalgia for highways jammed with broken heroes leading to lost frontiers of innocence, Neu!'s noise is dented with the reality of events. Shunning sentiment, it is triggered by the failures of 1968. Sick of being caught in street battles grown static, of the surging, groaning masses of demonstrators straining against the immovable weight of the State, Neu! are driven forward and outward. Their music is less a confrontation with authority than a running skirmish with traffic cops, a race to the city limits against increasingly sophisticated police surveillance techniques in a bid for the relative freedom of the Autobahn. Even so, Neu!'s noise doesn't sell the illusion that liberty equals no speed limits.

This point about speed limits marks the crossroads where American and German road dreams meet. Springsteen wrote his retro anthem "Born To Run" as if the highway could still provide an escape route from the daily grind. Paradoxically, the escape route opens up with the recognition that there's no way out. Neu!'s "Hero" (from *Neu! 75*) achieves the impossible release from the illusion of escape via its tremendous opening scream, *"BACK TO NOWHERE"*, as the *"just another hero"* of the title charges off on an odyssey through a city night scarred with 1968-era graffiti like *"The only crime is money"* and *"Fuck the harmony"*.[1]

Where does this great Neu! noise come from? Is there any significance in the fact that Unterwegs music originated in Düsseldorf? What is it about that city which seeded the constellation of groups clustered round Kraftwerk with dreams of leaving? Düsseldorf itself, a compact module of fast mode and moneyed modernity, is a desperate muse. It is more fruitful to speculate that the vehicles transporting the Dromomaniacs out of the city helped shape their various motoriks. Perhaps their progress can be traced through the upgrading of their cars, their upward mobility charting their gradual slide into respectability.

It's easy to imagine Neu! driving a battered green Citroën, their rhythms deriving from the hammering engine and the rush of wheels hugging the road. An American rock cassette, MC5 maybe, is barely audible above the blur of speed and the wind whistling through the rust. Subjected to the centrifugal tug on the wheels, the melody follows the camber of the road, broadening out into the exhilarating sweep of the long Autobahn curve. Like the Citroën, Neu!'s production values are a

---

[1] During separate interviews with Neu! members Michael Rother and Klaus Dinger in 2001, it transpired that I had been mishearing Dinger's song "Hero", from *Neu! 1975*, for the past 25 years. Far from being the dromomaniac anthem described, "Hero" is an intensely personal song that condenses Dinger's problems relating to his then girlfriend's return to Norway – prompting the song's opening roar *"Back to Norway!"* – and his arguments over money with his record company. Consequently, he spits *"Fuck the company!"*, not *"Fuck the harmony"*. On balance, I stand by my incorrect Dromomaniac reading of the lyric.

little pinched. But the battering it takes from the elements makes driver and passengers feel very much alive.

Harmonia cover similar ground, but in a secondhand Mercedes, possibly a 1966 black or white model, whose age displaces its original status as a bulwark of bourgeois respectability with a sense of style. The better protection it affords against the wind and the rain produces a sturdier music. Its improved suspension is apparent in more buoyant rhythms, rounded melodies played on organ and electronic keyboards buffing the scything edge of Neu! guitars. Sealed off from the outside, you can hear your own thoughts and thus can let them run through the landscape flashing by. It is more reflective than speed-reflexive, its way marked by moments of melancholy and drowsiness.

Such comfort is not to be sneezed at; but it does seem to reduce the physical responses to the world of those who can afford it. Michael Rother solo is the sound of the Dromomaniac contemplating his first Audi or BMW. Properly insulated, electronic windows push-buttoned up, the swish of silk on leather upholstery – in this motion, in perfect silence, Rother's music takes shape. The melodies recall those elevated Autobahns crossing valleys and clinging to the sides of mountains in Bavaria or the Black Forest. The rhythm is regulated by the pattern of sunlight flickering through the trees onto the windscreen. Rother's cartwheeling motorik is slower and sweeter than Neu!'s driven version. The driving urge is diminished; movement is no longer a pattern of life, the music not so much a transport elsewhere, as a lifestyle accessory. But every so often you get the impression that Rother looks out of his Audi, or BMW perhaps, and wistfully recalls the old Neu! Citroën.

Rother might envy his Neu! co-driver Klaus Dinger's later vehicle, La Düsseldorf. Whatever Dinger does, it bears all the bumps and scars of the intransigent rocker. The first and best La Düsseldorf album (1976's *La Düsseldorf*) is locked in a perpetual night network of striplit urban rings and inner city Autobahns. Great, gaudy and garish, La Düsseldorf are the Flying Dutchmen of motorik – condemned for all eternity to patrol that no man's land between the city and the airport in a vain race against time to catch a flight. The roar of rising jets periodically envelops their invigorating rushes of sound. Yet even as it signals their failure, it cannot negate their irresistible equation of speed and vitality.

Just because La Düsseldorf haunt the airport approaches like a JG Ballard disease, seeing the future trajectory of speed rising out of their reach and fighting to arrest their seeming obsolescence in a closing crash at the end of the runway, doesn't mean the Dromomaniacs are ready to admit it's over: anyone who has passed through an airport knows that flight means stricter bodychecks, less freedom of movement.

So long as they steer clear of State borders, the Dromomaniacs can nurture a sense of freedom. The Autobahn goes on forever, or at least as far as Kiel or Aachen or Germany's pre-unification border with the DDR... Proximity to the border seals this sense of freedom. Such a tension, derived from the closeness of control and uninhibited movement, stiffens Wim Wenders's great Wanderjahre (wandering years) movies of the 70s: *Wrong Movement*, *Alice In The Cities* and *Kings Of The Road*. When French speed baron Paul Virilio says, "In the end cinema imposes a kinetic uniform on the eyes", his intersection of cinema and speed might well be Wenders's point of departure.

"If only the poetic and the political could be one," worries the Wilhelm Meister character in *Wrong Movement* (adapted from Peter Handke's cine-novelisation of Goethe's original Unterwegs novel, *Wilhelm Meisters Wanderjahre*). The Dromomaniacs come close to tying the two strands, pre-empting Der Alte's reply to Meister: "That would be the end of longing and the end of the world." But the end is not yet in sight. The Dromomaniacs still speed up and down the Autobahn's lengths, seeking to resolve the tensions between the personal, the political and the poetic in perpetual movement, wrong or otherwise.

So the Autobahn goes on forever, its endlessness no doubt accounting for the fact that the Dromomaniacs' roads rarely seem to cross. Perhaps they are all heading for that distant Autobahn crossing point where they will finally meet. Each caught up in their own thoughts, they will not meet peacefully, but in an almighty pile-up that will mark the crucifixion of German Dromomania. Saints, martyrs or victims of speed? Whatever the answer, they will be venerated for their services to Autobahn and Unterwegs mythology. And even if they finally locate that elusive moment of true feeling, their greatest achievement will have already preceded them. Operating in an era subjected to ever more sophisticated surveillance techniques and traffic regulations calculated to bring everyone to a standstill, the German Dromomaniacs taught the world to think on the move.

CODA

WIth the unification of West and East Germanies in November 1990, the Autobahn network once again reached its eastern border with Poland at Frankfurt An Der Oder, where it connected with the Polish E11 highway and all points east. But even before the collapse of the Iron Curtain had opened up a trail across the Eurasian landmass all the way to the Pacific, Germany's pioneering Dromomaniacs had devised ways to keep on keeping on in defiance of the former Bundesrepublik's ever tightening traffic regulations, enforced through greater surveillance, closed circuit TV and computerised links with a central criminal investigation agency in Wiesbaden. When Kraftwerk took to the road in support of their 1981 album *Computer World*, they kept extending "Autobahn" by daily incorporating their itinerary into the lyrics, climaxing on their latest stop. Kraftwerk's enthusiasm for cycling kept them on the road for a 12" maxi single, "Tour De France". But thereafter Kraftwerk's output slowed to a trickle, as they have increasingly concentrated on digitally remaking their analogue classics. But the updating of "Autobahn" on 1991's *The Mix* anthology of newly digitised Kraftwerk standards ironically renders it obsolete in the act of electronically preserving it.

Neu! guitarist Michael Rother has kept in constant motion, carving crop circles in the German countryside with an ever-evolving sequence of cartwheeling instrumental albums. He has intermittently played out live with Harmonia's Dieter Moebius, who in the 1980s released a pair of albums exploring speed and velocity. He made *Zero Set* (1982) with producer Conny Plank, which sounds like its motor was kickstarted by Plank's desire to customise the electronic body music of his then highly successful clients Deutsch-Amerikanische-Freundschaft (DAF) for the open road. Moebius's duo album with Gerd Beerbohm, *Double Cut* (1983), is a much more convincing, not to mention thrilling electronic transcription of motorik's speed trajectories.

The post-Neu! career of Klaus Dinger has progressed in fits and starts. Internal squabbles ultimately stalled his commercially successful La

Düsseldorf group. But in the 1990s, he found generous backers in Tokyo label Captain Trip, through which he has deluged the world with a mass of erratic albums, including two Neu! archive sets disowned by Rother. The guitarist was also irritated by Dinger attributing many of his Captain Trip releases to La! Neu?, especially as most of them are highly erratic. But the best of them, *Year Of The Tiger*, regenerates the motorik momentum of his La Düsseldorf debut. And in 2001 Dinger and Rother finally resolved their differences to agree to the first official CD reissues of Neu!s three albums – hitherto broadly available as bootlegs – finally consolidating the enormous influence their motorik has exerted during the 25 years since they were made. David Bowie has always acknowledged Neu!'s impact on his *Low* and *Heroes* albums, recorded during his last great, sustained burst of recording activity in West Berlin in the late 1970s, when he also midwifed Iggy Pop's two fine albums, *The Idiot* and *Lust For Life*. Possibly under the influence of Bowie's iced Neu! enthusiasms, Iggy reconciled the pace and poise of Neu!'s motorik with its roots in his own Detroit Motor City homebase on the latter album's "The Passenger". One of the greatest Unterwegs songs to spring from German soil, Iggy's passenger economically narrates the kind of driven yet seemingly aimless and emotionally detached passages between cities that occur in Wim Wenders's great 70s road movies. Only the Iggy character is left bemused by the existential dread that renders Wenders's protagonists glum. Neu! motorik was also a factor in Sonic Youth's reclamation of American road culture for a more nihilistic age. Not only did they homage the Germans on Ciccone Youth's "Two Cool Rock Chicks Listening To Neu!", their "Expressway To Yr Skull" (on the *Evol* album) comes out of the other side of Neu!'s nihilistic immersion in speed for speed's sake, opening onto a nightsky of shimmering harmonics.

In Germany, meanwhile, successive generations of drivers have taken up the pioneering Dromomaniacs' lines of physical enquiry like they were pathways to the soul. In the 1980s, "How Do You Like My New Dog?", by the now defunct Berlin group Malaria, traced longings for the Mediterranean sun. Frieder Butzmann's "Wolfsburg" pointed to the drudgery of those lives spent in VW city Wolfsburg servicing the Dromomaniacs' desire for speed, montaging Beatles puns (*"Baby you can drive my VW"*), *Swan Lake* and production line counts. Another decade on, and a new generation of German speedfreaks, from Basic Channel through Chain Reaction, from Tresor's 3 Phase to the Austrian artist Gerhard Potuznik, whose Mego disc *Amore Motore (... Autobahn)* earns him honorary citizenship in motorik's realm of speed, have transcribed the flows of energy circulating the Autobahn networks as blips and beats coursing the electronic highways of Techno. In an age of computerised surveillance, these Techno outlaws stay one step ahead of the law precisely by not going anywhere. Cruising the Internet's digital highways instead, their computers are the prosthetic limbs with which they extend their reach way beyond geographical borders.

But the greatest motorik anthem to emerge since the 1970s heyday of dromomania is Berlin group Einstürzende Neubauten's "NNNAAAMMM", from their 1996 album *Ende Neu*, whose title is an onomatopoeic echo of the electronically simulated driving noises on Kraftwerk's motorik milestone "Autobahn". Here Neubauten not only reopen the fevered white line of enquiry laid down by the heroes of 70s German Dromomania, but the group's Blixa Bargeld also connects it with the restless, wandering urges of the German Romantics from 200 years earlier with his engine-turning mantra, *"The song sleeps in the machine"*. Together with the group's thousand engines a-hammerin', Neubauten's mantra and mesmerising rhythm power motorik's drive into the future. It shows no sign of stopping yet.

ROCK CONCRÈTE

COUNTERCULTURE PLUGS IN TO THE ACADEMY

BY EDWIN POUNCEY

One May evening in 1967 at San Francisco's Matrix club, Steppenwolf's bass player Nick St Nicholas got up on stage, plugged his guitar into an amplifier and Echo-lite unit and proceeded to experiment. Urged on by St Nicholas's freeform freakout, the rest of the group mounted the stage, picked up their instruments and joined in. "Before we knew it we were more or less improvising," reflected the group's leader John Kay two years after the event, "jamming, squeezing and shaping a musical thing which lasted for 20 minutes and broke finally into "The Pusher", which astounded us and the audience at how well it came off." Kay attributed this early improvisational rendering of what was to become one of Steppenwolf's most popular songs to a range of influences, from the electroacoustic compositions of Edgard Varèse to "the French semi-electronic symphonic school of music".

That a biker-favoured outfit like Steppenwolf were willing to push their primal brand of rock 'n' roll towards the more academic ideals of experimental music and musique concrète adds a hidden dimension to the lyrics of their greatest hit: musically, they really were (re)born to be wild.

"We did "The Pusher" every night and the intro part just kind of evolved as a time for us to do whatever we wanted," remembers drummer Jerry Edmonton. "People started talking about the band after that. "The Pusher" got people saying, 'There's this band from Canada and they're way out there'."

As with countless other 60s groups, the main ingredient that made Steppenwolf sound so out there was lysergic acid diethylamide, the hallucinogenic potion that had seeped out of the US government's own secret laboratories. Once it hit the streets, via the proselytising efforts of Timothy Leary and Ken Kesey, it inadvertently became the creative tool for a generation hellbent on opening up heaven, while bringing the establishment crashing down around them. The other ingredient was, of course, the music itself, which – along with attitudes towards sex, fashion, art and the ongoing Vietnam war – was ripe for transformation.

Rock music and the academy have rarely had anything useful to say to each other, either before or after the 60s, and it would be too glib to attribute the dialogue going on between them to the special openness that characterised that purportedly class-free decade. Besides, the academy had begun its end of the conversation way back at the beginning of modernism, which itself was breach-birthed at the turn of the century during the cataclysm of the Industrial Revolution. On one level, modernism was an artistic response to the deepening sense of alienation that resulted from the rapid industrialisation of town and country, and of work and leisure. Within academic music, it flowered most brightly in the post-war experiments happening in electronics, electroacoustic composition and musique concrète. Indeed, it could be argued that modernism's themes, of the fractured and disconnected self, found their fullest expression in musique concrète – a musical form defined by fragmentation and discontinuity. Based on recombining cut-up chunks of sound, and heard to best effect in the pioneering compositions of Frenchmen Pierre Schaeffer, Pierre Henry and Luc Ferrari, this music took full advantage of the plasticity of sound once it had been enshrined on the physical medium of magnetic tape.

In the 60s, the fragmentation that had been made concrète in musique concrète discovered a likeness, if a not wholly accurate reflection, in the distorting-mirror music of the LSD generation. But whereas musique concrète seemed to perma-fix the very process of fragmentation, psychedelia frequently charted an Edenic search for childlike wholeness. When concrète composers and psychedelic rock got to look each other in the eye during the 60s, they didn't necessarily see the same thing. But in psychedelia, the more utopian of the concrète composers possibly caught a fleeting glimpse of restored wholeness, while in the fragmentation of concrète, psychedelia's more farsighted cosmonauts were gifted with a method for expressing the consciousness-splintering aspects of an acid trip. In the process, those with good ears noticed how concrète's juxtapositions of ill-matched tones and timbres could also approximate the intense, physically ravishing aspects of the acid experience.

No wonder, then, that The Grateful Dead, the West Coast group that totally absorbed acid culture as a means of enlightenment and expression, embraced academic methods when, on their second album *Anthem Of The Sun* (1968), they attempted a musical recreation of an acid trip. For their projected assault on reality, they brought in keyboardist Tom Constanten at the invitation of his friend, Dead bassist Phil Lesh, who was himself a composition student of the Italian Luciano

Berio. Despite guitarist Jerry Garcia's formidable command of volume and feedback, The Dead felt that their first, self-titled album had failed to capture the essential mindwarp element of the group live, and thus sought to extend their sonic armoury in the studio with techniques picked up from the academic avant garde. With the enthusiastic participation of Garcia and Lesh, Constanten applied prepared piano and tape montage methods to the latter part of "That's It For The Other One". Collaged from superimposed performance tapes, his experimental symphony suddenly folds into a bout of musique concrète that falls somewhere between Varèse's *Déserts* and the respective keyboard deconstructions of John Cage and Conlon Nancarrow. Constanten created one effect by diving into the piano, having first pulled the string on a gyroscope and placed it against the sounding board. "The sound," he revealed, "is not unlike that of a chainsaw being taken into it."

All of which was a long way from the kind of upbeat rock 'n' roll which The Beatles had brought over to America for their appearance on *The Ed Sullivan Show* in 1963. Three years later, the group's moptop innocence had given way to a hairier, acid-burned recalcitrance. Both John Lennon and Paul McCartney were equally fascinated by music's 60s avant garde, and much to the muted disapproval of producer George Martin, they began to assemble tapes that attempted to mirror LSD trips and which they would then splice into the arrangements of their songs. Thus the backwards tape treatments and Indian war whoops on "Tomorrow Never Knows", the clanging tram car sound hallucination on the end section of "Strawberry Fields Forever", the tumbling calliope tape loop collage that runs through "Being For The Benefit Of Mr Kite", and the blurred, *Through The Looking Glass* radio effect that haunts "I Am The Walrus" were mechanically aided flashbacks to their acid dreams (and nightmares). This approach reached its zenith (or nadir, depending on which side of the fence the listener chose to sit) with "Revolution No 9", a slab of pure musique concrète that was included on *The White Album*. Unfortunately, only Lennon and his new bride Yoko Ono carried on where "Revolution No 9" left off, with their pair of 'Unfinished Music' albums, *Two Virgins* (1968) and *Life With The Lions* (1969). Before the couple met in October 1967 at London's Lisson Gallery, Yoko Ono had already been an active participant in George Maciunas's radically mischievous, neo-dada art group Fluxus, and had performed with John Cage, David Tudor and Toshiro Mayuzumi. Cage's crude 1940 prototype for concrète composition, *Living Room Music* – where household objects, furniture and even parts of the architecture where it was being performed were given the status of musical instruments – had since been remodelled in Western Europe, beginning with Pierre Schaeffer's musique concrète approach, and it was probably this version that (together with Ono's Fluxus schooled influence and Lennon's surreal Goonish humour) formed the basis for what one rock encyclopedia has described as "perhaps the most skipped-over track on any Beatles album".

Many of the groups who subsequently fed found sounds into their songs were blissfully unaware of such musique concrète pioneers as Cage, Schaeffer, Pierre Henry or Karlheinz Stockhausen. They were merely following The Beatles' example by adding the appropriate 'psychedelic' effects to an otherwise standard pop song. Although it is doubtful whether The Lovin' Spoonful realised what they were creating in 1966 by introducing a tape of traffic noise and road drills during the instrumental break of "Summer In The City", they ensured that the song would be remembered in the breach rather than the strict observance of its cheerfully lazy harmony. Regardless of the group's – or producer's – motivations, the sudden intrusion of the atonal noises of the outside world ripping through its tiny rent in the fabric of pop alerted radio audiences to a wholly other reality. (Conversely, they signalled a way back to reality for fazed, confused or lost day trippers.)

Other notable pop and rock musique concrète flirtations from this period include Alex Chilton's pre-Big Star unit The Box Tops' 'sampling' of the sound of a jet passing overhead on "The Letter" (1967); Beach Boy Brian Wilson's atmospheric, evocative and lonesome-sounding train and dog barking session on "Caroline, No" (1966); and the earthshaking A-bomb blast at the centre of Love's wired punk anthem "Seven And Seven Is" (from 1967's *Da Capo*). Apart from the obvious anti-war reference, this explosion commemorated the moment when rock 'n' roll innocence was permanently blown away, clearing the way for the massive changes that would rise up out of the ruins. As the war in Vietnam dragged on, politically engaged groups honed rock into a weapon of protest aimed at tipping the balance of popular opinion against US involvement. By detonating their sound bomb on the radio, Love were announcing that a collective finger had pushed the button. Just as 80s rappers would sample the shocking sounds of drive-by shootings for exploitative and journalistic purposes, so 60s rock musicians were using the sounds of combat and consumerism gone mad both to excite/incite their listeners and to drive their protests home.

FREAKY ÉLECTRONIQUE

Those who knew and were passionate about music's postwar avant garde incorporated its methods into their own work with more care and deliberation. Frank Zappa's early introduction to the music of Stravinsky, Holst, Ives, Webern and, more importantly, Edgard Varèse (mingled with his love for 50s doowop and R&B) had a profound effect on his interpretation of modern rock music. When Varèse died on 6 November 1965, Zappa composed "The Return Of The Son Of Monster Magnet (Unfinished Ballet In Two Tableaux)" in his memory. The piece took up an entire side of The Mothers Of Invention's debut album, the four-sided *Freak Out!*, which was released the following year. "[This] is what freaks sound like when you turn them loose in a recording studio at one o'clock in the morning on $500 worth of rented percussion equipment," Zappa wrote in his sleevenote. "A bright snappy number. Hotcha!" The resulting "snappy" mix of electronics, Varèse-inspired percussive sonorities, and strange spoken word exchanges between Pamela 'Suzy Creamcheese' Zarubica and the notorious Los Angeles producer, musician and eccentric Kim Fowley, was to become one of the earliest recorded examples of what can be loosely termed 'rock concrète'. Central to his music, however, was Zappa's William Burroughs-tinged sense of humour. Zappa subliminally incorporated Burroughs's cut-up tape recording techniques into such 'rock concrète' pieces as "Nasal Retentive Calliope Music" and "The Chrome Plated Megaphone Of Destiny", which concluded The Mothers' 1968 album *We're Only In It For The Money* (the listener was instructed to read Franz Kafka's short story *In The Penal Colony* before playback). "The Chrome Plated Megaphone..." apparently refers to a voicebox found between a toy doll's legs; but alongside its 'freak' humour, you can also detect warped echoes of Varèse's *Poème Électronique* and Stockhausen's breakthrough work of electronic tape mutation, *Gesang Der Jünglinge*, bubbling under and eventually breaking the surface. For the album sleeve, Zappa hired the graphic artist Cal Schenkel to satirise the Carnaby Street, pop art sentimentality of Peter Blake's cover for *Sgt Pepper's Lonely Hearts Club Band*. It misled many critics into assuming that "The Chrome Plated Megaphone..." was a cynical swipe at Lennon and McCartney's "A Day In The Life", the last track on *Sgt Pepper's*, when in fact Zappa was fine-tuning his personal art of noise. The culmination of Zappa's commitment to contemporary classical and electronic music was unleashed one month later as *Lumpy Gravy*, an orchestral work recorded in New York with the 50 piece Abnuceals Emuukha Electric Symphony Orchestra & Chorus, a few stray Mothers and various cohorts from his entourage of freaks. *Lumpy Gravy* is a crucial work for the way it combines classically motivated interludes, electronic abstractions and rambling spoken word compositions within a basic rock structure. Whereas other 'rock stars' frequently toyed with vague notions of musique concrète and experimental music, Zappa incorporated them into a medium that extended his musical repertoire and pushed the prowess of The Mothers Of Invention to new heights of skill and endurance.

Among those to take Zappa's experimental music approach seriously were the rebellious 60s West Coast superstars Jefferson Airplane, who approached him to produce their third album, *After Bathing At Baxter's* (1967). Zappa declined the offer due to pressure of work, but he eventually teamed up with the group's vocalist Grace Slick on 5 June 1968 to record a freeform composition which they had co-written entitled "Would You Like A Snack". It is a typically erratic keyboard and percussion dominated Zappa number, complete with deviant sexual vocalising from Slick in operatic diva mode. This short piece sends the imagination racing over what might have occurred had Zappa taken control of the Airplane for a whole flight. Even without Zappa's involvement, however, the extended soloing of guitarist Jorma Kaukonen and bass player Jack Casady on *Baxter's* is clearly enriched by the example of Zappa's forays into the avant garde, and their psychedelic protest rock is transformed into something more substantial and enduring than a 'plastic' soundtrack for the corporate 'Flower Power' counterculture.

CONCRÈTE IN THE LIMELIGHT

By the late 60s and early 70s, even a lethargic music industry was beginning to wake up to the realisation that the boundaries of rock were expanding, and soon the hunt was on to sign up any group that strayed beyond the familiar guitar, bass, drums and vocals line-up. One label that attempted to educate the hippy hordes, while shamelessly cashing in on the current craze for electronic and experimental music, was the Mercury Records subsidary Limelight, whose catalogue of musique concrète, electronic music and classical Indian ragas was described as "The Total Experience In Sound". Packaged in elaborate gatefold sleeves, their abstract artwork mirrored the coloured oil lightshows which were a major feature of any rock concert at the time, Limelight set out to introduce the music of such experimental composers as Pierre Henry, Kagel, Eimert, Ligeti, Berio, Ferrari and Xenakis to audiences who, until *Anthem Of The Sun* hit the racks, were probably unaware of Henry's equally mind blowing *Le Voyage*, an electronic score based on the Tibetan Book Of The Dead. Limelight also signed the electronic rock group Fifty Foot Hose, who recorded their lone *Cauldron* album for the label before sliding into obscurity (until that is, they were given the kiss of life in the 90s by the same fanbase that had helped to resurrect the career of The Silver Apples).

Unlike the many who were only just discovering his work through the Limelight label, Pierre Henry was no stranger to psychedelic rock. In 1967 he had collaborated with Michel Colombier on a series of electronic pieces based around pop and rock themes. The resulting *Messe Pour Le Temps Présent* marked a dramatic change of direction for Henry. With compositions such as "Psyché Rock", Henry's joyous demolition of the rock 'n' roll standard "Louie, Louie", he made contact with rock audiences, which discovered correspondences between the disintegrating logic of his rock concrète and their own hallucinogenically fuelled visions of the world. Two years after the release of *Messe Pour Le Temps Présent*, Henry was contacted by Gary Wright from the British group Spooky Tooth, with a view to collaborating on an electronic mass called

Ceremony. When the album was released, full page adverts were taken out in the rock press, describing it as 'Electronique Fantastique'. But Spooky Tooth's leaden Progressive rock dirge, once plugged in to Henry's accompanying electronic squeal, sounds unconnected and toothless: more mess than mass.

An experimental composer who left a more significant mark on 60s rock was Joseph Byrd. Working with his 'electronic rock' group The United States Of America, Byrd narrowed the gulf that separated 'serious' music from rock 'n' roll. Recording in 1967, he combined the psychedelic social attack of Zappa's Mothers and the neon-lit starkness of The Velvet Underground (The USA's singer, Dorothy Moskowitz, bore a passing resemblance, both vocal and physical, to Nico) with his own Morton Subotnick-influenced sheets of ring-modulated and synthesized sound to produce the (still undervalued) American answer to Henry & Colombier's *Messe Pour Le Temps Présent.*

EUROPE GOES LOOPY

Across Europe too, rock was going through radical changes. In Germany, the beat boom of the early 60s had been replaced with a musical aesthetic that critiqued the country's post-war industrial rebirth while looking out towards the cosmos for inspiration. Labelled 'Krautrock' by the British music press, one of the first and most influential of these groups was Can. Filled with the spirit of change, the group's first recording session in June 1968 included a recording of the riots which had brought Paris to a standstill the previous month (the tape was made by David Johnson, one of the founders of the group). The same year, Holger Czukay and studio engineer Rolf Dammers (under the pseudonym of the Technical Space Composers Crew) created the cosmic concrète masterpiece "Canaxis V", which rivalled the best electronic work of Czukay's former teacher Karlheinz Stockhausen. Czukay's 'acoustic sound painting' layered tape loops of a Vietnamese boat woman singing and gamelan styled guitar over a repeated electronic choral background to create a 'worlds within worlds' effect that is as alien as it is familiar. Sounding like it could have been beamed down from a distant galaxy, rather than a tape montage of electronics and a shortwave radio transmission, Czukay's message seemed to be that not only earth but also the cosmos beyond could be brought into earshot at the turn of a dial.

The nearest British equivalent to Can was Pink Floyd, whose post-Syd Barrett shows were equipped with quadraphonic sound systems that blasted out such sound effects as UFOs taking off and giant footsteps walking above the heads of the audience. Of course, Pink Floyd also encouraged a strain of pomposity to enter the rock arena which gradually took centre stage once the 60s had burnt itself out.

When William Burroughs maintained that the future, as well as the past, bleeds through the ruptures opened up in the cut-up process, he could have been describing the work of today's selfconsciously postmodern sampling composers. The 'plunderphonic' hybrids of John Oswald have built one of the most enduring bridges connecting the pioneer spirit of the 60s with the relentless referentiality of the next generation. His psychedelic plunderphonics piece *Grayfolded* (1995) was directly inspired by the experimentation that produced *Anthem Of The Sun*. Oswald spliced together live selections from various locations of recordings of The Grateful Dead's "Dark Star" to create a telescopic, sonic time tunnel. Oswald's simultaneous celebration and extension of The Dead's musical legacy shows that the song might remain the same, but the way of singing it has been irretrievably altered.

DECK WRECKERS

THE TURNTABLE AS INSTRUMENT

BY PETER SHAPIRO

"The basic principle of scratching is to take a record and pull it back and forth," explains Rob Swift of legendary New York turntable crew The X-ecutioners. "You can incorporate the fader of a mixer and cut the sound off and on. But you can just move it back and forth in rhythm, on beat to a song that's playing. That's what scratching is. The motion is like scratching, but it also has a double meaning because people used to go, 'You're gonna scratch the record if you do that'."

Of course, turntablism is more than just dragging a record back and forth under a stylus, or segueing two tracks together nice and smooth. HipHop is very like the British class system: it's not so much *what* you say that matters, but how you say it. This is as true of the DJ as it is of the MC and graffiti tagger. Thus, turntablism recognises that the best music is a complete triumph of style over substance; everything's been said already, so why bother listening unless the speaker's got some serious chutzpah? In fact, the DJ's style is the very substance of turntablism. All of which serves to explain HipHop culture's infatuation with kung-fu flicks: when everyone is using the same basic materials, style – whether it's drunken boxing and Shaolin shadow boxing or flaring and beat juggling – becomes all important.

For all of the ubiquity of the record during the 20th century, it's quite remarkable that so few people managed to make anything out of it as a tone- and texture-generator rather than a playback device until the HipHop virus struck everything around it. The first person to envision the turntable as a musical instrument was John Cage. In his 1937 essay "The Future Of Music: Credo", Cage writes, "With a... phonograph it is now possible to control... any one of these sounds and give to it rhythms within or beyond the reach of imagination. Given... four phonographs we can compose and perform a quartet for explosive motor, wind, heartbeat and landslide." Cage just about succeeded with *Imaginary Landscape No 1*, which he composed in 1939. Originally written to be performed in a studio by a pianist, a Chinese cymbal player and two turntablists playing Victor frequency records, *Imaginary Landscape No 1* was a kind of proto-musique concrète piece that took advantage of the turntable's ability to switch gears from 33 1/3 to 78 in order to manipulate recordings of constant tones. In a 1958 recording of the piece, the rising and falling tones generated by the turntables sound uncannily like the theremin glissandi from Louis and Bebe Barron's soundtrack for *Forbidden Planet*. While several composers took up Cage's challenge by scoring pieces for other electronic reproduction apparatus like the radio and microphone, the possibilities of the turntable as an instrument in its own right lay dormant until Kool DJ Herc transplanted the Jamaican sound system to New York's Bronx in the early 70s.

Kool Herc was a Jamaican DJ who had emigrated to the USA in 1967 and set up his own sound system in the Bronx. When his reggae records failed to move the crowd at the block parties, he turned to funk, but the only part of the records he would play was the short section where all the instrumentalists dropped out except for the percussionists. The 'break' was the part of the record that the dancers wanted to hear anyway, so he isolated it by playing two copies of the same record on two turntables – when the break on one turntable finished, he would play it on the other turntable in order to keep the *beat* going. At the same time, in clubs much further downtown like the Sanctuary and the Tenth Floor, DJs like Francis Grasso and Larry Levan were developing the disco DJing style that depended on superimposition and segueing to keep the *groove* going.

Herc's breakbeat style laid the foundations for HipHop, but it was another DJ, Grand Wizard Theodore, who created its signature flourish in 1977 or 1978. Purely by accident, Theodore stumbled across scratching when he was practising in his bedroom with two copies of Ralph McDonald's "Jam On The Groove" and had his attention diverted by his mother banging on his door, asking him to turn that noise down. The sound of a record being rubbed across a stylus is HipHop's equivalent of the guitar solo – the climactic moment of intensity that everyone wants to emulate – but the techniques developed by Grandmaster Flash are HipHop's riffs – the less obvious facets, but the genre's very foundation.

Inspired by another HipHop pioneer, Pete DJ Jones, whose chopping technique was similar to the downtown disco DJs beat matching, Flash brought DJing to a new level of sophistication by introducing the techniques of backspinning and cutting. Flash came up with the idea of punch-phasing: taking a stab, lick or riff from a record on one turntable and 'punching it in' over the top of another record on the other turntable. Flash combined the blend with the break; he was the pioneer of the crossfader, cutting back and forth between records, slicing and dicing them and overloading the mixer's channels with brilliant, arrogant noise. With his phonographic flights of fancy, Flash truly made DJing something other than just spinning records and proved that the audio montage could be more than just the smart-ass shenanigans of the Dickie Goodmans and Bill Buchanans of this world.

HipHop may have had its premiere on vinyl with The Fatback Band's "King Tim III" and The Sugar Hill Gang's "Rapper's Delight" in 1979, but Flash announced its true arrival with 1981's "The Adventures Of Grandmaster Flash On The Wheels Of Steel". A collage of The Sugar Hill Gang's "8th Wonder", Queen's "Another One Bites The Dust", Blondie's "Rapture", Chic's "Good Times", The Sequence & Spoonie Gee's "Monster Jam", Grandmaster Flash & The Furious Five's "Birthday Party", The Incredible Bongo Band's "Apache", a *Flash Gordon* record and a mock children's story from an album called *Singers, Talkers, Players, Swingers & Doers* by The Hellers, "Wheels Of Steel" was done live on the decks; if Flash messed up, he erased everything and started from scratch. It took him about three hours, but he nailed it on the tenth take.

Of course, "Wheels Of Steel" was more than just a simple collage – it was a cut-up that was *on beat* for the track's full seven minutes. Flash showed that, despite its normal usage, the turntable was really a percussion instrument with a tonal range and expressive capability far beyond that of drums, woodblocks and marimbas. As audacious, assertive and aggressive as anything coming from downtown's art-punk fringe (check the vicious scratch that serves as the bridge from the children's story to "Birthday Party"), "Wheels Of Steel" was (and remains) HipHop's greatest feat of derring-do. Nobody since The Sex Pistols had so boldly and so authoritatively claimed new turf and no one until NWA would mount such a vigorous challenge against the status quo. You couldn't escape "Wheels Of Steel" in New York in 1981 even if you wanted to: every other subway car and every other street corner was occupied by someone with a boombox trying to shake down Babylon's walls with its massive sound. While the Big Apple was shaking to its core, the rest of planet rock was sleeping and "Wheels Of Steel" achieved prominence largely in hindsight.

Even more underground, both in terms of its provenance and the number of people who actually heard it, was Afrika Bambaataa's *Death*

Mix. Released on former doo-wop impresario Paul Winley's self-titled label, *Death Mix* lacks the highwire-act sense of danger and possibility of "Wheels Of Steel", but as the bootleg of Bambaataa and Jazzy Jay playing a party at the James Monroe High School in the Bronx, it is even more raw and, in its way, just as immediate. It has diabolical fidelity – the cuts and scratches sound terrible – but it only adds to the feeling that *Death Mix* is HipHop's equivalent of cave painting. It not only sounds older than the late 70s or early 80s, but since you can't hear the crowd, there's an eerie, palpable sense of ghostly absence in the record. There's no recording date, but *Death Mix* was released in 1983, two years after "Wheels Of Steel", and sounds like not just its predecessor, but its distant ancestor. Since *Death Mix* is more concerned with keeping the beat going than with anything as arty as Flash's montage cuts or the bold strokes of his scratches, it is probably the closest any document will come to capturing the original style of Herc.

While Flash and Bambaataa were using the turntable to explore repetition, alter rhythm and create the instrumental stabs and punch phasing that would come to characterise the sound of HipHop, Grandmixer D.ST was becoming the Dizzy Gillespie to Grand Wizard Theodore's Louis Armstrong. Having already established his deck skills with his 1982 single for Celluloid, "Grandmixer Cuts It Up", D.ST made the turntable the electric guitar of the next decade with his scratching on Herbie Hancock's 1983 single, "Rockit".

"Rockit" only reached number 71 on the American charts, but its moderate crossover success (and heavy airplay on MTV) meant that it would become probably the most influential HipHop track of them all. Cited by nearly every turntablist as the reason they started DJing, "Rockit", even more than "Wheels Of Steel", established the DJ as the star of the record, even if he or she wasn't the frontman. Produced by Bill Laswell, "Rockit" is a dense assemblage of Fairlight keyboards, Oberheim DMX drum machines and vocoders that manages to move with a dexterity that belies its rump of steel skin. However much detail might be packed into it, everything is superfluous aside from D.ST's scratching – it's what you listen to and what you listen for. Epitomising the HipHop-jazz metaphor far more than any Roy Ayers-sampling Pete Rock track, D.ST approaches his solo as if he was playing at a cutting session at

Minton's Playhouse in the 40s. Nearly as in your face as "Wheels Of Steel", D.ST's scratching (according to David Toop's book *The Rap Attack*, he was using a record of Balinese gamelan) trashes Hancock and tells him to go back to the 70s because "this is our time now".

If D.ST cut 'real' musicians on their own turf, then West Street Mob's "Break Dancin' – Electric Boogie" (also from 1983) was punk negation. Only DJ Code Money's brutalist record mangling on Schooly D's early records can match the cheesegrater note-shredding of "Break Dancin'". As great as "Break Dancin'" was, though, it also highlighted the limited tonal range of scratching which was in danger of becoming a short-lived fad like human beatboxing until the emergence of Code Money's DJ brethren from Philadelphia in the mid-80s.

Despite New York's continued pre-eminence in the HipHop world, scratch DJing was modernised 90 miles down the road in Philadelphia. While Schooly D's DJ Code Money created the rawest, most vicious scratching ever recorded, other denizens of the City of Brotherly Love were creating the climate for the return of the DJ by inventing transformer scratching. Developed by DJs Spinbad, Cash Money and Jazzy Jeff, transforming was essentially clicking the fader on and off while moving a block of sound (a riff or a short verbal phrase) across the stylus. Shortkut, a Bay Area DJ formerly allied with The Invisibl Skratch Piklz, explains 'transforming' as "rapidly cutting off the sound, like how you play with the off and on. It's like a light switch, you know how you play with it to make the lights flash on and off. It's the same thing as far as transforming but you're moving it to a rhythm."

Skratch Pikl DJ Q-Bert adds, "Ever heard of the cartoon *Transformers*? When they transform they make that sound [imitates a wah-wah guitar]. You're messing with the whole sound from beginning to end. If the word was *"hello"*, it would be like, *"h-he-he-ell-ell-lo-o-o-o"*. If you were cutting, you'd be getting the beginning of the note: *"h-h-he-he-he-hello"*."Expanding the tonal as well as rhythmic possibilities of scratching, the transformer scratch epitomised the 'chopped-up' aesthetic of HipHop culture.

The only problem with the Philly DJs was their timing. HipHop was starting to become big money and the cult of personality started to take over. HipHop became very much at the service of the rapper; Cash

Money and DJ Jazzy Jeff were saddled with B-list rappers like Marvelous and The Fresh Prince and were only allowed to get busy on perhaps one track (check the bonus disc of scratch tracks from DJ Jazzy Jeff & The Fresh Prince's second album *He's The DJ, I'm The Rapper* or Cash Money's extraordinary "The Music Maker"). While they could shine at DJ battles like the DMC World DJ Championship, they were pushed to the sidelines when it mattered most.

Of course, it was only a matter of time before the DJ tracks spread out of Philadelphia: LA's Aladdin and Unknown DJ, Florida's DJ Crash, Magic Mike and Mr Mixx, and New York's Prince Paul and DJ K La Boss all produced tracks that would become classics of on-the-fly cut 'n' paste. Probably the most influential of all these DJ tracks was "DJ Premier In Deep Concentration" from Gang Starr's 1989 debut album. More than just a collection of Mach 1 scratches to display Premier's deck dexterity, "Deep Concentration" was an emotive sound assemblage that took in Kool & The Gang's "Summer Madness", Double Trouble's "Double Trouble", Billy Stewart's ululation from "Summertime" and the buzzing horn hook from Freda Payne's "Unhooked Generation". It was the loop of the piano intro from "Summer Madness", though, that made the track the best turntable montage since "Wheels Of Steel". Undoubtedly influencing 90s turntablists such as DJ Shadow and Peanut Butter Wolf, Premier was able to incorporate a sense of melancholy into a genre normally associated with content-free thrills and spills.

Not only did these DJs create new scratches and expand HipHop's tonal and emotional palette, but they once again reinvented the use of the turntable. "In 1988 I became aware of DJs like Cash Money, Aladdin, Jazzy Jeff who were actually not just scratching, but taking two turntables and juggling, juggling noises and sounds and beats," says Rob Swift. ""Aladdin's Shuffle" was where he'd be shufflin' his shoulders, going behind his back, breaking each piece of a beat or a groove down which is like... Let's say a record is playing, with your fingers you tap the record gently on beat, so you're breaking down each noise on the record. You're breaking down the kick, the hi-hat, the snare. It's like everything is slowed down... In 1990 Steve D is credited with actually taking records and rearranging them like a sampler; making beats and stuff like that. Back then, DJs were mostly just going fast, doing speed like *"Rock the bells, bells, bells, bells...*". But Steve would take [LL Cool J's] "Rock The Bells" and make it sound funky and not just fast and 100 miles per hour. He would do patterns and beats with it."

While HipHop DJs were becoming more virtuosic on the turntables, the avant garde was becoming increasingly fascinated with mistakes. With his background at the Massachusetts College of Art, Christian Marclay, unlike Flash or even D.ST, was almost certainly aware of the conceptual antics of Cage and Fluxus. Inspired by the 'Social Sculptures' of German artist Joseph Beuys, Marclay's brand of turntablism was an intervention into consumerism's cult of the object. Using mass culture flotsam like ancient Califone turntables hijacked from local high schools and 50 cent records that he literally and figuratively cut up and rearranged, Marclay represented the selfconsciously conceptual flipside of HipHop's 'necessity is the mother of invention' readymades.

Accentuating the natural erosion of vinyl through use, Marclay constructed collages out of the skips and pops and hiss of discarded thriftstore records. By foregrounding surface noise, Marclay attempted to jolt the listener out of the reification created by the medium of recording. His 1985 *Record Without A Cover* – which was exactly what the title said it was – and *Footsteps*, the product of a gallery installation in which 3500 records lined the floor for six weeks for people to trample on and were then packaged as regular albums, were not dissimilar to the autodestructive art of Gustav Metzger, and drew attention to the sounds and noises of the record itself rather than the music imprinted in its grooves. This idea has since been taken to its logical conclusion by British art terrorists Project DARK, who construct 7" singles out of sandpaper, biscuits and Edam cheese.

As clever as Marclay's art pranks were, his original music and DJ sets are better. *Records* is a stunning collection of his collages made during the 80s and a recording of a short set he performed on Hal Willner's sorely missed television show, *Night Music*. The only problem with *Records* is that Marclay is just as much a performance artist as he is a sound manipulator and you miss him callously throwing the objects that he has created out of abused records into the crowd or onto the floor at gigs, actions which form an integral part of his set. Nonetheless, pieces like "Brown Rain" (1982) and "Black Stucco" (1986) are wondrous collages of steel drums, pingpong-ball rhythms, string crescendos and rainforests of unidentifiable sounds as densely and organically layered as one of Henri Rousseau's painted jungle backgrounds. An excerpt from a live performance, "His Master's Voice" is a more typical collage of a preacher railing against rock 'n' roll damnation with *"Push, push in the bush"* disco, Wagnerian chorales, Metal guitar spin-outs and the Hawaiian kitsch of Don Ho flitting in and out of the mix. Unlike too many avantists, Marclay's more conceptual pieces like "Groove", an eight-track layer of the same skipping record that produces a faltering drone; "Phonodrum", a piece composed by dragging a guitar string attached to the stylus across records and wooden discs studded with nails to produce rhythms; and "One Thousand Cycles", which was made from the reconstituted records he made by cutting records up and then gluing them back together, work just as well as his more 'mainstream' compositions.

The real masterpiece here, though, is "Jukebox Capriccio" from 1985, which is as whimsical as it is brilliant. Featuring squelching scratches, the synth hook from Soft Cell's "Tainted Love", kitschy xylophones, free jazz freakouts, ice-rink organs and cop show percussion (to describe the more discernible elements), "Jukebox Capriccio" imagines what Looney Tunes composer Carl Stalling would have sounded like as a DJ, and is one of the surprisingly few turntablist pieces that take advantage of the reality that the entire history of recorded music is available for use.

Hugely influenced by Marclay, but using his techniques and style to explore the ghost world created by vinyl's gradual dissolution is British musician/composer Philip Jeck. Crucially, though, Jeck was equally influenced by New York's masters of the megamix, DJs like Walter Gibbons, Larry Levan and François Kevorkian. Rather than splatter sound like Jackson Pollock, Jeck uses the broad brushstrokes of Mark Rothko. His masterpiece is 1993's *Vinyl Requiem*, an epic multimedia composition for 180 turntables, nine slide projectors and two movie projectors that was a lament for vinyl in the face of the digital juggernaut.

While scratching may be, as has often been noted, an aesthetic challenge to the concepts of ownership and copyright, the use of turntablism as an affront to the sanctity of the work of art is largely the preserve of one man – Otomo Yoshihide. HipHop might mutate and refocus the energies of old music in order to create something new, but with the possible exception of The Bomb Squad's productions for Public Enemy, there is a reverence for the Old School – HipHop may rewrite tradition, but it never rejects it.

For a different approach, check out "WJAZ-1" on the self-titled debut album by Otomo's Improv group Ground Zero. Otomo uses the turntable as the foundation for a savage de(con)struction of the classic jazz mentality. With John Zorn dripping sarcasm as he imitates a sanctimonious boho jazz radio disc jockey, Otomo subdues a Coltrane lick with shredding scratching before laying down a Jimmy Smith Hammond groove for Zorn to blow ballistic over. A sustained, barbaric bleat of guitar feedback extracted via the turntable from a pillar of classic rock and spun back over itself until grinding to a sputter, "Massacring" is even more ferocious. Emerging contemporaneously with Rage Against The Machine, who do something very similar, Otomo's scratch-imitating guitar patterns on "Sniper XR" are a potentially even more radical challenge to rockist orthodoxy.

Unlike HipHop DJs who operate largely within the framework established by Herc, Flash and Theodore, Otomo is a free jazz autodidact whose only reference points are ethnomusicology and an encyclopedic knowledge of musique concrète. Thus, as is the case with Marclay and Jeck, Otomo employs sound for sound's sake even more purely than the HipHop DJs. Using the turntable to bolster the claustrophobia or mania his bandmates create, the idea of the break is superfluous to Otomo: there is no need for a groove or for anything to drop out just as long as it's noise, so a snippet of Trouble Funk emerges from the din on "Chronicle-2", music blurs into cross-faded static on "Silanganan Ingay" and note-shredding axemen leap out of the stylus on "Euthanasia Drive" and "I X Love II B.S. M-Project 2".

Although he doesn't dive headlong into the spin-outs of information overload that Otomo does, Canadian turntablist Martin Tétreault uses a similar approach in which the stylus is the passageway to tundras of sound buffeted by gusts of howling static and populated with melting stalagmites and brittle icicles. On records like *Île Bizarre*, a collaboration with Ikue Mori and Dianne Labrosse, and *Dur Noyau Dur*, a duet with guitarist René Lussier, Tétreault's primal scratching is performed with tiny gestures that evoke the invisible and inaudible microscopic worlds that exist in barnacled rock crevices, while his turntable tableaux are barren acid washes of denuded horns and strings.

When the HipHop DJ track spread from the East Coast, it landed most forcefully in San Francisco's Bay Area. The Bay Area had an enormous mobile DJ scene in the mid-80s, particularly among the sizeable Filipino community. In a fashion not dissimilar to the Philly DJs who first turbocharged the wheels of steel, these Filipino DJs were largely ostracized from the HipHop scene and made their mark by working out hyper-dextrous tricks on their Technics. While many DJs who performed live were taking turntablism into the realm of showbiz by scratching with their noses or other body parts, the Bay Area DJs were only interested in one thing: skills. It was here that the art of DJing became a spectacle of those magnificent men and their spinning machines, where the gymnastics were replaced by a flurry of crabs, flares, orbits, strobes, twiddles and hydroplanes.[1]

With turntable chops so awesome that they've been banned from the competitions that are the lifeblood of the turntablist scene, the most famous of the Bay Area's Filipino DJ crews, The Invisbl Skratch Piklz (including at various times DJ Q-Bert, Mixmaster Mike, DJ Apollo, Shortkut, DJ Disk, DJ Flare, Yoda Frog) heralded the return of the DJ as a self-contained group. Emerging as a force in 1992 by taking the DMC World DJ Championship away from the odious DJ Dave from Germany (who, as John Carluccio's excellent film *Battle Sounds* showed, actually air-scratched and performed handstands on a moving turntable), The Skratch Piklz brought turntablism back to the basics of scratching and cutting and away from the grandstanding showmanship that it had largely become.

---

[1] In the vernacular of turntablism, the crab is where you tap the fader using all of your fingers in sequence against your thumb (like fingers drummed on a table), producing extremely fast speeds. The flare is similar to the transformer scratch, but with more speed and noise because you're literally bouncing the fader off of the edge of the fader slot. An orbit is essentially a scratch that is performed both forwards and backwards, most often used in tandem with the flare. Strobing is a beat-juggling technique where you're separating each beat on two records by tapping them to keep them in sync. The twiddle is similar to the crab, but using only two fingers. And a hydroplane is where you lightly touch the record while it's spinning to get a frictive sound.

While turntablism was meant to be heard (and seen) live, it probably works best in the mixtape format where the DJs' propensity for indulgent scientifical madness is reined in by the high thrills-per-minute ratio that is crucial to the medium. Tracing its roots back to *Death Mix* and popularised by New York radio DJ Kid Capri, the mixtape is emblematic of HipHop's basic guiding principle: the flow and juxtaposition are everything. If history is indeed over, then the aesthetic of the mixtape (along with the samplescape) has become post-history's overarching narrative and turntablists the epic poets.

The *Odyssey* of HipHop mixtapes, and very likely the greatest of them all, is Q-Bert's utterly devastating 1994 mix *Demolition Pumpkin Squeeze Musik*. Inspiring the approach of the *King Of Diggin'* mixtapes by Japanese DJ Muro, Q-Bert (with some help from fellow Skratch Piklz Shortkut and DJ Disk) unleashes his untouchable deck skills on HipHop's treasure trove of breaks that are so Old Skool that Q-Bert calls them "Pre-Skool". Where Flash and Herc created HipHop out of the syncretic readymade of the breakbeat, Q-Bert colonises and infests the break with his scratches and blocks of viral noise. With what are now rudimentary turntable skills, Flash's journey on the wheels of steel was more like an adventure in the record crates. With the break merely the catalyst for Q-Bert's wildstyle jamming, *Demolition Pumpkin Squeeze Musik* is a true adventure on the wheels of steel through fantastic George Lucas-style mindscapes where the scratches sound like the shapeshifting video game charcters of Q-Bert's imagination.

Demolition Pumpkin Squeeze Musik starts off with Q-Bert duetting with guitarist Alex Lifeson as he scratches over Rush's "Tom Sawyer" before quick-cutting to Eddie Bo's New Orleans funk classic "Hook & Sling". He proceeds to travel through "Tramp" (Lowell Fulson's version), Banbarra's "Shack Up" and Rhythm Heritage's "Theme from SWAT", transforming them all with the crossfader and peppering them with dozens of snippets of *Style Wars* and *Wildstyle*. The highlight, though, is the way he stretches out Bootsy Collins's bassline on James Brown's "Give It Up Or Turn It A Loose" and then breaks it down along with the guitar riff into The Blackbyrds' "Rock Creek Park".

The emergence of crews like The Skratch Piklz, The X-ecutioners and The Beat Junkies dovetailed with the developing independent HipHop movement to establish a flourishing 'real' HipHop culture that stood in opposition to the crass materialism, stupid violence and talentlessness of what they disparagingly called 'rap'. Where mainstream rap was a comfortable collusion with the established practices of the record industry, the turntablists looked back to HipHop's origins as a street-culture with its own language and code of practice. As the intro to Z-Trip's "U Can Get With Discs Or U Can Get With DAT" (which is featured on *Return Of The DJ Volume 1*) said, *"Ignoring the DJ in HipHop is like ignoring the guitar in rock 'n' roll"*.

The *Return Of The DJ* records, compiled by David Paul, editor of the *Bomb Hip-Hop* zine, effectively announced that a DJ could be a band. Originally released in 1995, *Return Of The DJ Vol 1* was, incredibly, the first album to be devoted exclusively to the HipHop DJ. Although *Volume 1* remained strictly underground, *Volume 2* caught the leftfield zeitgeist and indeed heralded the rise of turntablism.

While *Volume 2* had brilliant tracks like Radar & Z-Trip's manically tense "Private Parts", Kid Koala taking B-boys ballroom dancing on "Static's Waltz" and Z-Trip's "Rockstar", a glorious condensation of the dope-addled experiences of the white American teenage male, *Volume 1* was the better of the two. Picking up on an idea from Q-Bert (and John Cage), who used to play tunes like "Mary Had a Little Lamb" on the turntable by manipulating a recording of a pure tone with the pitch control lever, Rob Swift's "Rob Gets Busy" uses the pitch control adjustment on the Technics turntable to mutate the Moog riff from The JBs' "Blow Your Head" before embarking on an exposition of the beat juggling techniques developed by Steve D in 1990. The Skratch Piklz show off their battery of flare and crab scratches on "Invasion Of The Octopus People", while Mixmaster Mike invoked the ghosts of Double Dee & Steinksi on "Terrorwrist". It wasn't all excitement and flash, though. Peanut Butter Wolf's "The Chronicles (I Will Always Love HER)" was similar to "DJ Premier In Deep Concentration" and DJ Shadow's records in that it was a melancholic journey through HipHop's short history that showed both how much had been gained and how much had been lost.

Given the prominence of the DJ on the pop cultural landscape, it seems that this melancholic nostalgia proved nearly universal. There's a DJ everywhere you look nowdays: not only do those great white hopes of the Steve Lamaq set, Ash, and the current rock antichrists, Limp Bizkit, have spinners in their midst, but so does, wait for it, Billy Ray Cyrus. Perhaps even more surprisingly, The X-ecutioners could be found in the UK Top Ten in March 2002 with "It's Goin' Down", a collaboration with Nu Metal dorks Linkin Park. *Spin* magazine summed up turntablism's fairly uncomfortable relationship with the mainstream when they asked: "Who's using who more?"

PART FOUR

FREEDOM

DESTROY ALL MUSIC

THE FUTURISTS' ART OF NOISES

BY MARK SINKER

No more painters, no more writers, no more musicians, no more sculptors, no more religions, no more republicans, no more royalists, no more imperialists, no more anarchists, no more socialists, no more Bolsheviks, no more aristocrats, no more armaments, no more police, no more countries, enough of all these imbecilities, no more, no more, no more, no more, no more
Louis Aragon, *Manifeste Du Mouvement Dada*

In his introduction to a 1954 French reprint of Luigi Russolo's 1913-16 manifesto *L'Arte Dei Rumori* (*The Art Of Noises*), pioneer Lettrist Maurice LeMaître charged all known heirs of Futurism – apart of course from the Lettrists – with both plagiarism and betrayal. Betrayal, that is, of a certain past's dream of the future, not by ignoring this dream, but elaborating on it. "Examine a history of music and you will not find... even a mention of [Russolo's] name. Such an injustice cannot be tolerated at a time when the neo-Russoloans like John Cage, [Edgard] Varèse and Pierre Schaeffer are boasting with impudence," he wrote. LeMaître praised Russolo's systematisation, and scorned Schaeffer's. Futurism had birthed dada, he said, and dada had inspired Erik Satie, and since "Satie's dadaism already existed, Schaeffer justifies badly what his predecessors had done well not to justify."

The Lettrists were a furious little post-surrealist Parisian sect, at war with the oppressive building blocks of language itself: they wanted to turn the alphabet itself into a kind of weapon. LeMaître was responding to Schaeffer's 1952 treatise *À La Recherche D'Une Musique Concrète*, which laid out his proposal of a coming music fashioned from collages of disc (and later tape) recordings, of any sound whatever, from pianos to steamtrains. In fact, Schaeffer *had* mentioned Russolo – just before attributing all of the Italian painter-turned-inventor's detailed proposals about the shape of music to come to self-obsessed loudmouth Filippo Tomasso Marinetti, founder and spokesman of the Futurist movement and exactly the type that always walks off with the spoils of half-baked history's regard. The Futurists issued some 50 manifestos between 1909 and 1916, on poetry, painting, sculpture, theatre and music, and Marinetti is yet again wrongly credited for the work of Russolo, who was surely Futurism's most self-effacing and diligently persistent figure. The twist is this: while Schaeffer, the inventor of musique concrète, was notoriously self-effacing and persistent, LeMaître his denouncer was a voluble pedant with a gift for shock-tactic careerism and not much more. These days hardly a month goes by without some excitable young muso announcing the new true break with all the dead past, invoking Russolo or Marinetti or both, in a noisy muddle of marketable vision and bad education. Such is Futurism's odd legacy.

CHRONOLOGY #1

1909 The Futurist Manifesto announces the death of the past, a Year Zero for Italian art and heritage: "Turn aside the canals to flood the museums!" A claque of impatient young Italian painters and poets publish manuals exalting dynamism over the familiar, an end to imitation and 'taste', the celebration of pride, speed and shock. They glory in machines, and call for the transformation of all culture.
1910 Balilla Pratella writes a *Manifesto Of Futurist Music*.
1911 Pratella publishes a *Manifesto Of The Technics Of Futurist Music*. Music must "represent the spirit of crowds, of great industrial complexes, of trains, of ocean liners, of battle fleets, of automobiles and aeroplanes. It must add to the great central themes of the musical poem the domain of the machine and the victorious realm of electricity." In the Libyan war – a colonial spat between Italy and Turkey – soundpoet Marinetti turns war correspondent: "Every five seconds siege cannons disembowel space with a harmony ZANG TUMB TUUMB mutiny of 500 echoes to seize it with its teeth. . . Attention! Courage! what joy to see hear smell everything everything taratatata of the machine guns to scream at the top of one's voice under bites slaps traak-traak lashes pic-pac-pum-tumb... ZANG TUMB TUUMB toc-toc-toc-toc... crooc-craaac..." And a Futurist music followed. Jannelli's *Sintesi Delle Sintesi* contains gunshots, screams and laughter. The performers in Balla's *Macchina Tipografica* mimic a printing press. And to replace the conventional orchestra, Russolo designs and builds his infamous intonarumori – Heath Robinson boomboxes of canvas and wood, cousins of the football rattle and the siren, some powered by small electric motors, all flaring into

bullhorn mouths – for his 'compositions' *Awakening Of A City* and *Meetings Of Automobiles And Planes*.

1913-16 Russolo writes *The Art Of Noises*: "Noise has the power to bring us back to life." If by 'life' he means hostile audiences hurling vegetables, he is not wrong.

1913 The Victor recording of James Reese Europe's proto-jazz ragtime dance band playing "Castles In Europe" features Buddy Gilmore's trap drum impression of a machine gun. A second recording, "Castle Walk", includes Gilmore's imitation of pistol shots.

1916 In Zurich, soundpoet Hugo Ball founds the Cabaret Voltaire, and dada is born. Ball is joined by Tristan Tzara, Richard Huelsenbeck and others.

1918 Tzara writes the dada manifesto: "I want nothing; I am against manifestos: I am against principles." Within a year dada goes international, and Tzara heads for Paris, to fashion an endless career out of nostalgia for a brief daring moment.

Insurrection is an art, and like every art it has its rules.
Leon Trotsky, *The History Of The Russian Revolution*

"Italian Futurists," asked Edgard Varèse in 1921, "why do you merely reproduce the vibrations of our daily life only in their superficial and distressing aspects? My dream is of instruments that will obey my thought – and which, by bringing about a flowering of hitherto unsuspected timbres, will lend themselves to combinations it will please me to impose on them and bow themselves to the demands of my inner rhythm."

Varèse was "the only musician of the dada years", wrote Louis Aragon, many years after he had put Paris dada and its self-promoting offshoot Surrealism behind him, when he became a moralising cheerleader for the French Communist party. The remark combines admiration with a hint of regret, implying correctly that Varèse stood above the dreary factionalism and relentless avant garde grandstanding of the late teens and 20s.

Varèse was ally of all and toady to none. Surrealist composer he was not, for Surrealism anathematised music. André Breton, its tireless ideological policeman, idolised the late Jacques Vaché, a war veteran who liked to pull a gun on concertgoers. In Breton's reckoning, the only music acceptable to a Surrealist was the random, repeated pistol shot into a passing crowd. The aesthetics of such an event depended, evidently, on neither sound texture nor formal structure. Its significance was as sociopathic conceptual art, and – like many Surrealist gestures – the idea went round the world as astonishingly effective hype.

Yet if anything, when it came to music, dada had been even more dismissive. Breton's absolutism at least reflected his suspicion of music's power to move, his fear of its routine techniques, and human susceptibility to them. At the Cabaret Voltaire you could hear the sounds of Chicago and the Congo, as contemptuously imagined by young white artists ignorant of either: that is, grunts and howls and clumsy drumming. At issue was the sanctification of rubbish. After all, with aged Europe turning its Gatlings on its youth – and Marinetti's prophecies on their heads – wasn't the very notion of culture a cretinous joke? "We were for the war and dadaism today is still for war," argued Huelsenbeck in later years. In 1916, putting cloudy red water between the Zurich mob and the Italian Futurists (who had been Hugo Ball's inspiration), he had written that dada was "decisively opposed to the future". In 1919 dada composer Georges Ribement-Dessaignes would insist that, "for the purposes of political morale", music be forbidden and musicians hanged. Evidently he had exempted himself from his own diktat – he continued to write cheery dance tunes by throwing dice.

The Futurists had gone to the front eagerly, mostly entering a new-fangled motorcycle corps. In essence, they became victims of their own brilliant propaganda. Dada – a collective of draft-dodgers – used hype as a blizzard of shock and contradiction to undermine itself; Surrealism used it to promote itself, with great style and curiously little substance. But the Futurists alone earnestly set themselves the task of living up to their own apocalyptic demands. The problem was that their ability to stage provocative spectacle – such as the symphonies of aeroplane propellers – was everywhere occluding awareness of their theoretical and practical breakthroughs. Hence Varèse's attitude.

By the late 20s, the Surrealists' battleground was no longer bad faith in radical art, over the corpse of dada, but bad faith in radical politics, over the corpse of Bolshevism. When mutual bickering palled, Tzara and Breton would unite to excoriate Marinetti, whose work had cleared the space both of them lived in, an Oedipal spasm viewed by most historians through a highly PC lens. Because the Futurists gave vocal if adolescent support for the Fascisti, many Futurist innovations have been consigned to subaltern status: their explosive typographical experiments are treated as premature constructivism, while their paintings are treated as a subgroup within cubism.

And Russolo's music? Badly wounded in the war and living on an inadequate veteran's pension, the composer had quietly distanced himself from the never-ending Marinetti show. By the late 20s, he and Varèse (who never hid his left wing sympathies) were friends. The evidence of their similar outlook can be read in his pre-war publications. As the closing words of *L'Arte Dei Rumori* insist, while "the characteristic of noise is that of reminding us brutally of life", the Art of Noises "should not limit itself to an imitative reproduction. It will achieve its greatest emotional power in acoustical enjoyment itself."

Futurist music was to be a sensual exploration of noise as a continuum of detail, structured by contrast and juxtaposition. Its symbolic status as pure irruption – the unbiddable negation of all harmony – was at best an optional bonus, and very possibly a misleading distraction. As proof, share the pleasure this librarian of enharmonic frottage found in acoustic variation by repeating to yourself the names of Russolo's machines: ululatori, rombatori, crepitatori, stropicciatori, scoppiatori, ronzatori, gorgogliatori and sibilatori.

Their abrupt English translations – howlers, roarers, cracklers, rubbers, bursters, hummers, gurglers, whistlers – may make us miss the point. If Futurist music is an insurrectionary art, it demands a refined, analytic technics: "Here are the six families of noises of the Futurist orchestra that we will soon realise mechanically: (1) roars, thunderings, explosions, hissing roars, bangs, booms (2) whistling, hissing, puffing (3) whispers, murmurs, mumbling, muttering, gurgling (4) screeching, creaking, rustling, humming, crackling, rubbing (5) noises obtained by beating on metals, woods, skins, stones, pottery, etc (6) voices of animals and people: shouts, screams, shrieks, wails, hoots, howls, death rattles, sobs."

This is a revolution grounded not in easy and abstract shock gesture but in close attention to material reality: "Among the different motors, electric motors are the quietest... At first it might even be believed that they have no rhythm. As everyone knows, the electric motor produces a beautiful and characteristic purr, which is musically very close to a fifth held by a harmonium. This hum is continuous, but if studied attentively, it will be perceived every two or three seconds to have a slight variation of pitch or intensity... The rhythmical movements of a noise are infinite. As with tone, so with rhythm; there is always one which is predominant, but around this predominant rhythm numerous other secondary are also perceptible."

CHRONOLOGY #2

1912 Painter and microtonal composer Nikolai Kublin is the first to propose an "emancipation of dissonance", in Die Blaue Reiter's *Almanac*. Mayakovsky signs the Russian Futurist manifesto, *A Slap In The Face Of Public Taste*.
1913 Matyushin, Kruchenykh and Malevich stage *Victory Over The Sun*, a quartertone opera played on an out-of-tune piano.
1917 Diaghilev stages Satie's ballet *Parade* in Paris, featuring a libretto by Cocteau, set design by Picasso and instrumentation by Russolo; that is, until Satie rescores it for typewriter, revolver, ship's whistle and siren.
1918 The word "Surréaliste" first appears, in Apollinaire's programme notes to *Parade*. Futurism is nowhere mentioned.
1919 Mayakovsky's Kom-Fut movement declares that the birth of a revolutionary art demands the rejection of all bourgeois culture, a claim denounced by Lenin and Lunarcharsky.

CHRONOLOGY #3

1913 Varèse attends the riotous premiere, at the Théâtre des Champs-Elysées in Paris, of Stravinsky's *Rite Of Spring*.
1916 He sails to New York, where, with Picabia and others, he establishes New York dada and denounces Futurism for its superficial machine mimicry, and destroys all his own compositions to date.

1921 The Futurists stage a show in Paris at the Théâtre des Champs Elysées, with Varèse again in attendance – he signs *Dada Soulève Tout*, denouncing Marinetti and Russolo.

1923 Georges Antheil plays – at the same theatre, to the usual riot – works by Stravinsky, Schoenberg, Milhaud, Auric and his own *Airplane Sonata*, *Jazz Sonata*, *Sonata Sauvage* and *Mechanisms*.

1924 Varèse stays with Léger, whose film *Ballet Mécanique* inaugurates avant garde cinema. Antheil's soundtrack requires tamtam, bass drum, two pianos, pianola, three xylophones and three propeller mechanisms. The same year Breton publishes the first *Surrealist Manifesto*, denouncing Tzara, while Satie and Picabia stage their opera *Relâche*, and René Clair's movie *Entr'acte*, scripted by Picabia, starring and scored by Satie, is screened during the interval.

1928 Russolo moves to Paris, where movie studios show an interest in his intonarumori.

1929 Varèse's *Amériques* is performed in Paris, its sirens now replaced with Ondes Martenots. After the usual riot, Tzara needs four stitches, while Russolo shyly hands Varèse an inscribed copy of *The Art Of Noises*.

CHRONOLOGY #4

1915 The Futurist Pratella uses intonarumori in his opera *L'Aviatore Dro*.

1918 For Azari's *Aerial Theatre*, Russolo builds a modified aeroplane engine, able to vary its timbre.

1922 Marinetti uses intonarumori in his play *Il Tamburo Di Fuoco*.

1923 Nikolai Foregger devises a Noise Orchestra – broken bottles, packing cases, metal sheets, whistles and percussion – for G Smetanin's *The Factory* and his own *Machine Dance*, with music hall and human mimicry of running machines, which later influences The Tiller Girls and Busby Berkeley.

1918–24 In Nizhny Novogorod, Petrograd, Baku, Moscow and elsewhere, Arseni Avramov stages citywide spectacles with fireworks, factory and ship sirens, flags and pistol shots, and featuring simultaneous sound and action from artillery, the navy, infantry, tanks, a machine gun division and hydroplanes.

1928 Giovanni-come-lately Futurist Prampolini uses intonarumori in the mimed ballet *Santa Velocità*.

A virtuoso is always a spectacle, just as an engine is always a rhythm. A stroke of the bow is a chronicle, a grating is always melodious.
Luigi Russolo

Superficially subversive, art gestures challenge the easily challenged. Such gestures enter history because they're so easy to translate and domesticate. Nothing explains Russolo's expulsion from mainstream avant garde history better than the very fact that wins him an eternal footnote in it – his invention, for *Awakening Of A City*, of the graphic score. Futurism taught its successors to be typographically alert. Russolo's music script – ordinary staves, but with thick black lines instead of dots – was no mere concession to the approximate pitch of the intonarumori, but a conscious celebration.

The Lettrist assault on Pierre Schaeffer was arguably no more than a bid by the newest little post-war French avant garde to make its name on the back of the one just established and canonised: Futurism was cultural news again in the early 50s, and – courtesy of Marinetti's links with Mussolini – a bit naughty. Schaeffer's citing of it as a precursor had been scholarly and bland, almost content-free except in the loosest sense, and fairly unexceptionable: now, stung by LeMaître's assault, he would shift in the mid-50s to ground musique concrète in two ways that Russolo had indeed anticipated: first, by focusing ever more obsessively on empirical research into the manifold facts of acoustics; second, by attempting to devise a music script, a written documentation, to encompass all possible noise. But it was in the US that the graphic score flourished, under Cage (the virus for it was probably ferried back from Lettrist Paris by Robert Rauschenberg). The Cageian metagraphic accepted explicitly what Schaeffer's system seemed unable to grasp: that a written music simply cannot find a new symbol for every possible different noise. Shortcuts and abstractions will eventually by necessary: this is what writing is. At the heart of concrète's total soundworld is a dream of full concrete particularity, everything in the world as materials for music, each item as valid as any other. To write this is to reintroduce a symbolic order: and this order may gently reinstate everything pallid and past that the embrace of material particularity – of engine noise as the root of harmony and rhythm, for example – was intended to reject.

Writing is a bid for permanence, a paper trail leading forwards towards a coup on the future, a message in a bottle drifting implacably towards the invisible legions of academics, teachers, freelance researchers and performers responsible for music transmission, education, analysis and explanation. It's this that transforms the score into reaction's most subtle fifth columnist. For the Lettrist movement, which was fascinated by the machinery of cultural production considered as machinery, the solution was the demolition, brick by brick, of the prisonhouse of all extant symbol systems. Every atom of written or spoken language, every grunt or letter, must be rendered unstable, revolutionary. LeMaître loved Russolo's intonarumori because, as undomesticated novelty instruments, they demanded a neo-technicity that would destroy musicianly habit and dissolve the bonds of history. Russolo insisted that the orchestra had to be exploded timbrally from within, broadening the field of sound towards unknown vistas of noise and terrains of uncolonised detail, necessitating new maps on which new emotions and new social possibilities could be located.

In his 1959 essay "Russolo And The Futurists", Pierre Schaeffer took Russolo's famous eight part manifesto point by point, in reverse order, to demonstrate that the only intonarumori which could deliver both a full tonal expansion of music and an appropriately expanded musicianly understanding were records used as instruments. In other words, LeMaître's peevishness notwithstanding, musique concrète was Futurism undiluted.

But where Cage, Schaeffer and the Lettrists came untied from Russolo – and, born before his time, he had far greater excuse than they – was in failing to recognise that the record, as its very name declares, would itself stage a coup on the future, diminishing paper music's dominion forever. Dada had of course long recognised mass culture's implicit radical-critical potential, and had freed some of it, via the jumpcut. But where the collage of the visual or the written was easily effected in 1916, the effective performance of music collage – as with Satie's 1924 score for *Entr'acte*, a flurry of random cut-ups entitled

Cinéma – was beyond the skills of any performer then living. Marinetti's 1914 *Un Paesiggio Udito* features phonographs playing recordings of water and fire; in 1928 Surrealist Luis Buñuel would soundtrack *Un Chien Andalou* with alternating recordings of Wagner and Argentinian tango (actually an art formalisation of routine moviehouse practice in the silent era, but one that the film itself gave some kick to). But it was the 7" microgroove 45, mass manufactured the world over from the late 40s on, that made writing unnecessary to any noise-filled new music's access to the future. It proved that Futurism had never needed Futurists to get into people's heads – it just needed those heads to have ears.

For all their energised glory, the graphic scores of the Cageans (like the métagraphies of the Lettrists, and thus exactly like pre-Futurist scores) demanded a priestcraft to ensure their authentic interpretation. Cage might argue that all sounds were equal, but he was fiercely opposed to the anything-goes school of Cage performance. Unlike Cage, Russolo failed to found a coherent school of Futurist performers. So his scores (only one survives), his recordings (ditto) and his concerts, too spectacular for their own good, taught hardly anyone to love that soft engine purr for what it was.

CHRONOLOGY #5

1932 Varèse and Antonin Artaud plan a great spectacle, a sci-fi disaster epic to be called *The Astronomer*, or perhaps *The Firmament Is Gone*. The composer intends to build several Futurist instruments, but Artaud is unwell and the project languishes.
1934 Russolo returns to Italy and painting. His machines remain in Paris, where they will eventually be destroyed by Nazi bombs.
1946 With his *Introduction À Une Nouvelle Poésie Et À Une Nouvelle Musique*, Isidore Isou founds the Lettrists and makes a name for himself by accusing surviving Surrealists and dadaists of plagiarism before the fact. In 1948, a radio broadcast of Artaud's *Pour En Finir Avec Le Jugement De Dieu* (drums, gongs, sound effects, human noises) is banned at the last minute. The avant garde establishment protests, and Artaud dies a month later.
1949 John Cage rediscovers Satie's furniture music.

1951 Isou wins the Avant Garde award at Cannes for *Treatise On Drool And Eternity*.

1952 The year Guy Debord's Lettriste Inernationale splits from Isou's and LeMaître's movement, briefly co-opting it in order to expel it (for betrayal of its own principles), LeMaître's *Is The Feature On Yet?* (symbols scribbled directly onto celluloid, with audience movements and comments fed into its soundtrack) vies with Debord's *Hurlements En Faveur De Sade* (a patchwork of fragments of dialogue, blank screen and long, long, long silences) for the same honour. At Black Mountain college in North Carolina, the first 'happening': Cage reads a lecture from a stepladder, Charles Olson and Artaud scholar MC Richards read poems, Merce Cunningham dances, David Tudor plays piano, painter Robert Rauschenberg plays scratchy records on a wind-up phonograph, his infamous all-white paintings hanging all round, while movies and slides are projected.

1957 Jamaican DJ Sir Coxsone Dodd establishes himself and his legendary Downbeat sound system, a control tower of turntables, amplifiers and speakers, on Love Lane and Beeston Street, Kingston.

1965 La Monte Young, Tony Conrad and John Cale incorporate a turtle aquarium motor into the tuning system used by The Theater Of Eternal Music.

1966 Andy Warhol incorporates The Velvet Underground into his Exploding Plastic Inevitable.

1968 Valerie Solanas, excluded Factory hopeful and author of *SCUM Manifesto*, empties a non-Surrealist pistol into Andy Warhol, ending neo-dada, birthing punk.

1974 Kraftwerk make *Autobahn*.

1975 Lou Reed makes *Metal Machine Music*.

THE LIMITS OF LANGUAGE

TEXTUAL APOCALYPSE: MERZ, LETTRISM, SOUND POETRY

BY JULIAN COWLEY

Words are an arbitrary communication unit and any sound could do as well. An exquisite sonnet could be conveyed in bestial snarls and grunts once the units were established
William S Burroughs

Poets are meant to liberate words, not chain them in phrases. Who told poets they were supposed to think? Poets are meant to sing and to make words sing
Brion Gysin, "Cut-Ups Self-Explained", reprinted in *The Third Mind*

In his book *Reports From The Present*, Glaswegian poet Tom Leonard offers an account entitled "How I Became A Sound Poet". During the early 1960s he heard a radio broadcast of Bob Cobbing's poem "Are Your Children Safe In The Sea?", where that question is repeated with changing vocal inflections and sliding sense: "It was very menacing, very daemonic – and very funny." Leonard thought it was great.

Around the same time he heard Brion Gysin's recently composed poem "I Am That I Am", where that closed statement is opened out revealingly, through a process of permutation plus mild electronic treatment. "I fell out of bed beating time to it. This was a response usually reserved for Berlioz and the last movement of Bruckner symphonies." Gysin, primarily a painter, secured a place in literary history when he introduced William Burroughs to the cut-up method, a randomised collage technique which helped the novelist to produce some of his most incisive texts. Around 1968 Leonard decided to join the fray, and in 1975 he participated in one of Cobbing's annual sound poetry festivals in London. "My Name Is Tom", prepared for the occasion, pulverised the title's unassuming statement into its component parts and worked permutations, with the aid of a two-track tape recorder over which the poet declaimed further materials: a conversation between fictional air-ace Biggles and his pal Ginger, "a dialogue on the metaphysics of the naming process". Simultaneously Leonard raised placards, adding a dimension of visual textuality. The piece was a modest excursion into mixed media, typical of late 1960s adventures in the arts. It also had clear precursors in the history of sound poetry.

There is a wealth of timbre in the spoken word which no orchestra possesses. Nature has endowed the magnificent instrument, the human voice, with subtle tone qualities for which music has no equivalent
Luigi Russolo, *The Art Of Noises*

In 1914, shortly before the outbreak of World War One, Filippo Marinetti, flamboyant promoter of Italian Futurism, performed a poem at a London gallery. The poem evoked sensory bombardment experienced in a besieged city. The Fascist iconoclast marched around the room, reciting furiously and gesticulating, in accordance with his theory of dynamic declamation. Novelist and painter Wyndham Lewis witnessed the event and reported that the English artist Christopher Nevison "belaboured a gigantic drum" to accompany Marinetti. "But it was a matter of astonishment to me what Marinetti could do with his unaided voice. He certainly made an extraordinary amount of noise. A day of attack upon the Western Front, with all the 'heavies' hammering together, right back to the horizon, was nothing to it." A few years later, dada activist Tristan Tzara could be seen in public places erupting into random outbursts punctuated with loud ringing from an electric bell. Marinetti celebrated the energies unleashed by warfare; Tzara protested against orchestrated slaughter in the trenches – radically differing perspectives, yet the extended language of sound poetry appeared to both men the appropriate response to contemporary conditions. While fellow Futurist Luigi Russolo extolled the rich resources of the human voice and affirmed noise to be an inescapable factor in 20th century life, Marinetti conceived "parole in liberta" (words in freedom), ditching conventional syntax, approaching the printed page as an arena for typographical dynamism, and using words to mimic the sounds of the world as directly as possible, to reproduce "the countless noises of matter in motion". Newspaper reporting of World War One concealed physical suffering; it debased words. Dada poet Hugo Ball set out to put an end to conventional language "ravaged and laid barren by journalism". But even prior to the war Russian Futurist poets sought a new voice that would revitalise a jaded world. The secret was to shed received meaning and cleanse expression by returning it to stark utterance.

In 1913, while Igor Stravinsky caused a sensation with the pulsating primal rhythms of *The Rite Of Spring*, a group of his Russian compatriots, including avant garde poets Alexei Kruchenykh and Vladimir Mayakovsky, issued a manifesto, "Declaration Of The Word As Such", promoting the physical properties of language and specifically its existence as sound. Kruchenykh, with Vladimir Khlebnikov, had been developing transrational or 'zaum' poetry, using an invented language that resembled infantile babble, the outpourings of the insane or occult utterances not mediated by the conscious mind. The goal was immediate communication of intense feelings. Both Italian and Russian Futurists regarded poetry as essentially performative, best delivered in contexts that matched the ebullient and irreverent spirit of circus and music hall.

Total pandemonium. The people around us are shouting, laughing and gesticulating. Our replies are sighs of love, volleys of hiccups, poems, moos, and miaowing.
Hans Arp, *Dadaland*

In February 1916 Hans Arp and other members of the dada group established the Cabaret Voltaire in Zurich. As poets recited deliberate nonsense, drums were pummelled and pianos were hammered. Dada was uncompromisingly anti-art, yet its anti-poetry and anti-music were as serious as life itself. Arp recalled that "while the thunder of the batteries rumbled in the distance, we pasted, we recited, we versified, we sang with all our soul." Dada sound poetry assaulted the rational structures of modern European culture which perpetrated technologised slaughter and negated the value of the human body. Hugo Ball felt that dada was "fighting against the agony of the times and against an inebriation with death". In July 1916 Ball performed "O GADJI BERI BIMBA", a poem made in a language of his own invention, patterned sound, calculatedly non-Western. Its intrinsic musicality was acknowledged decades later when Talking Heads recorded the poem as "I Zimbra" on their Eno-produced album *Fear Of Music* (1979).

Inventing words was an established poetic strategy. Some sound poets have claimed ancestry in Lewis Carroll's "Jabberwocky" in *Through The Looking Glass* (1872), Christian Morgenstern's semantically opaque "kroklokwafzi" (around 1890) and Paul Scheerbart's poem "kikakoku!" (1897). In 1967 Henri Chopin composed "Frogs Of Aristophanes", acknowledging sound poetry elements in ancient Greek drama. In 1970, Morgenstern's poem supplied the title *Kroklok* for a visual and sound poetry magazine initiated by monastic concrete poet Dom Silvester Houédard. Another strategy brought existing languages into collision. Dada's "simultaneous poems" created an auditory vortex, words swirling like dirty water sucked into a plughole. Music, theatre and poetry fused in high-energy, decentred multivocal performances such as "L'Amiral Cherche Une Maison À Louer" ("The Admiral Seeks A House To Rent"), composed by Tristan Tzara with fellow dadaists Richard Huelsenbeck and Marcel Janco. Three illogical texts in three different languages are disrupted further by shrill whistle blasts, with ratchet and drum deployed as percussive irritants. Other explorations of language as noise were being conducted elsewhere. Henri Barzun, initiator of Orphism, had already investigated the potential of simultaneity, and Pierre Albert-Birot, editor from 1916 of the magazine *Sic*, was conducting polyphonic experiments. Swiss-born French concert violinist Arthur Pétronio formulated 'verbophony' in 1919, proposing a symphony of noises to be realised by multiple voices and instruments. As late as 1953 he formed a 'verbophonic choir'.

In Holland, in 1921, Theo Van Doesburg, founder of the De Stijl movement, addressed the need for trained listening. He published three "letter-sound images" under the pseudonym IK Bonset, declaring: "To take away its past it is necessary to renew the alphabet according to its abstract sound values. This means at the same time the healing of our poetic auditory membranes, which are so weakened that a long-term phono-gymnastics is necessary."

Fümms bö wö tää zää Uu,
pögiff,
kwii Ee
Kurt Schwitters, *Ursonata*

In 1932, in his journal *Merz 24*, Kurt Schwitters published the text of his "Sonate In Urlauten" or "Ursonata" ("Primal Sonata"), written throughout the preceding decade. Curious combinations of vowels and consonants are assembled into extended musical form. Schwitters made his own recording of this lengthy piece, but there have been numerous other realisations, notably flautist Eberhard Blum's 1991 version. A brief excerpt formed singer George Melly's contribution to a collection entitled *Miniatures* (an album that also boasts a brief Rabelaisian encounter between Bob Cobbing and Henri Chopin); Melly tells that recitation of these sounds once saved him when cornered by thugs. Brian Eno mixed a snippet of Schwitters's performance into "Kurt's Rejoinder" on his *Before And After Science* (1977). Schwitters was an associate of the core dada group, including Raoul Hausmann. Initial impetus for the "Ursonata" came from a poem constructed in 1918, when at Hausmann's instigation, a printer randomly set letters of the alphabet and punctuation marks to form:

**fmsbwtözäu
pggiv-..?mü.**

The beginning of Schwitters's epic takes its lead directly from this assemblage, although Hausmann disapproved of the classical mould into which the subversive implications of his act of provocation had been channelled. Schwitters could be far less elaborate. Novelist and publisher Stefan Themerson recalled such an occasion: "Kurt Schwitters, in 1924, shows the audience a poem containing only one letter [W] on a sheet of paper. He starts to 'recite', slowly raising his voice. His consonant changes from a whisper to a howling sound until he ends with a shockingly loud bark of a dog."

A wider audience was reached in 1933 by Marinetti and Fortunato Depero when Radio Milan made the first phonetic art broadcast. Marinetti issued a manifesto, "The Radio", embracing interference as well as "the geometry of silence" surrounding words, in the service of a "universal, cosmic human art".

Believing that the use of words in poetry is antiquated, our movement proposes a purer and profounder element, namely the letter.
Isidore Isou, *Lettriste Statement*

In the wake of the Second World War, a movement known as Lettrism emerged in Paris during under the guidance of Isidore Isou, like Tzara a Romanian. Isou proposed a totally new lexicon for vocal performance in order to galvanise and renew the entire social world. Words were to be pulverised to produce new particles for poetic use. Raoul Hausmann had accomplished as much in 1918; Isou and his followers taunted the older man as a plagiarist. Greil Marcus gives more details in *Lipstick Traces*, his secret history of the 20th century, which traces a trajectory from Dada through Lettrism to punk. Marcus memorably remarks that "Isou played Chubby Checker to Tzara's Fats Domino". François Dufrêne left the Lettrist movement to pursue his own vision of "ultra-lettrism". From 1953 his intensely physical and emotive "cri-rhythmes" took sound poetry into a knottily expressive world of grunts, howls and groans. In a more concentrated way than any poet before him, Dufrêne developed a vocabulary of breathing in and out, tongue clicks, farts and whistles, sucking, kissing, lip-smacking and spitting. Bob Cobbing commented: "One thinks of primitive song on hearing François Dufrêne. His cri-rhythmes employ the utmost variety of utterances, extended cries, shrieks, ululations, purrs, yarrs, yaups and cluckings, the apparently uncontrollable controlled into a spontaneously shaped performance."

A related phenomenon was Gil Wolman's conception of "Megapneumes". From 1950, he strived for communication based in the particulars of human respiration, the energy of the lungs inhaling and exhaling. Cobbing felt that Dufrêne and Wolman had ventured "back where poetry and music began... back beyond the word, beyond the alphabet to direct vocal outpourings which completely unified form and content". Their poetry had been anticipated by Antonin Artaud, who in November 1947 incorporated sound poems and violent screeching in *Pour En Finir Avec Le Jugement De Dieu* (*To Have Done With The Judgment Of God*), a radical project realised in the Paris studio of Radiodiffusion Française. Broadcast of the piece was immediately prohibited.

Today our acoustic technology is beginning to restore the ancient union of words and music, but especially the tape recorder has brought back the voice of the bard.
Marshall McLuhan, *Counterblast*

Wolman and Dufrêne used tape primarily as a recording medium, although from 1963 Dufrêne investigated superimposition and used reverb and echo effects. But as Cobbing noted in 1970, sound poetry had evolved along two complementary paths: one scientific and technological, seeking "the humanisation of the machine, the marrying of human warmth to the coldness of much electronically generated sound"; the other, a "return to the primitive, to incantation and ritual, to the coming together again of music and poetry, the amalgamation with movement and dance, the growth of the body to its full physical powers again as part of the body, the body as language."

The technological route had been signposted by composers Pierre Schaeffer and Pierre Henry who started making musique concrète in the late 1940s, redeploying materials already in the world. Their collaborative *Symphonie Pour Un Homme Seul* (*Symphony For A Man Alone*, 1949-50) inventively weaves various manifestations of the human voice amongst noises and instrumental sounds. Such concrete physicality had previously been an aspiration of sound poets, but recognition that tape machines could be a means of composition rather than merely documenting a performance proved a crucial development.

Bob Cobbing concurred with McLuhan that "the invention of the tape recorder has given the poet back his [sic] voice. For by listening to their voices on the tape recorder, with its ability to amplify, slow down and speed up voice vibrations, poets have been able to analyse and then immensely improve their vocal resources. Where the tape recorder leads, the human voice can follow." Tape recorders promised extension of human expressive resources, enabling the body to transcend its own performative limits. Foremost among poets unleashing the potential of this medium has been Henri Chopin. In common with Schaeffer and Henry, but independently, Chopin understood that "the sounding world had become concrete... after centuries of writing".

Chopin endured great personal hardship during the Second World War.

In 1943 he was arrested by the Nazis and deported to perform forced labour. He refused and was interred in concentration camps in Czechoslovakia and Germany. Meanwhile, members of his family who remained in France were murdered by the occupying forces. In 1945 he served as a nurse in the USSR, and in 1948 spent a brief period of military service in Indochina. He became determined to find a creative response to totalitarian barbarism and its supporting rhetoric.

In 1967 he proclaimed the existence of sound poetry quite distinct from "simple recitations of phonetic poems"; this poésie sonore "finds its sources in the very sources of language and, by the use of electromagnetics, owes almost nothing to any aesthetic or historical system of poetry". As editor of the sound poetry magazine *Cinquième Saison* between 1958-61, and of the international audio-review *OU* from 1964-72, Chopin became, in Cobbing's view, "the most important influence in propagating knowledge of concrete sound poetry throughout the world".

In 1955 he commenced his technologically assisted attack on the tyrannies of conventional language, which had proved incapable of responding adequately to events Chopin had witnessed under Nazi occupation. Soon he abandoned even the vestiges of words, instead utilising "micro-particles" of vocal sound which he subjects to close scrutiny. The premise of his audiopoems is that the tape machine enables us to "listen to our infinite vocal vibrations", which letters of the alphabet scarcely begin to suggest.

Technology has enlarged the voice immeasurably. Henri Chopin captured barely audible vocal sounds using extremely sensitive microphones so that, as Cobbing has remarked, "one mouth becomes an orchestra". In interview with John Hudak in 1990 (published in the booklet to the CD collection *Les 9 Saintes-Phonies*), Chopin suggested that poésie sonore has restored the link between music and words which existed for medieval troubadours and which was severed as literature, the printed word, lapsed into silence. Placing a microphone inside his mouth, Chopin discovered the body to be "like a factory that never stops. The body ignores silence. It is always a big factory".

In performance, Chopin augmented playback of recorded poems with on-stage vocalisations. As critic Larry Wendt has described, Chopin was inclined to "molest" the machine, "applying pressure to various parts of its mechanism to alter and distort the sound". Visceral impact is heightened by extreme volume; as late as 2000, he gave a performance in Leicester, England that was reported as "ferociously loud".

Action Poetry is born from the moment the poem is torn from the page.
Bernard Heidsieck, "Notes Convergentes"

In 1964 Chopin performed at London's Institute of Contemporary Arts, which was staging an exhibition of concrete and visual poetry at the time. Other participants were Brion Gysin and Bernard Heidsieck. In 1955 Heidsieck had launched his poèmes-partitions pieces, scores employing typographical variation and spacing on the page to steer performance. During the 1960s he integrated the tape recorder into his "action poetry", collaging words and phrases, including quotations from newspapers, with recordings of environmental noise. His goal was to shed light on daily reality in ways that words alone fail to achieve: "Poetry is open. Now. To the world." Found texts, contrapuntal superimposition and tape manipulation were deployed "to animate our mechanical and technocratic age by recapturing mystery and breath". Heidsieck's intense live realisations involved interaction between prerecorded material and real-time activity, sometimes using props such as a telephone.

Sound poetry dances, tastes, has shape.
Bob Cobbing, *Concerning Concrete Poetry*

Bob Cobbing has for nearly half a century been the most vocal, visible and unassimilable presence in British visual and sound poetry. Open to all performance options, he started in 1954 by exploring the form and texture of words and their physical expression with his poem "Worm", still performed with evident relish. He has worked with tape recorders and computers, but it's his deep personal reservoir of expressive resources that makes Cobbing's physical realisation of visual cues so distinctive. He has performed alone, collaborated in duets with Chopin,

Dufrêne, Welsh poet Peter Finch and composer Annea Lockwood, in vocal trio with the group Konkrete Canticle, with David Toop and Paul Burwell in abAna, and more recently with guitarist Hugh Metcalfe in Birdyak, often augmented by Lol Coxhill's soprano saxophone and dancer Jennifer Pike. During the 1980s Cobbing worked as Oral Complex with poet Clive Fencott and sound engineer John Whiting, an electronics specialist who has also worked with musical luminaries such as Luciano Berio and The Kronos Quartet. Fencott had previously been heard in the trio JGJGJG with Lawrence Upton and Cris Cheek. Cheek has subsequently worked with the group Slant.

Paula Claire, Cobbing's colleague in Konkrete Canticle along with Michael Chant and, later, Bill Griffiths, has favoured the role of catalyst: "The poems are for participation, for living in rather than for communication... Poetry is becoming once again a folk art. It is for everyone." Aspiring to ensure relevance to all, Claire's poems return to basics, jettisoning typography and using prints of woodknots, cabbage leaves, stones and other textured surfaces. "The sounding of pattern is a basic skill which we must constantly revive if we hope to maintain the energy flow from the 'innermost alchemy' [Hugo Ball] of the word into the main body of the language."

Since its inception in 1963, Cobbing's Writers Forum has been an exemplary instance of uncompromisingly radical independent publishing. One of its rare retrievals of previously published work is Jack Kerouac's *Old Angel Midnight* (1959), showing that Gysin was by no means the only bridge between sound poetry and Beat writing. Michael McClure roaring beast-language tantras at caged lions forms another part of that picture. The Kerouac connection touches upon another relevant line of vocal activity, audible through the rhapsodic account of jazz absurdist Slim Gaillard in *On The Road* (1957): "Then he slowly gets up and takes up the mike and says, very slowly, 'Great-orooni... fine-ovauti... hello- orooni... bourbon-orooni... all-orooni... orooni... vauti... ooronirooni...' He keeps this up for fifteen minutes, his voice getting softer and softer till you can't hear." Collective improvisation was an important element in performances by Canadian quartet The Four Horsemen, formed in 1970 by bpNichol, Steve McCaffery, Paul Dutton and Rafael Barreto-Rivera. According to McCaffery, the group aspired to nothing less than "a claiming of the transient, transitional, ephemeral, the intensity of the orgasm, the flow of energies through fissures, escape, the total burn, the finite calorie, loss, displacement, excess: the total range of the nomadic consciousness". It rejected all technological intervention and favoured a direct and animated approach, as did another Canadian quartet, Owen Sound.

Dutton has more recently meshed his voice with Michael Snow's piano and John Oswald's saxophone in the group CCMC. Jazz and improvised music have provided some fertile contexts for sound poets. The impressively gruff Ernst Jandl, who appeared at London's Albert Hall in 1965 alongside Allen Ginsberg, Gregory Corso and Lawrence Ferlinghetti, has recorded with vocalist Lauren Newton and other Vienna Art Orchestra members. Saxophonist Steve Lacy collaborated with Gysin. During the 1970s the group Area offered a freeform rock backdrop for the explosive articulations of voice artist Demetrio Stratos. Australian Chris Mann has done extraordinary work with Machine For Making Sense, as has Dutch vocal acrobat Jaap Blonk with Splinks. And Cecil Taylor's glossolalic fusion hovers luminously on the periphery.

The sound poem appears to me as a homecoming for poetry, a return to its source close to the spoken word, the rhythm and atmosphere of language and body, their rites and sorcery, everything that centuries of written verse has replaced with metaphors and advanced constructions. The sound poem is perhaps also a way back to contact with a larger public such as transmitted the tradition of poetry in ancient times.
Sten Hanson

Approaches to sound poetry have been multiple, demonstrating the expansiveness and diversity that comes with exploration, throwing up internationally distinctive figures such as Franz Mon, Gerhard Rühm, Paul De Vree, Patrizia Vicinelli, Arrigo Lora-Totino and Ladislav Novàk. The five CD box released by Milan's Cramps label in 1978 remains the most comprehensive documentation of this variety. Group identities have formed however, nowhere more clearly than in Sweden. As early as 1953 Swedish Fluxus artist Öyvind Fahlström made a significant connection between concrete music and text in "A Manifesto For Concrete Poetry". In the same year, Rune Lindblad realised his first concrete sound works in Gothenburg. In 1964-65, composer Bengt Emil Johnson produced *Through The Mirror Of Thirst*, a sophisticated polyphonic word-soundscape in which ornate electronically generated sounds are organised around textual fragments. Other notable workers in the field have been Sten Hanson, Lars-Gunnar Bodin, Åke Hodell and Christer Hennix Lille. Lille's forward-looking work used computerised synthesizer to simulate speech, an activity paralleled in the United States by composer Charles Dodge.

Hanson rejects historical accounts tracking contemporary text-sound composition (the preferred term in Sweden) back to Futurism, dada and Lettrism. Like Chopin he argues that "Sound poetry grew as a result of new working tools and new media: the tape recorder, the electronic music studio, the LP record, the radio". Nonetheless, he believes it to be essentially "a means of bringing the body, its rhythm, the orality and non-semantic communication of spoken language back into poetry".

In April 1968 the Fylkingen Centre for Experimental Music and Art, together with the Literary Unit of the Swedish Broadcasting Corporation, sponsored the first International Festival of Sound Poetry at the Museum of Modern Art in Stockholm and started issuing a series of important recordings. The Festival became an annual event, moving in 1974 to London, where Cobbing had initiated a Sound Poetry Workshop at the National Poetry Centre in 1969.

The music people don't consider me a composer and the poetry people don't consider me a poet, and I'm in no way disturbed about that.
Charles Amirkhanian

In America, sound poet Charles Amirkhanian played a pivotal role, travelling to Sweden for the 1972 festival and, discovering others working in the text-sound composition field, he started to explore independently in California. Soon afterwards he toured Europe in a station wagon, interviewing sound poets for later broadcast on Berkeley's KPFA Radio. In 1975 he curated *10 + 2*, a sound poetry anthology, released by baritone singer Tom Buckner's 1750 Arch Records, of the acclaimed concert series he ran in Berkeley. John Cage, who had by this time evolved his distinctive approach to text-sound in such works as *62 Mesostics Re Merce Cunningham* and *Empty Words*, features on Amirkhanian's compilation along with other composers Robert Ashley and Beth Anderson, painters Gysin and Liam O'Gallagher, and poets including Aram Saroyan and John Giorno.

Singular figures such as Jackson Mac Low had been active in the field for a long time; indeed Mac Low had travelled to London in 1975 for the 8th International Sound Poetry Festival. Still, *Open Secrets*, the title of his 1993 album with Anne Tardos for XI Records, comments wrily upon his status.

The *10 + 2* compilation crystallised sound poetry's identity in America, where works such as Steve Reich's important mid-1960s compositions *It's Gonna Rain* and *Come Out* have fallen on the music side of the interface, together with pieces by composers such as Roger Reynolds, Paul De Marinis, Meredith Monk, Kurt Nurock and Joan La Barbara. In 1980, Richard Kostelanetz edited *Text-Sound Texts*, the first book-form anthology of sound poetry in North America. Amirkhanian, Gysin and The Four Horsemen are included, so are Kerouac and Allen Ginsberg, but so are musicians Philip Glass, Kenneth Gaburo, Philip Corner, Tom Johnson, Ned Sublette, R Murray Schafer and John Oswald.

In Europe today, the dual role Amirkhanian has performed as practitioner and curator is being fulfilled by Italian Enzo Minarelli, who issued a "Manifesto Of Polypoetry" in 1987, endorsing the opportunities offered by electronic media and the computer, as well as the musicality, movement and dance of language, which must be free to extend to the pure noise, and to release its "manifold sonorities".

After taking shape in many forms across the 20th century, sound poetry appears to be experiencing rekindled interest at the beginning of the 21st. Henri Chopin's graphic poetry work featured in the Live In Your Head exhibition at London's Whitechapel Gallery in 1999; and both Chopin (now resident in East Anglia) and Cobbing surfaced at a Sound Poetry conference/event in Leicester a year later. There has been a series of reissues, notably from the Milanese Alga Marghen label, plus new releases such as Paul Dutton's *Mouth Pieces* (OHM Editions).

In Kostelanetz's book, sound poetry is defined as "language that coheres in terms of sound rather than syntax or semantics". Tom Leonard writes, "As to what the definition of 'sound-poetry' is, I've never heard a satisfactory definition yet, and it's not a question that interests me". Steve McCaffery jokingly suggests, "It's a new way to blow out candles". New listeners approaching the field from adjacent ground such as rap or electronica may find its real appeal encapsulated in McCaffery's more serious contention: that sound poetry is above all "a practice of freedom".

THE MUSIC OF CHANCE

MUSICAL DICE MEN FROM JOHN CAGE TO JOHN ZORN

BY ANDY HAMILTON

From John Cage's *I Ching* compositions and Karlheinz Stockhausen's 60s aleatoric experiments to John Zorn's game pieces and Brian Eno's oblique strategy cards, 'chance music' seems an essentially postmodern phenomenon. But with music like any other human activity, chance has always entered in. Though John Cage was the grandmaster of chance, he wasn't entirely its pioneer. The dice were already rolling in 18th century Vienna, where Mozart reputedly used them to decide the order of the sections in a minuet – reflecting a trend among his contemporaries made possible by the ornately symmetrical form of Rococo music. In a positively surreal contrast, in 1751 William Hayes 'wrote' the composition *The Art Of Composing Music By A Method Entirely New, Suited To The Meanest Capacity* by flicking ink at music manuscript paper.

Despite Mozart's dabbling, however, such early adventures in chance composition were the parlour games of minor composers, and could easily be dismissed as frivolous. The more pervasive dimension of chance has always been employed at the level of performance rather than composition, anyway. Indeed, it can be argued that the very notion of scoring music is a product of composers' attempts to minimise unwanted chance factors (such as accidental/wilful misinterpretation by ignorant/disobedient musicians) in the performance of their work. If in Bach's time the musical work was viewed as a partnership between composer and performer, by the later 19th century composers were asserting their dictatorial control. For Schoenberg, the interpreter is the servant of the work: "He must read every wish from its lips".

Yet a degree of ensemble imprecision was something that late Romantics such as Wagner and Richard Strauss took for granted. Indeed, the opening of Strauss's tone-poem "Don Juan" was intended as a cacophony of blurring lines. With improving orchestral standards, it could be argued, it is played too accurately and the music has become too transparent. Indeed, Stravinsky later complained that the bassoon solo which opens *The Rite Of Spring* had become "too easy" – he wanted it to sound dangerous and on the edge. With some composers, chance music was a way of regaining that blurred or dangerous effect. But one of Schoenberg's American students, John Cage, went much further. In rejecting the European concept of the genius-creator, he called for a complete uprooting of Western musical tradition – deliberately, by chance.

SATIE REARRANGES THE FURNITURE

Chance music wasn't entirely without modern precursors when Cage came to it in the 1940s. "It's not a question of Satie's relevance, he's indispensable," Cage wrote in 1958. The French eccentric's love of incongruity favoured the deliberate deployment of accident. There's a kind of graphic notation in *Sports Et Divertissements*, and Satie used a mosaic technique in *Prélude De La Porte Héroique Du Ciel*, reordering the sections of his piece until he found one he liked – which accounts for its strangely indeterminate succession of unrelated chords. This last piece was from his Rose+Croix period of the 1890s, when Satie believed his work was directed from beyond the grave by a fanatically pious medieval cleric – as his sister remarked, "My brother was always difficult to understand. He doesn't seem to have been quite normal".

While Satie's piece is fixed for the performer, in some of his scores Charles Ives went further and offered the performers themselves significant alternatives – while also making impossible demands on them through unrealisable notations. Ives pioneered a layering technique, using a collage of musical sources at different tempos – such as sounds from different brass bands. This resulted in a kind of "chance counterpoint", most extravagantly in the short orchestral piece *The Fourth Of July* (1911-13). Ives greatly influenced West Coast maverick Henry Cowell, described by Cage in his classic 1961 collection of writings, *Silence*, as "the open sesame for new music in America". Cowell experimented with what he called "elastic notations" in his *Mosaic Quartet* (1934), which included a selection of fragments to be assembled by the players.

ROARING SILENCES

But these were isolated experiments. Postmodern methods of collapsing the cultural hierarchies came later to music than other artforms. Through dada, Surrealism and Futurism, the set-in-stone certainties of literature and the visual arts had been disrupted by found objects, automatic writing, action painting, performance art and happenings, before music got more than a glimpse of such possibilities. Almost alone among composers, Cage was immersed in Surrealism and shared ideas with Marcel Duchamp, though unlike the Surrealists, he didn't seek out significance in his chance conjunctions. Maybe he was familiar with dada composer Georges Ribement-Dessaignes, who composed dance music by dice-throwing. But Cage's famous method of constructing pieces by tossing coins was generated by consulting the ancient Chinese book of oracles, the *I Ching* (or *Book Of Changes*). Introduced to the book by his student Christian Wolff, whose father had published an English translation, he applied the method in the last movement of his *Concerto For Prepared Piano And Chamber Orchestra*, then most dramatically in *Music Of Changes* for piano, both from 1951.

Cage's excursions into chance had begun a little earlier, in fact. In the late 40s and early 50s, he formed an unlikely alliance with Pierre Boulez – long before the latter had established himself as IRCAM's notorious autocrat. At this time, Cage and Boulez were two lonely, embattled avant gardists. The 'total serialism' Boulez was experimenting with involved trying to predetermine all musical parameters – not just pitch but rhythm and dynamics. But serialism and chance are two sides of one coin; it's often said that chance pieces and totally determined pieces – such as Boulez's *Structures I* for two pianos – come out sounding very similar and equally arbitrary. Boulez later recognised that his 'automatic' music engendered an entropic kind of anarchy – "chance by the back door". So the Cage-Boulez friendship wasn't the complete mis-encounter it looks like from a later perspective.

Gradually realising just how opposed his and Cage's viewpoints were, Boulez wrote in 1951, "The only thing, forgive me, which I am not happy about, is the method of absolute chance (by tossing the coins). On the contrary, I believe that chance must be extremely controlled...I am a little afraid of what is called 'automatic writing', for most of the time it is chiefly a lack of control..." This apologetic murmur turned into an ideological chasm between the two, since the abdication of control by the composer is at the heart of Cage's anti-aesthetic.

Even so, it's been argued, there's a sense in which Boulez owed total serialism to Cage, and Cage owed chance to Boulez. The depersonalisation of *Structures 1* is closer to a concept of chance than Cage had reached at that time. But while still using chance elements, for instance in his *Piano Sonata No 3*, Boulez drew back from it. As Cage later bitterly complained, "Boulez was promoting chance, only it had to be *his* kind of chance" – influenced now by the French Symbolist poet Mallarmé, not Cage. If Boulez required discipline with a little freedom, Cage characteristically mixed anarchy and discipline. Cage sets up systems in order to produce unpredictable results. 'Chance' for him was more than just a compositional tool. It was a part of the liberating ideology he set out in *Silence*, a philosophy of artistic non-intention, dissolving the difference between art and life.

A famous piece in the *Silence* collection is "Indeterminacy", a "lecture on composition which is indeterminate with respect to its performance" (as it repeatedly describes itself). *Music Of Changes* is not indeterminate in this way, Cage claims. "The function of the performer... is that of a contractor who, following an architect's blueprint, constructs a building. That the *Music Of Changes* was composed by means of chance operations identifies the composer with no matter what eventuality. But that its notation is in all respects determinate does not permit the performer any such identification: his work is specifically laid out before him. He is therefore not able to perform from his own center... [It] is an object more inhuman than human, since chance operations brought it into being. The fact that these things that constitute it, though only sounds, have come together to control a human being, the performer, gives the work the alarming aspect of a Frankenstein monster." But, Cage argues, this is essentially no different to the masterpieces of Western music.

Music Of Changes is an extreme example of chance determinism, and in order to tame this "monster", Cage soon extended his chance operations. He went beyond "chance determinism" – the dice-throwing method where the work is composed by chance – to "chance indeterminism", or chance at the level of performance, where the score deliberately makes room for chance occurrences, or choices by performers. But in fact real choices for performers were never really on Cage's agenda. He didn't yield them any autonomy, and remained a control freak.

He wrote for the unpredictable output of radio sets in *Imaginary Landscape No 4* (1951). *4'33"* (1952) – in which a performer sits at the piano for the set duration – is unpredictable simply because ambient sounds are unpredictable. *Atlas Eclipticalis* (1961) experimented with random contact mics. When the players of The New York Philharmonic, after learning their devilishly difficult parts, discovered that only a proportion of the mics were to be switched on at any one time during the performance – decided by chance – they rebelled, and had to be disciplined by conductor Leonard Bernstein. All of these pieces involve chance occurrences in performances, rather than choices made by performers.

A popular method of chance indeterminism is graphic notation, which was Cage's chosen weapon for *Fontana Mix* (1958), where the score consists of transparent sheets to be superimposed on each other like a series of map overlays. Graphic devices had already been used by Satie, Ives and Cowell, and most radically in Morton Feldman's *Projection 1* for solo cello (1950), whose score, as with other early Feldman compositions, looks like an abstract painting. The *Concert For Piano And Orchestra* of 1957-58 is Cage's masterpiece of indeterminacy in that it has no 'master score'. The conductor's role is purely theatrical, and each player works through their part independently, without coordinating with others.

Cage hadn't forgotten about dice-music though. In 1968 Lejaren Hiller assisted him in the multi-media composition *HPSCHD*, using a computer to produce a large number of alternative realisations of Mozart's musical dice game. In the early 50s Hiller had collaborated with Leonard Isaacson in writing computer programs that used random generation to produce a series of notes, and then filtered out sequences which sounded too idiomatic. From the 70s onwards, with the exception of the wonderful late 'Number' pieces, Cage returned to chance determinism.

The 'Number' pieces did admit performer choice – leaving parameters of pitch or rhythm open while specifying duration – but only in terms of the Western classical tradition could these pieces be regarded as free. Whether the performer picks a B flat or C sharp, or when, is still governed by strict parameters – and it's relatively insignificant for the ultimate direction of the piece. In "Two^6" for violin, for instance, Cage asks for impossibly high harmonics – at some point out of the performer's control the note inevitably cracks. (The 'number' refers to the number of players involved, the superscript to the place of the work in the series of pieces for that number of players.) Ironically, in denying individuality to the performer, Cage ended up agreeing with his teacher Schoenberg. He regarded interpretation as a kind of improvisation, and did his damnedest to eliminate it.

That wasn't the attitude of Cage's student, Christian Wolff, whose consistent vision has been to use the force of hazard to shape his distinctively spare works. "Chance is used as a way of discovering things," Wolff declared in a 2001 interview. "You could call it a heuristic device. Cage once said he looked forward to performances to discover what he'd composed, to be surprised by it. I recall somewhere in Tolstoy's *Anna Karenina* the story of a painter who got stuck while working on a painting. He gave up on it, put the canvas away in some corner of his studio. Some months later coming back to it he noticed a grease spot or smudge had appeared on it, and then he knew just what to do to finish the picture."

In 1957, through a collaboration with his near-contemporary, the composer and pianist Frederic Rzewski, indeterminacy made a significant appearance in Wolff's output. But his use of it has been individual; and also unlike Cage, he's been sympathetic to free improvisation, for instance in his pieces *Edges* and *Burdocks* (1970-71). As he explained: "[Cage] made a composition which was then performed the way it was written, it was fixed... But what I became interested in introducing wasn't even chance so much any more, but the element of what we called indeterminacy – not at the point of composition but at the point of performance. So my scores might be made without using any chance procedures at all, but they were made in such a way that when performers used them, unpredictable events would take place."

Cage's use of chance indeterminism didn't allow any autonomy to performers. Wolff, in contrast, collaborates with the performer in what he calls "working actively with contingencies". Whereas in Cage's music, each player works through the musical events prescribed in the score regardless of what other players are doing, Wolff focusses on the unpredictable possibilities that arise from each performer attending to what the others are doing. As he commented: "My composition might consist of time spaces – so many seconds, and fractions of them, within which various kinds of material are indicated. Say, a choice of three pitches from a collection of seven, two dynamic markings and some colour articulation like a pizzicato. The performer then has delimited choices, as well as areas that might be quite free – for instance, the spacing of the sounds within a given time space.

"Mostly there are several performers," he continued, "so that what they do will partly combine by chance, though when they listen to each other, this may affect how they each make their choices, and so they too collaborate, which again is not a matter of chance." Contrasts between Cage and Wolff are spelled out usefully in Michael Nyman's *Experimental Music*. Nyman points to an interesting paradox in Wolff's music: "In performance the players seem to be in a state of perpetual crisis, yet the music sounds calm, relaxed and unruffled, unlike the avant garde variety which often sounds as though it is actually the expression of crisis."

Cage's championing of openness and indeterminacy resonated throughout the 60s. He wrote in *Silence*: "As contemporary music goes on changing in the way I am changing it what will be done is to more and more completely liberate sounds... I am talking and contemporary music is changing." Among those falling under his influence at this time were Cornelius Cardew, La Monte Young and many minor neo-dadaists.

BACK TO EUROPE: THE TEXTURE COMPOSERS

The European avant garde were mostly more cautious when it came to taking chances. Boulez and Stockhausen evolved methods of indeterminacy within strictly defined parameters, such as the 'mobile form' pioneered by Ives and Cowell. On Stockhausen's *Piano Piece XI* (1956), the performer's freedom is fairly limited; they select the order of movements and have some say over internal arrangements, tempo and dynamics. His *Momente* also permits alternative orderings of material. But *Ylem* and *Aus Den Sieben Tagen* are much more open. Clarinettist Anthony Pay reported: "He invites you, for example, [simply] to play in the rhythm of the molecules that constitute your body. Or in the rhythm of the universe. There's a story of a second violin player who said, 'Herr Stockhausen, how will I know when I am playing in the rhythm of the universe?' Stockhausen said, with a smile, 'I will tell you'." He's probably still waiting for the nod: by 1970, Stockhausen had returned to exact notation – his most radical work already completed.

Xenakis's 'stochastic composition' was not really chance. But he did write three pieces based on mathematical game theory: *Duet* (1958-59), *Stratégie* (1962) and *Linaia Agon* (1972-82). *Duel* is a game between two orchestras, with the conductors as active contestants. Xenakis drew comparisons with competitive situations in folk music – he could also have referred to 'cutting sessions' in jazz. Nouritza Matossian suggests that the psychological roots of his interest was the feeling that his own life had been saved in Athens, during the wartime Nazi occupation, only by chance.

Xenakis is sometimes bracketed with Lutoslawski, Penderecki and Ligeti as a 'texture composer', dealing in sound-masses rather than individual tones – and it could be argued that, in fact, this attempt to capture a natural phenomenon is the opposite of chance. Polish composer Witold Lutoslawski's *Venetian Games* was directly inspired by Cage's *Concert For Piano And Orchestra*. Sections are divided by a fixed percussion signal, and within each section there's a 'collective ad lib'. As the score says, "When the sign for the end of the section is given, the performers must interrupt playing immediately. If by this time a player has already played his part to the end, he should repeat it from the beginning of the section". The result is an "aleatory (ie chance) counterpoint" – the exact coincidence of individual lines left to chance. (The word aleatoric, by the way, comes from alea, Latin for dice.) This is the same concept that Ives deployed, but with a very different effect. Ligeti's *Poème Symphonique* for 100 metronomes from 1962 was a more radical, completely mechanical example of the same idea, while in his *Requiem* he writes lines for the chorus which are too difficult to coordinate, resulting, like *Venetian Games*, in random counterpoint.

But for Lutoslawski, the composer had to be left in control: "I firmly believe in a clear delineation of duties between composer and performers," he said, "and I have no wish to surrender even the smallest part of my claim to authorship of even the shortest passage." Cage badmouthed such "experimenting within tradition". In a 1962 interview he complained that "It doesn't seem to me to radically alter the situation from the familiar convention. It simply takes these new ways of working and consolidates them with the old knowledge... I think we are in a more urgent situation, where it is absolutely essential for us to change our minds fundamentally." But even limited chance was too much for high-culture modernist Elliott Carter: "Aleatoric pieces with any degree of free choice," wrote the American composer, "are simply demonstrations of certain general styles or methods of composition without ever becoming concrete individual works in which every detail... contributes some way or other to the total effect." Evidently he didn't understand that, for the texture composers, blurrings were an essential part of that total effect.

A genuine radical, no more part of the academy than Cage himself, was self-taught Argentinian composer Mauricio Kagel. Influenced by dada and Surrealism as well as Cage, his *Match* (1964) features a musical contest between rival cellists, refereed by a percussionist. Like Cage, Kagel rejects "the pure doctrine of improvisation – if indeed this ever existed". Essential to his work is "strict composition with elements which are not themselves pure". In *Exotica*, the performers have to try to master the techniques of the non-Western instruments as best they can; they're left to furnish the prescribed rhythms with pitches in any register. Kagel exploits the fact that where instruments and other sound-producers are unfamiliar to the performer, this will also introduce an element of unpredictability – any untried instrument is a little 'aleatory' at first. In a way that recalls the roots of the Cage-Boulez mis-encounter, Kagel commented about his *Saint-Bach Passion* that "totally planned things [as in serialism] and totally arbitrary ones have a similar place" in the shaping of a piece.

AMATEUR HOUR: SCRATCH ORCHESTRAS AND RUINED PIANOS

As Kagel's music shows, unpredictable results follow from asking players to perform beyond their capabilities. For this reason some composers experimented with amateur ensembles, such as Gavin Bryars's Portsmouth Sinfonia from the early 70s, which famously murdered Tchaikovsky's *1812 Overture* and other popular classics. Bryars encouraged his naive and incompetent amateurs to take their roles seriously and play with heart, even though he was probably quietly laughing at them himself. If Bryars had a serious point it probably wasn't shared by his performers – the Sinfonia was an exercise in both dadaism and sadism.

British composer Cornelius Cardew also chose to work with amateurs, but out of a high-minded political impulse as much as a musical one. Cardew started out as a disciple of Stockhausen, before falling under the spell of Cage. For a brief period in the 60s he opted for the total Improv of AMM, then in 1969 formed The Scratch Orchestra from both professional and amateur musicians, to perform didactic works such as *The Great Learning*, for which he supplied both the building blocks of sound and some loose architectural plans. It wasn't just the final outcome that was valuable; how the groups of players variously negotiated his designs itself formed a model of social and musical organisation. Cardew became a Maoist and repudiated his mentors. He was killed by a hit-and-run driver in 1981 before he had a chance to explain the contradictions between his utopian interpretation of the Great Helmsman's thoughts, and their rather more restrictive application in Mao's China. His AMM improvisations aside, one of the few chance pieces to survive his death is the 193-page *Treatise* in graphic notation.

The so-called New Complexity composers have also been concerned with demanding the impossible of performers, only in their case only professional players need apply. In his piano-piece *Tilt*, composer Chris Dench asks the performer to make a 'tilt' at the right notes, which are technically impossible to obtain; Brian Ferneyhough's works also encourage a "desperate virtuosity". Michael Finnissy has explored the layering technique pioneered by Charles Ives. Australian composer Ross Bolleter, in contrast, places excessive demands on instruments rather than performers. 1990's "Nallan Void" is a conventional parlour piece, except that it specifies the use of an out of tune "ruined piano prepared by its environment" at an outback sheep station. Booming bass notes and clunks where notes don't sound give little indication of the complexities hidden in the score; a different ruined piano would give a completely different result.

CARD SHARPS: ENO AND ZORN

Chance operations aren't limited to the 'contemporary classical' tradition. With the painter Peter Schmidt, Brian Eno in his Roxy Music period famously evolved a deck of oracle cards called "Oblique Strategies", which helped David Bowie out of his coke-blocked impasse when he recorded *Low* and *Heroes* in Berlin (both 1977). The cards were modelled on – you guessed it – the *I Ching*. He wrote aphorisms on the cards and placed them round the recording studio, to kickstart or refloat the creative process; examples include "Retrace your steps", "Don't break the silence", "You are an engineer", "Turn it upside down". Eno wasn't appealing to anything as exotic as supernatural forces: "You can believe that they work on a purely behavioural level, simply adjusting your perception at a point, or suggesting a different perception." Like improvisation, they were a method for altering the dynamics of a creative situation in a way that compositional logic couldn't manage.

But isn't improvisation itself a game of chance? It can seem that way when improvisors aim for the previously unheard and unplayed – perhaps when, like Ornette Coleman, they aspire to play "without memory". But for most improvisors, improvisation is more risk than chance. Improvisors are always looking for ways of maintaining unpredictability. Conductions by George Lewis with The London Jazz Composers Orchestra, among others, have used numbered cards in a 'mosaic technique', a jazz equivalent of the Boulez/Stockhausen mobile form.

Though Cage condemned the Western classical tradition, it didn't stop John Zorn from bracketing his work with the "dead, lifeless music" of the "boring old farts". For Zorn, who's as much an improvisor as a composer, Cage is an anti-type. Zorn's game pieces take their titles from sports and board-games such as *Lacrosse*, *Archery*, *Pool* and *Cobra*. These pieces are 'composed' insofar as they're performed to a score consisting of a series of hand signals, each corresponding to a type of interaction from quickly-traded bursts of sound to longer free-for-alls. As 'conductor', Zorn simply relays changes to the rest of the players with a hand signal. But the players are permitted to try to wrest control from the conductor by 'guerrilla tactics' – an antagonism reminiscent of Xenakis's *Duel*, though Zorn himself more often mentions Mauricio Kagel as an influence. The cue card system fits with Zorn's 'block structure' or filmic technique of fast-moving juxtaposed sections.

Cage moves towards obliterating the creative will – Zorn tries to engage it differently. Cage, notoriously, wasn't interested in improvisation. At a performance of the late Number piece *Five* in 1990, the players sustained their notes rather than the silences because, evidently, they felt they had too little to play. "They weren't supposed to improvise!" Cage complained – he didn't like the limited instructions he gave to be disobeyed. He wasn't interested in the idea of performers expressing themselves, because *he* wasn't interested in expressing himself. His denial of self-expression is the outcome that chance ultimately leads to. But few composers or improvisers are egoless enough to follow the Zen Master the whole way. Art, and the intention that goes with it, proves almost inescapable.

SMILING FACES SOMETIMES

SOUL MUSIC'S GRINNERS VERSUS THE BACKSTABBERS

BY PETER SHAPIRO

In December 1963, at the beginning of a long New England winter, graphic artist Harvey Ball was commissioned by the State Mutual insurance company of Worcester, Massachusetts to design a feelgood campaign to boost morale amongst the workers. What Ball came up with was two dots above an inverted arc on a vivid yellow, circular beaming sun background. The company initially printed up 100 badges, but they proved so popular that Worcester was soon overrun with these caricatures of vacant cheerfulness. Ball's fee for designing what is probably, aside from the cross and the swastika, the world's most iconic symbol: $45 (even adjusted for inflation, that ain't much more than a couple of hundred dollars).

However, despite the local success of Ball's smiling face and its subsequent use in numerous advertising campaigns across the US, Smiley was truly born seven years later, a few hundred miles away in Philadelphia. In September 1970, two brothers, Bernard and Murray Spain, were looking for a way to make a quick buck. With America entrenched in the Vietnam War and riven by protests, generational conflict and racial unrest, Bernard stumbled upon the image that summed up America's Nixonite reaction to the 60s in some old ad campaign. Bernard put the Smiley on a badge and Murray came up with the slogan "Have A Happy Day", which soon mutated into "Have A Nice Day". Echoing such mantras of bland optimism as "turn that frown upside down" and "a day without a smile is like a day without sunshine", the "Have A Nice Day" campaign swept a country that was desperately trying to put the 60s behind it and was looking more and more like the dehumanised futures depicted in films like *The Stepford Wives*, *Logan's Run* and *Dawn Of The Dead* every day. The Spain brothers hooked up with New York button manufacturer NG Slater, and the Smiley face became the fad to end all fads, replicating the Worcester craze on a national level. By 1972, some 50 million Smiley badges had been produced, not to mention all the other paraphernalia the image appeared on.

But as Smiley was zombifying the country, narcotising it with an empty, blissful grin, a group of musicians recognised the symbol as the pernicious little yellow devil that it was. After centuries of betrayals and lies, the smile, handshake and pat on the back are no longer ways of sealing a social contract. Instead, they become things to fear, temporary placations mollifying rage and resentment until the inevitable u-turn, retraction and cutback comes. For African-Americans in the early 70s, the Cheshire Cat grin was all that was left of the promises of the 60s – the substance of which had long since vanished into thin air, gone up in smoke like the ghettoes of Watts, Detroit and Pittsburgh.

Instead of turning their frowns upside down and grinning and bearing it, soul artists of the early 70s engaged in a remarkable conversation centred around the 'smiling faces' trope, an imagistic minefield that played confidence games with centuries of caricatures, the beaming faces of the white liberal establishment promising civil rights and integration, Nixon's Dirty Tricks gang and, yes, Smiley himself. Invariably, these smiling faces told lies, but rather than being simple protest shorthand for the duplicitousness of the oppressor that worked in a similar way to other pop music tropes – like, say, stoner/doom rock's 'Witchfinder General' trope derived from the great Vincent Price flick of the same name, which attacks the hypocrisy of squares and Moral Majority types – it is infinitely more complex and confusing, filled with self-loathing, and hectors any number of targets. Whether the central theme of the song or merely an apparently thrown-away line, the trope of 'smiling faces' was universally wrapped up in some of the tensest music ever made in the stunning succession of soul records that used it, creating the ultimate expression of paranoia and elevating the answer-song tradition above the level of kitsch.

Motown producer extraordinaire Norman Whitfield was perhaps the first to see Smiley as the lobotomised, jaundiced, signifyin' so and so that he really was. In 1968 he pretty much defined the strain of paranoid soul that dominated black radio in the late 60s and early 70s with Marvin Gaye's version of "I Heard It Through The Grapevine". He redefined this sub-genre, though, when he wrote "Smiling Faces Sometimes" in the late 1970 with his regular songwriting partner Barrett Strong. "Smiling Faces Sometimes" first appeared on wax as a 12 minute mini-epic on The Temptations' *Sky's The Limit* album, which was released in April 1971. However, it was first recorded by a vocal trio that Whitfield formed almost as a sketchbook for his studio experimentation. When their (much better) version was finally released as a single in July 1971, The Undisputed Truth (Joe Harris, Billy Rae Calvin and Brenda

Joyce Evans) had their first and only US Top Ten hit with their first record. Despite the uncompromising lyrics, the debut's chart success was no surprise: with massed chorales, percussion that imitates both a ticking clock and a rattlesnake, swooping strings, the refrains of *"Can you dig it?"* that Isaac Hayes would borrow for "Theme From Shaft" and palpably gargantuan brass and woodwind sections, "Smiling Faces Sometimes" was the most fully realised orchestral soul production up to that point.

However, this was no Hugo & Luigi, Easy Listening, crossover appeal for Sam Cooke or The Stylistics. The first four seconds let you know all you needed to figure out what was to come. "Smiling Faces Sometimes" begins with a horn fanfare from some hyperspace where Vegas, Bob & Earl and Charlton Heston biblical epics conjoin, only to be compounded by a heroic wah-wah echo that bounces around the soundfield like a Rabelaisian Ricochet Rabbit. In the third second the scything strings that would become blaxploitation's other signature slice the production in half, leaving a dangling guitar lick and doomy, insistent maracas. Lush arrangements straight off Isaac Hayes's *Hot Buttered Soul* follow, but the instrumental richness is denser, thicker, more claustrophobic – the sweetening becoming ever more cloying and fulsome, like false praise. When lead singer Joe Harris comes in, he sings like a mourning Levi Stubbs: you can hear his power held in reserve as if he is subduing his hectoring tone because he has resigned himself to the fatalism the song describes.

And what a brutal vision the song relates: *"Smiling faces sometimes pretend to be your friend/Smiling faces show no traces of the evil that lurks within/Smiling faces, smiling faces sometimes they don't tell the truth/Smiling faces tell lies and I've got proof... Beware of the handshake that hides a snake/Beware of the pat on the back/It just might hold you back."* On the surface it seems a pretty clear indictment of the white establishment who failed to deliver civil rights while promising the world. In a song written by Al Bell, The Staple Singers saw things pretty much the same way. 1972's "I'll Take You There" contained the refrain: *"I know a place/Ain't nobody crying/Ain't nobody worried/Ain't no smiling faces/Lying to the races."* Rarely had a popular African-American record ("I'll Take You There" was number one on the R&B chart for the entire month of May as well as being a pop number one) been so direct about its protest.

However, "I'll Take You There" – along with War's "Get Down" from 1971's *All Day Music* (*"Police and their justice laughing while they bust us"*) – was the least ambiguous of all the records that used the 'smiling faces' trope, perhaps because Al Bell was a minister who had become the president of Stax Records and there was no room for equivocation in his vision of paradise. But that line about the handshake in "Smiling Faces Sometimes" – which has resonances with the Black Power movement and its numerous soul handshakes and hand signs – seems to indicate that it's not only Whitey who'll cheerfully rob you blind. It wasn't alone.

On the amazing "Don't Call Me Brother" from The O'Jays' 1973 album *Ship Ahoy*, lead singer Eddie Levert breaks into a sermon: *"Just the other day, when I was hanging out down on the main drag/I went in to get me a small, teeny weeny toddy for the evening/And when I come out, I got a bad case of the blues when I saw my tyres gone/I open up the door and there was my glove compartment all torn out from the dashboard/And here you come, here you come, skinnin' and grinnin', skinnin' and grinnin'/Here you come – I know you did it – with the power sign/Talkin' about, 'My man, solid on that, my brother'/I said I don't like it, how can you really, really mean it?/I know about ya, I know what you're really good for..."*

Following the even more incredible "Back Stabbers", "Don't Call Me Brother" was produced by Philadelphia International's Kenny Gamble and Leon Huff, who were the main instigators of a whole series of records from that city that seemed to interrogate traditional roles of black masculinity (see also former associate Thom Bell's productions of the helium harmonies of The Delfonics and The Stylistics who took falsetto into the realm of the castrati). Before Levert's sermon, The O'Jays take that enduring symbol of black male camaraderie, the street corner doowop group, and turn it into a savage indictment of black masculinity. Over some of the ripest music of Gamble & Huff's opulent career (but just as in "Smiling Faces Sometimes", the unctuous vibes and zinging strings reinforced the song's message), The O'Jays ask some ne'er-do-well, *"How can you call me brother when you don't respect my woman? How can you call me brother when I can't even trust you behind my* back?" But it's that sermon and its *"skinnin' and grinnin'"* line, *"power sign"* detail and even that bit about *"a small, teeny weeny toddy"* that give the song its force. Given that Kenny Gamble was a black Muslim, it seems strange that the character we're meant to identify with is drinking and criticising at least the trappings, if not the substance, of the movement. Was this Gamble questioning his faith? Or was the sermon improvised by Levert who was taking a camouflaged potshot at his boss? Or were the details simply coincidence?

Given the swirling paranoia of "Back Stabbers", it's hard to imagine that they were merely coincidence. Beginning with what must surely be the greatest intro of any pop song save maybe "Johnny B Goode", "Back Stabbers" is the the tale of a man whose friends want to steal his woman. The first song written by the duo of Gene McFadden and John Whitehead (with input from Leon Huff) who would later find fame with "Ain't No Stoppin' Us Now", "Back Stabbers" is just that: the story of a guy whose relationship is going south trying to fend off the opportunists and scavengers putting the final nail in the coffin. But those roiling piano chords that introduce the record create a drama too big to be contained by the merely personal. The heavenly strings that gradually fade in the mix, trying desperately to get the upper hand on the relentless, insistent beat only to be undone by the punchiest horns in the Philly lexicon, turn "Back Stabbers" into a huge, Shakespearean saga.

"What they doin'? They smilin' in your face/All the time they want to take your place/The back stabbers." While the music speaks volumes, to really hear "Back Stabbers" as the crucial part of the smiling faces conversation, you need to listen to it as part of the album with the same title. *Back Stabbers* begins with an almost mocking James Brown horn riff before modulating into a hard funk groove called "When The World's At Peace" that borrows heavily from Sly Stone in both musical and lyrical tone. The first verse goes, *"I can see the day when it's safe to walk the streets/When we'll learn to care for those lost in poverty/There'll be no need for our sons and daughters to march up and down the streets singing "We Shall Overcome""*, and its civil rights reference places "Back Stabbers" in context. The next line is *"When the world's at peace will it still be in one piece?"*, and the song soon slows down to a disoriented crawl.

"Back Stabbers" emerges from this percussion fog. It reached number one on the American R&B chart on 9 September 1972, six days before E Howard Hunt, G Gordon Liddy, James McCord, Frank Sturgis, Bernard Barker, Virgilio Gonzalez and Eugenio Martinez were indicted for their role in the Watergate break-in. Released at a time when the full scale of Nixon's treachery was just beginning to be revealed, at a time when The O'Jays and Gamble & Huff still believed that people needed to sing "We Shall Overcome", at a time when liberal Senator Daniel Moynihan was blaming the cycle of poverty on African-American men, "Back Stabbers"'s refrain of *"Smilin' faces sometimes back stabbers"* resonated with a significance that went far beyond the tale of a man whose friends want to steal his woman. Coupled with the eerie piano, screeching strings and off-kilter percussion, the air of spooks, dirty tricks and double-crossing is unmistakable.

One year later, as John Shaft was doing his thing in Africa, former Motown cogs The Four Tops were wailing, *"There's not a street that you can walk/You gotta watch just who you're talking to/They're out to get ya/Can't turn your back on a smiling face/Next thing you know, there ain't no trace of you... Gotta keep your eye on the passers by, better watch your step/'Cause you never know where the knife will go and they ain't missed yet"*. Produced by Chicago soul stalwart Johnny Pate for the *Shaft In Africa* soundtrack, "Are You Man Enough" was largely pro forma blaxploitation: surging Hollywood strings, gratuitous wah-wah, handclaps and a wonderfully cinematic intro.

For the most part, the lyrics are pretty pro forma as well. Except for two remarkable passages that add more layers of meaning to the conversation, where the above lines merely reiterate the terms of the debate. If "Back Stabbers" was all suggestive metaphors and uncanny timing, "Are You Man Enough" was unquestionable intent: *"There's no pretending it goes away, with every step that you take you're paying your dues/And I ain't lying/You got to struggle to see the light because someone's looking to steal your right to choose/And they don't stop trying."*

If Nixon was the perfect symbol of the changing same of Afro-America (has a 30 year old song ever been more appropriate?), then *"Someone needs a friend just around the bend/Don't you think you should be* there?/Are you man enough when the going's rough/Is it in your heart to care?" is a plea for new paradigms, echoing the critique implied by The O'Jays and forcefully stated by The Temptations and Norman Whitfield on "Papa Was A Rolling Stone".

Long before Harvey Ball ever dreamed up his little yellow face, America was full of even more pernicious smiling caricatures. The pickaninny was a depiction of a black child with nappy hair, bulging eyes, enormous lips, a wide mouth usually being stuffed with watermelon and, almost infallibly, a huge, stupid grin. Most scholars date the origin of the pickaninny to Harriet Beecher Stowe's Topsy character from *Uncle Tom's Cabin*, but Topsy was a solemn girl meant to symbolise the brutality of slavery. The caricatures, both literary and figurative, that followed, however, universally depicted 'good-for-nothing gator bait' pickaninnies as mirthful and more than happy with their lot. The pickaninny was a fixture in American popular culture until very recently, with such notable examples as *Little Black Sambo*, Buckwheat from the Our Gang films and numerous minstrelsy characters. In 1932 Cab Calloway recorded a version of the old minstrelsy number, "There's A Cabin In The Cotton": *"I got a feeling so sentimental/And I see a smile so gentle/When I think of old Virginnie/And my pickaninny days."*

Almost 40 years later, Sly Stone was slightly less sentimental when he sang, *"You caught me smilin' again"* on his 1971 album *There's A Riot Goin' On*. Sly & The Family Stone's early music was among the greatest music of the 60s because it actually practised what it preached. A mixture of rock and soul, pop and funk, whites and blacks, men and women, Sly & The Family Stone represented the words of the 60s dream made flesh. While the rock community paid lip service to tolerance and loving each other (probably only because they thought they could raise their groupie quota), The Family Stone were living it. The protest singers filled their songs with a self-righteousness that made their world a drag to live in, but The Family Stone made a joyful noise out of collectivity.

By the end of 1969, though, Sly & The Family Stone was no longer the voice of a shiny, happy, new, integrated America. 1970's "Thank You (Falettinme Be Mice Elf Agin)" was a snarling record that intimated that Woodstock, and the group's triumph there, was a sham: *"Thank you for the party, but I could never stay."* The group's new album was endlessly delayed, Sly wasn't showing up for concerts, he was wrestling with drug addiction, there were rumours that black nationalist leaders were trying to force him to make his music more radical, he was getting death threats. When *There's A Riot Goin' On* finally emerged in November 1971, the joy, the gorgeous mosaic of voices and the *"different strokes for different folks"* tolerance were all gone. In their places, were scorn, derision and dead spots so vast you felt like you'd just fallen off the end of the world. The deadest spot of all was the title track, which clocked in at 0'00". While Marvin Gaye was making *What's Goin' On* as an article of faith in the power of pop music, Sly was highlighting his pessimism by sardonically pointing out that nothing was going on.

With Sly turning to cataloguing the betrayals of the 60s dream, America needed a new black icon to make it feel good about itself. Instead of someone who still believed in the possibilities of the American experiment, this new icon was an 11 year old boy who didn't know any better. While Michael Jackson was electrifying the world with his innocent charm, Sly was retreating into himself because he knew a lot better. "(You Caught Me) Smilin'" was a sketchy, slo-mo groove with deconstructed and incomplete JB horn charts, too wasted to try to fight their way through the narcotic haze – like Sly & The Family Stone in dub, or maybe in photo-negative. Sly gurgled and wailed like a hungry baby, and sang like he was talking to his chest, railing like an incoherent drunk against the prevailing notion that ignorance is bliss. The song was a kiss-off – both to a lover and to his old constituency who didn't want him to stop smiling; he had been dragged through the ringer and he was going to take you with him.

The protagonist of The Persuaders' 1971 hit, "Thin Line Between Love And Hate", had also been left for dead. With Douglas 'Smokey' Scott's overenunciated lead vocals and the old fashioned melodrama of the arrangement, "Thin Line Between Love And Hate" is a pretty standard cautionary tale. Until the last verse, where the put-upon wife exacts her revenge and sends the cheating bastard to the hospital. As the record fades out, Scott gets on his knees and belts, *"Every smiling face in a happy world...",* like he's got old-time religion. Unlike Willie Hutch's 1974 "Theme From Foxy Brown", which contrasts Foxy's smiles and *"foxy looks"* to portray a sex bomb who's not to be trifled with, it's not too much of a leap to suggest that "Thin Line Between Love And Hate" can also be seen as a warning about what lurks behind the goofy grin.

The summer of 75: Nixon had been pardoned, stagflation had set in, the leaders of the Black Power movement had been rounded up, exiled or had retreated into academia, Van McCoy's "The Hustle" was heralding the disco era. However, replacing "The Hustle" at the top of the R&B charts was the last gasp for overtly political black music until The Furious Five's "The Message". "Fight The Power" was The Isley Brothers' second biggest hit, and, of course, everyone remembers it for the *"all this bullshit goin' down"* line. If the record company had got their way, however, it would only have been heard in a bowdlerised version. Yet, even if the DJs didn't ignore the biz's advice, the chorus made the point just as forcefully; so forcefully in fact that Public Enemy would borrow elements from it more than a decade later: *"Time is truly wasting/There's no guarantee/Smiles in the making/Fight the powers that be."*

The Isleys may have closed the smiling faces chapter of soul, but Smiley himself inevitably continued to haunt popular culture like Casper The Friendly Ghost. *Watchmen* – Alan Moore and Dave Gibbons's savage critique of the 80s under the cartoonish leadership of Reagan and Thatcher – used the image of Smiley extensively. During Britain's Acid House boom of the late 80s, Smiley was first spotted at the Shoom club, and was popularised by a designer called Barnsley who made it all the rage once again for a year or so. But Aciiied wasn't really about disguising pain behind the camouflage of a smile: *"Gurning in their place/All they want to do is get off their face"* doesn't really cut it as a metaphor. In 2000, though, New York rap trio Antipop Consortium brought a HipHop perspective to the smiling faces trope. With HipHop inverting the soul paradigm, Anti-Pop's *"motto is show no teeth"*. Never let 'em see you smile, never say, "Have a nice day".

FRAMES OF FREEDOM

IMPROVISATION, OTHERNESS AND THE LIMITS OF SPONTANEITY

BY DAVID TOOP

"**When Niggers make** the revolution," wrote the black, French Caribbean-born poet Aimé Césaire, "they start by uprooting gigantic trees from the Champ de Mars they hurl them at the sky's face like howlings in the warmest air they take aim at pure streams of cool birds and fire blanks at them... and the Niggers go searching in the dust – with jewels in their ears singing loud as they can – for the shards which mica is made from which moons are made from and the lamellated slate from which sorcerers construct the intimate ferocity of the stars." This extract from Césaire's collection, *Solar Throat Slashed*, first published in 1948, anticipates by more than ten years a glossolalic surge, a volcanic shout for freedom, that finally found its true voice in breakthrough recordings of the late 1950s and early 60s by Cecil Taylor, Ornette Coleman, John Coltrane and Albert Ayler.

Césaire's poem was a form of automatic (or semi-automatic) writing, drawing upon Surrealist techniques but projected onto a more specifically political canvas: his conception of negritude. A notion of freedom that predated the Surrealist movement, écriture automatique had been enshrined by André Breton in 1924 as a method for accessing "the superior reality of certain forms of association heretofore neglected, in the omnipotence of the dream, and in the disinterested play of thought". Breton went so far as to suggest that this was the "true function of thought" and that all other psychic mechanisms would be permanently destroyed. Replacing reason, aesthetics and morals with pure psychic automatism would lead, he claimed, to "the solution of the principal problems of life".

This intoxicating prescription, clearly flawed on many levels, implied a broader history of automatism, encompassing outsider art, spiritualism, occultism, divination, somnambulism, post-Freud and Breuer 'hysteria', and other forms of apparently subconscious expression. "Automatism should be differentiated from various so-called spontaneous literary techniques, such as the well-known 'stream of consciousness' writing and the similar method popularised by Céline and later used by several 'Beat' writers," wrote Franklin Rosemont in his breathless hagiography of Breton, *André Breton And The First Principles Of Surrealism*. "Surrealist automatism has affinities with shamanistic and other trance states. Its aim is to escape the dust storms of all immediate frames of reference; to release the mind's wildest beasts and set them roaming far and wide; to permit the innermost dawn to embrace and conquer the outermost obscurity."

Rosemont's articulation of this quest in the crude terms of nature versus culture is telling. As Breton suggested, this was a search for the real, yet all versions of the real differ. Other forms of automatism thrived before Surrealism, some of them ancient forms of accessing otherness, such as Tibetan drum divination and late Sung Dynasty fu chi automatic writing; some of them emerging from interstices between art, occultism and psychoanalysis. South London based occult artist Austin Osman Spare, for example, privately published *The Book Of Pleasure (Self-Love): The Psychology Of Ecstasy*, in 1913. "Automatic drawing," he wrote, "is a vital means of expressing what is at the back of your mind (the dream-man) and is a quick and easy means to begin being courageously original – eventually it evolves itself into the coveted spontaneous expression and the safe omniscience is assured."

Despite this early 20th century upsurge of interest in tapping the subconscious, evident in the drawings of André Masson, the frottages of Max Ernst and the transcribed trance utterances of Robert Desnos, music seemed strangely immune to the concept of unfettered spontaneity. Assaults on textual logic pioneered by the Free Words of FT Marinetti and Tristan Tzara were mirrored by an interest in noise, a pursuit of new sounds that expanded the instrumental and structural constraints of the concert tradition, yet there is little evidence of any musician – whether in the context of orchestra, jazz band or avant garde performance – throwing away the rules with the abandon of a Masson or Kurt Schwitters.

This may partly be explained by the available means of documentation. During the period of acoustic recording, from the last years of the 19th century up until 1925, the music industry was dominated by commercially viable recordings that suited the limitations of the medium at that time. "Large numbers of performing musicians could not be recorded at all," wrote Timothy Day in *A Century Of Recorded Music: Listening To Musical History*. He asks the question why the record catalogues were filled with "a succession of operatic potboilers and popular salon pieces and hackneyed ballads" during "an epoch of intense musical creativity, one of the richest periods in the history of Western music." The answer lay with economics and technicalities. Markets had to be created, records were expensive to produce; sonically, the recording process was not yet capable of capturing anything beyond the obvious.

With a few exceptions, extreme experiments in spontaneous sound vanished into the aether, preserved only in excitable written accounts which we are forced to trust. Noise of smashing glass and struck metal accompanied Nikolai Foregger's *Mechanical Dances*, performed in Russia in 1923, and some form of semi-improvised bruitism played a part in performances at the Cabaret Voltaire in Zurich around 1915-16. Important as they were, solo recitations by Hugo Ball or the simultaneous poems of Richard Huelsenbeck, Marcel Janco and Tristan Tzara all began and ended with transformations of literature – exploded, interrupted, rendered into nonsense – yet still tied to human vocal utterance. In an atmosphere of chaos, Mary Hennings sang her songs, Huelsenbeck banged relentlessly on a big drum, Janco bowed an invisible violin, Ball played the piano; there was so-called Negro music (undoubtedly something embarrassingly primitivist) and when Ball recited his sound poem, "Karawane", in 1916, he imitated the chanting of the Catholic mass in order to give his recitation more mystique and power.

The impression left from written accounts suggests that these moments of sonic anarchy were almost an afterthought, a dive into infantilism that flooded the proceedings with extra mayhem. Poets or visual artists raised an undisciplined racket without having to confront problems of embouchure, intonation and fingering or the absence of a score. From what we can gather, no individual musician was deconstructing performance with the same demonic verve as the poets, though new instrumental techniques, compositional forms and sonic technologies were being invented every day. This view may change when the history of sonic art matures enough to move beyond its current emphasis on European and American trends and embrace research into avant garde art movements elsewhere. In other countries, the synthesis of local initiatives and a mixture of foreign influences may have produced a different balance. The charismatic central figure in the Japanese Mavo artists group, Muruyama Tomoyoshi, absorbed the influence of German expressionist dance in early 1920s Berlin, seeing Mary Wigman dance her *Heroic Parade* to Beethoven's *Symphony No 5*. "While attending the Düsseldorf Congress of Progressive Artists," writes Gennifer Weisenfeld in *Mavo: Japanese Artists And The Japanese Avant-Garde 1905-1931*, "he witnessed an impromptu dadaist performance by the Dutch couple Theo and Nelly Van Doesberg, who sang and yelled while dancing half-naked on tables and chairs. The combination of expression and provocation fundamental to expressionist and dadaist performance pervaded Muruyama's, and later Mavo's approach to drama."

In 1924, Muruyama and Okada Tatsuo performed *The Dance That Cannot Be Named* at the Tokyo Imperial University Christian Youth Hall. Weisenfeld reproduces a newspaper photograph of this event in her book. Dressed in women's clothes, they are contorted into expressive poses of ambiguous sexuality that clearly indicate a connection with the Butoh dance imagery developed by Tatsumi Hijikata, Mitsutaka Ishii and Min Tanaka more than four decades later. "The news article accompanying this photograph," she writes, "describes their writhing movements and identifies Takamizawa Michinao as providing the music, playing unusual instruments constructed out of tin cans, a spinning wheel, oil cans and logs. Takamizawa rubbed these various objects together to produce sounds, calling them 'sound constructors', undoubtedly a reference to the instruments of the same name used by the Futurist Luigi Russolo in Italy. There were two types of sound constructor, 'wind sound constructors' and 'broken instrument constructors'." As with the majority of comparable contemporary events, the totality of the performance has to be imaginatively constructed from anecdotal description and a grainy photograph. Despite that limitation, *The Dance That Cannot Be Named* implies a more consistently avant garde fusion with sound than Mary Wigman's use of Beethoven and a more considered approach than the Doesbergs or any other dadaists (except Kurt Schwitters).

Perhaps the relationship between musicians and their technology accounted for a relative lack of abandon, an interest in liberating techniques and systems rather than the goal (or mirage) of total freedom. By the 20th century, most of the musical instruments commonly used in European and American musics had developed into externalisations of the tempered system of tuning. With the exception of certain wind instruments – the trombone, to some extent – and untuned percussion, instruments were tools that forcibly imprinted the rules of the system they represented through the necessary process of learning their mechanics. Implicit in virtuosity was an acceptance of the matrix – the ability to play in tune within the tempered system, to understand the rules of harmony and the language of notation, to articulate the machine of sound. Within this context, only jazz and blues musicians were developing a radically progressive approach to instrumental virtuosity that challenged these rules without discarding them entirely.

For this reason, Edgard Varèse praised the jazz band as a tiger. To his ears the symphony orchestra had degenerated into a dropsical elephant.

Density 21.5, the solo for flute he composed in 1936, anticipated the advanced techniques catalogued and published in the mid-1960s by John C Heiss and Bruno Bartolozzi. Though the piece implies an unfamiliar freedom, a continuation of the potentiality unlocked by Debussy's flute solo of 1913, *Syrinx*, the differences of emphasis are greater than the 23 years that separate them. Originally called *Flûte De Pan*, *Syrinx* is a languorous piece of symbolism, an evocation of the randomness of reeds sounded by wind (Toru Takemitsu wrote about something similar in his 1971 essay, "A Single Sound": "Now we can see how the master shakuhachi player, striving in performance to re-create the sound of wind in a decaying bamboo grove, reveals the Japanese sound ideal: sound in its ultimate expressiveness, being constantly refined, approaches the nothingness of that wind in the bamboo grove."). *Density 21.5*, on the other hand, is named after the density of platinum, the metal of George Barrère's flute. Between reed and platinum lay a cavern of horrors: the brutality of World War One, with Fascist and Nazi activity signalling the imminence of a second. Varèse's solo is full of tension and uncertainty, sudden stops and abrupt leaps, shrill high pitches and labyrinthine structure. After composing this piece, he devoted ten years to unrealised projects, searching for further advances in sonic production that would express any thought at the speed of thought.

The epitome of a musical instrument embodying a utopian vision of freedom was Léon Thérémin's etherphone, patented and first demonstrated in Russia in 1921. Capable of emitting sweeping parabolas of sound, the theremin, as it came to be known, was operated by the musician's hand movements. Since the operator didn't actually touch the instrument, only gesturing close enough to interrupt an electromagnetic field, there was a suggestion of detachment from corporeality – the flesh of the trapeze artist floating on air currents. Thérémin envisaged all kinds of new possibilities: spontaneous music generated by the movements of dancers' bodies and a synaesthetic performance art that drew together all the senses.

Paradoxically, the absence of physical contact with the theremin's surface demanded even more control and concentration than a conventional instrument. Accurate intonation, articulation and particularly speed were so difficult to achieve that the theremin turned out to be a poor conduit for spontaneity. One or two genuinely progressive composers tried to use it. From 1932-34, Varèse worked on *Ecuatorial*, originally scored for two custom built theremins, an ensemble of acoustic instruments that included six percussionists and a bass voice, though the published score and later recordings have used Maurice Martenot's invention, the Ondes Martenot, in place of the theremins. "Varèse used the theremins for their timbre and the glissandi and long sustained notes he couldn't find on any other instrument," wrote Albert Glinsky in *Theremin: Ether Music And Espionage*.

Of the everyday matters they chatted about I understood very little. All I heard was the rise and fall of their voices, a kind of warbling such as comes from the throats of birds, a perfect fluting sound, part celestial and part the song of sirens.
WG Sebald, *The Rings Of Saturn*

Varèse was frustrated by what he called "the old Man-Power instruments". His use of these electronic prototypes mirrored the visions of Antonin Artaud, writing his first manifesto for *The Theatre Of Cruelty* in 1932. "Musical Instruments," wrote Artaud, "These will be used as objects, as part of the set. Moreover they need to act deeply and directly on our sensitivity through the senses, and from the point of view of sound they invite research into utterly unusual sound properties and vibrations which present-day musical instruments do not possess, urging us to use ancient or forgotten instruments or to invent new ones. Apart from music, research is also needed into instruments and appliances based on special refining and new alloys which can reach a new scale in the octave and produce an unbearably piercing sound or noise."

This was exactly the case in *Ecuatorial*, in which the electronic instruments soar to stratospheric pitches that are beyond the highest reaches of even the piccolo. Perhaps there was also a sense of otherness that drew him to electronics. Until the rebirth of the theremin as the aetherial voice of aliens, alcoholics and mad magicians in 1950s cinema, Thérémin's futuristic ideas about his revolutionary instrument were hardly borne out by its customary repertoire: recitals of Chopin, Rachmaninoff, Tchaikovsky, Mozart, Handel and Saint-Saëns. Varèse and Olivier Messiaen, who composed the eerie, weightless *Oraison* for an ensemble of Ondes Martenot in 1937, were exceptions. Both composed through a mystical glass: Varèse invoking an awe-inspiring future-past of pagan magic, alchemy and beast cries in the urban night; Messiaen synthesising Catholicism, Platonic love and the complex manifestations of nature into a music that was "more than a work of art, it was a way of existing, an inextinguishable fire". Messiaen, in fact, insisted that his approach was theological, rather than mystical. "Whereas mysticism seeks the annihilation of being, which in its perfection, is the contemplation of spiritual ecstasy and unites man to the Godhead," Robert Sherlaw Johnson wrote in 1970. "Messiaen's approach, on the other hand, is concerned with the truths of the Catholic faith which relate to God's acts of redemption in the world."

There is a connection here between weightlessness, ecstasy and free lines. Percy Grainger, of all the most improbable composers, gave some of the clearest reasoning as to why that should be so. Perhaps the first composer to use the expression 'free music', Grainger believed (along with his teacher, Busoni, Henry Cowell and Harry Partch), that sound was trapped in the grid of 12 tone equal temperament. Cowell's composition of 1923, *The Banshee*, delved into the bowels of the piano, transmuting the rigid frame into a well full of spirits; Partch embarked on the monumental work of theorising a new approach to tonality, notation and musical purpose, then building the musical instruments to play it.

"Grainger thought that music was unique among the arts by its woeful dependence on the type of segmentation inherent in temperament," wrote Douglas Kahn in *Noise, Water, Meat: A History Of Sound In The Arts*. Grainger had been thinking about "nonharmony, gliding tones, total independence of voices, and what he called 'beatless music' as early as 1899, when he was seventeen years old," says Kahn. He quotes Grainger, from 1942: "Current music is like trying to do a picture of a landscape, a portrait of a person, in small squares – like a mosaic – or in preordained shapes: straight lines or steps."

Grainger comes close here to imagining into being the coming world of digital music, of zeros and ones and curves that reveal themselves as stepped straight lines under high magnification. His own inspiration was the movement of waves that he had seen as a young child, growing up in Melbourne, Australia. Always threatening banality as an image, waves in the ocean demonstrate a model of complexity, of infinity, of temporal division, endless variety and disintegrating curves. Music could only aspire to that infinite horizon of content. "There are a thousand ways of probing the future," said Olivier Messiaen in a 1958 lecture in Brussels. "I only wish that composers would not forget that music is a part of time, a fraction of time, as is our own life, and that nature – an inexhaustible treasure house of sounds, colours, forms and rhythms, and the unequalled model for total development and perpetual variations – that nature is the supreme resource."

Grainger put his faith in the construction of machines, believing that humans would never be able to rise to the potential of a superior machine (perhaps inventing the computer in his mind, though building his own machines from a bizarre collection of utilitarian flotsam). Messiaen turned to birdsong, which also displayed an infinitude of parabolas, pitch relationships, rhythmic sequences, tonal variations, alien melodies and unpredictable juxtapositions. Finding inspiration in natural phenomena may be as old as music itself, not that anybody can be absolutely certain. But a wealth of documentation over centuries shows that animals and meteorological phenomena have always represented otherness, the mystery of communication that holds its meaning at a tantalising remove from human understanding. The distance between nature and culture, never entirely clear in any society, could break down in shamanistic communications with animal familiars, or in possession by spirits or demons in animal form.

Some artists courted this danger, or found their artistic visions of otherness and the extra-human liable to unravel into uncontrollable states of being. "Artaud was so entrenched in his own world," wrote Bettina L Knapp in *Antonin Artaud: Man Of Vision*, "so overcome by his 'other preoccupations' that the rapport with the 'normal' 'outer' world ceased." In this deteriorating condition, experienced in 1943, he would get down on his hands and knees, spit, belch in rhythm and make strange noises. "Hours were spent in articulating the words forcibly," wrote Knapp, "injecting each syllable with a kind of metallic ringing sound; treating words as something concrete, actual being possessing potential magic forces."

Artaud is particularly germane to any meditation on the limits of improvisation and its relationship to otherness. Knapp describes his behaviour during this period of madness, shortly before his incarceration in the asylum at Rodez, as a form of glossolalia, yet glossolalia (or speaking in tongues) tends towards stereotyping and repetition. In its Christian form, glossolalia represents baptism by the Holy Spirit. This phenomenon, a kind of acquired babbling expelled involuntarily during trance, replays the incident at the Feast of Pentecost after Christ's death, vaguely described in the New English Bible as a moment of "tongues like flames of fire, dispersed among them and resting on each one. And they were all filled with the Holy Spirit and began to talk in other tongues, as the Spirit gave them power of utterance."

Artaud's behaviour is more complex, subtler, since he was consciously seeking new forms of theatrical language, yet also subject to psychic disintegration which provoked an untangled chaos of theory and psychosis. "The theatre of cruelty necessitates a new form of language," writes Alan S Weiss in *Breathless: Sound Recording, Disembodiment And The Transformation Of Lyrical Nostalgia*, "the archetype of which is glossolalia: a performative, dramatic, enthusiastic expression of the body; language reduced to the realm of incantatory sound at the threshold of nonsense; speech as pure gesture. Such instances of glossolalia are not mere symptoms, as Artaud explained to Dr Ferdière at Rodez: 'Half of the chants in the Catholic church were exorcisms at the beginning of the

Christian era, and they have now passed into the liturgy of the faithful...'
Originating as a private speaking in tongues within Artaud's religious
delirium, this glossolalia was first transmogrified into an apotropaic
incantatory technique, a veritable curative magic, to protect him from the
gods and demons that tormented him; ultimately, it was raised, through
textual performance and production, to the level of poetry."

In an analysis of glossolalia based on fieldwork conducted among an
Apostolic movement in Mexico, anthropologist and linguist Felicitas D
Goodman came to the conclusion that glossolalia of this type "mirrors
that of the person who guided the glossolalist into the behaviour".
Contextualising this discovery within a general contemporary ambivalence
towards dissociative states, a fear of "chaos beyond the threshold of
awareness", she concludes that the opposite is true, that "beyond the
threshold of the conscious there is not disorder but structure".

In *The History Of Surrealist Painting*, Marcel Jean compared
automatism to the photographer-seaweed – "an aquatic plant which is a
kind of living magic lantern and whose functioning might symbolise the
return to consciousness of first memories" – in Raymond Roussel's
Impressions D'Afrique. "In Roussel's novel," wrote Jean, "the spectators
are fascinated at the beginning by the performance of the screen plant,
but in the end their attention wanders: the same cycle of images repeats
itself indefinitely. Habit tends to make a conscious action nothing less
than automatic and monotonous; inversely, it introduces a factor of
monotony, of real stereotype, into any too long prolonged or too often
repeated unconscious experience." As Jean points out, even the
Surrealists wearied eventually of Desnos and his endless monologues
dredged up from the depths of reverie.

This serious objection to spontaneous expression was more or less
John Cage's point of view whenever the subject of improvisation was
raised. "I've always been opposed to improvisation," he told Joan
Retallack, during the conversations collected as *Musicage*, "because you
do only what you remember." During the same conversation, less than a
month before he died, Cage admitted a change of heart. "I became
interested because I had not been interested," he said. "And the reason I
had not been interested was because one just goes back to one's habits.
But how can we find ways of improvising that *release* us from our habits?"

This suggests that Cage had not paid close attention to the kind of improvisation, from the 1960s onwards, that either began, or learned through practical experience, to do exactly that. Paradoxically, Cage's earlier rejection of improvisation can now be seen as a key – one of many – that unlocked the possibility for total improvisation in the 1960s. For Cage, indeterminacy and chance methods were strategies for asking questions without the necessities of also providing answers. Discussing a Mark Tobey painting with Joan Retallack, Cage says: "What's so beautiful is that there's no gesture in it. The hand is not operating in any way."

This sounds like an observation on the phenomenon of emergence, in which coherence will develop from apparently unrelated or undirected actions. In *Writings Through John Cage's Music, Poetry, + Art*, Alvin Curran, a member of the pioneering improvisation group MEV, talks about the formation of MEV in a similar way: "We found ourselves busily soldering cables, contact mikes, and talking about 'circuitry' as if it were a new religion. By amplifying the sounds of glass, wood, metal, water, air, and fire, we were convinced that we had tapped into the sources of the natural musics of 'everything.' We were in fact making a spontaneous music which could be said to be coming from 'nowhere' and made out of 'nothing' – all somewhat a wonder and a collective epiphany. And learning that Cage had done these things even ten years earlier was no shock, but a confirmation of a 'mutual' discovery."

The possibility of amplifying sounds inherent within inanimate material, a kind of aural microscopy, was made possible through the fast advances of electronic music. The intense struggle of Varèse to liberate sound from the custody of instrument technology, heard so clearly on *Density 21.5*, was answered by tape music and live electronics. As a partial answer to harmonic limitations in so-called Western music, percussion had become increasingly important in 20th century music, whether through jazz, the influence of musical practice from regions outside European/American hegemony (the vastness, diversity, sonic richness and structural complexity of African and Asian music, in particular), or the rejection of equal temperament. Although electronics appeared to offer a solution to the challenges of ultimate control posed by serialism, the consequence of electronically generated and manipulated sound was a greater freedom to abandon control, particularly in collective settings.

In 1946, John Cage began composing his *Sonatas And Interludes*, an extended cycle for prepared piano. As with other works he had been composing since the late 1930s, this developed ideas initiated by Henry Cowell, using objects within the piano's interior to radically alter its sonority and tuning. More significantly, since that battle had already been won, the piece addressed the structural problems of composing in long form for a solo instrument without resorting to conventions of harmony. In the same year, the New Orleans drummer Baby Dodds hauled his drum kit into a studio to record a set of solos for Folkways Records. Intended as an unpretentious document of the skills that lay behind a glittering career, working with King Oliver, Louis Armstrong, Jelly Roll Morton, Sidney Bechet, Bunk Johnson and Merce Cunningham, *Baby Dodds: Talking And Drum Solos* goes far beyond any other percussion showcase. Dodd's control of dynamics, sound and swing makes this 10" album the spiritual ancestor of many solo percussion records made by improvisors, from *The Milford Graves Percussion Ensemble With Sunny Morgan*, released on ESP in 1965, to Han Bennink's *Solo*, released on ICP in 1972 and containing, just like the Baby Dodds album, two tracks entitled "Spooky Drums". The major difference, from Milford Graves onwards, was that rhythm was explored microscopically, as pure sound, freed from the narrative of linearity.

Cold War politics, race politics and their portrayal through the global theatre of mass media tattooed indelible marks on the post-war generation. A strong undercurrent of resistance to technology (the weapons of total annihilation that stood ready) or access denied to all but the most successful of African-American jazz musicians, contributed to the overwhelmingly acoustic feel of so much early free jazz and free improvisation. Inside the studio, sound recording was beginning its experiment of physical and audio separation; beyond that, the sense of alienation in an increasingly mediated, commodified landscape was intensifying. "To feel is perhaps the most terrifying thing in this society," pianist Cecil Taylor has said. "This is one of the reasons I'm not too interested in electronic music: it divorces itself from human energy, it substitutes another kind of force as the determinant agent for its continuance."

Sun Ra's use of electronic keyboards was prophetic, not just because he was almost alone among free jazz musicians in using the Moog, Clavioline, tape effects and so on, but because his use of these instruments and techniques was so utterly liberated in comparison with the highly structured and theorised (or mytheorised) trajectory of the rest of his work. If hearing Sun Ra's Arkestra was an audio hallucination of the ballrooms of Chicago transplanted into the midst of verdant rainforest on a lonely planet where chaos was beauty, the effect of hearing Albert and Donald Ayler for the first time was like hearing the drum and fife music of Napolean Strickland and Othar Turner, the gospel saxophone of Vernard Johnson, the slide guitar moans of Blind Willie Johnson, the R&B tenor shriek and roar of Big Jay McNeely, the androgynous whooping and screaming of Little Richard, the New Orleans marches of George Lewis and The Eureka Brass Band, all refracted through the turmoil of civil rights, Malcolm X's assassination, the riots in Watts, the media futurism of the space race, the escalating war in Vietnam.

Just the titles of Albert Ayler's breakthrough albums – *Spirits*, *Spiritual Unity*, *Spirits Rejoice*, *Bells* – were clear signs of the elevated consciousness he brought to music. In 1964, Ayler had recorded a selection of gospel tunes with Call Cobbs, Henry Grimes and Sunny Murray. Gospel was the well-kept secret of African-American music at that time, the voices of Archie Brownlee, Julius Cheeks, Claude Jeter and Inez Andrews little known beyond the sanctified circuit, despite being the foundation of soul. These were voices that inhabited the body to a point beyond its corporeal limits, screaming to the spirit, rising through registers to a place beyond conventional existence. Ayler inhabited the saxophone in the same way, bursting through its mechanical and physical expression of equal temperament to otherness. It was as if all the individual acts of instrumental subversion in jazz, from Bubber Miley, Joe 'Tricky Sam' Nanton and Cootie Williams of the 1920s Duke Ellington Orchestra onwards, had now found a form through which their true meaning was understood.

From the mid-century, explorations in 'freeform' or 'abstract' music, improvised without a predetermined structure, were touched upon, or implied, by a small number of musicians: Lennie Tristano, Warne Marsh and Lee Konitz in 1949; Cecil Taylor and Steve Lacy in 1955, George

Russell and Bill Evans in 1956, Ornette Coleman and Don Cherry in 1959, Joe Harriott and Phil Seaman in 1960. At the time, the idea was shocking and while some quickly abandoned what later seemed an interesting diversion, a moment of madness, others recognised a lifetime faith. Faith was a requirement. Capitol Records treated the Lennie Tristano tracks "Intuition" and "Digression" as worker rebellion. The company refused to release one of the recordings and initially withheld payment for the recording date. From the mid-1960s onwards, European improvising groups such as AMM, Joseph Holbrooke, MEV, Gruppo Di Improvvisazione Nuova Consonanza, The People Band and Spontaneous Music Ensemble faced indifference or abruptly-terminated interest from established record labels. Perceived as a branch of the entertainment industry, improvised music survived within an environment that was economically harsh and intellectually impoverished.

One means of ingress to improvising without a map was to interact through counterpoint. This approach could be legitimised through the historical precedent of JS Bach and the Baroque. But the social movements and politics of the 1960s moved in two contrary directions – towards self-exploration on the one hand; collective action on the other – and this paradox finally shattered any need to legitimise art through bourgeois history or by exercising self-restraint. Some of the reasons why free improvisation was a logical development in musical history can be understood retrospectively through relatively recent scientific studies of complexity and emergence. Creating musical coherence, variety and beauty without the instructions of a director was possible through the skills of listening and response that many musicians already possessed. "This is the secret of cell assembly," wrote Steven Johnson in *Emergence*. "Cell collectives emerge because each cell looks to its neighbours for cues about how to behave."

At one level, improvisation can be compared with the ultimate otherness of an ant colony or hive of bees. Perhaps it was no coincidence that in the wake of drummer John Stevens and The Spontaneous Music Ensemble, certain strands of English improvised music were known, half-disparagingly, as insect music. In its earliest days, all of this music was classified under freedom: free jazz, free improvisation, or simply free music. The jazz musician's concept of playing 'outside' – outside the changes or metre – had moved one more step into anarchy. Eventually, as with any experiment in collectivism, the limitations of freedom began to assert themselves. Collective relationships in which hidden dynamics are not exposed are breeding grounds for covert tyranny. The best improvisors realised that their music demanded constant awareness. As the history of automatism shows, spontaneity attracts the inevitability of collapse into repetitious themes and behavioural tics, stasis and empty chatter.

"We're taught that music is something special," said saxophonist Trevor Watts, interviewed by *Melody Maker* in the early 1970s. "We intellectualise about it; that's how we're taught to function, so therefore it is necessary for us to have methods to cope with our environment, and yet play natural music." In a society increasingly dominated by a marketplace of synthetic materials, electronic communications and the inexorable spread of mass media, this struggle between pragmatic strategies and 'natural' music became desperate. By the mid-1970s, free jazz and free improvisation were being written off as outmoded 'genres' that had promised visions of a new kind of society yet failed to communicate to an audience or develop an aesthetic. The truth, however, was more complicated and more hopeful. The challenges of creating music that dispenses with any hand of authority would now be addressed as issues central to a long term project, rather than an expression of unfettered spontaneity and the utopia of freedom. After an extended experiment with absolutism, a new process was beginning.

GENERATION ECSTASY

NEW YORK'S FREE JAZZ CONTINUUM

BY TOM ROE

1999: The Little Huey Creative Music Orchestra is just finishing a robust afternoon performance at its homebase, the new artist-curated club Tonic, when suddenly the burly bassist William Parker takes it on himself to lead his big band still blaring into the streets. Watching Parker's dozen sweating musicians descend on Delancey Street, you can't quite shake the impression this scene has been played out before. The cast might have been different, and maybe the street corner was a few blocks away, but the feeling persists that today's spontaneous march past could have been scripted from an old New York jazz documentary.

Almost 35 years ago to the day, an earlier generation of musicians had congregated on the Lower East Side, declaring their independence from the city's jazz establishment at the now historic 1964 October Revolution In Jazz, a series of concerts held at the Cellar Cafe and organised by trumpeter Bill Dixon. Over six nights, the likes of Sun Ra, John Tchicai, Roswell Rudd, Paul Bley and Milford Graves loudly proclaimed their manifestos for a new music, at once proving its vitality and its viability as a force outside the mainstream (the concerts were sold out). Down the years, their stance has inspired likeminded spirits across the city to pick up and develop their initiative into artist-run labels, self-supporting networks and communities. At the beginning of the 70s, the likes of drummer Rashied Ali and saxophonist Sam Rivers bypassed the tight circle of promoters, agents and money men running New York's lucrative club circuit by staging concerts and art events at home, in the large, spacious lofts of the Lower East Side, which was then a cheap property district where a sizeable colony of artists had gravitated. Ali's Alley and Studio Rivbea, the loft run by Rivers and his wife Beatrice, were as much 'head space' as physical architectural conversions, where outsider musicians could develop their own signatures free of the pressures to please that had come to preoccupy nightclub promoters with more expensive rents to consider.

Back in real time, Parker's exuberant troupe is just spilling out into the New York afternoon crowd. The knowledge that they're walking in the giant steps of earlier generations of jazz dissenters, through streets haunted by the ghosts of Albert Ayler and all the other great practitioners of free music, living and dead, from John Coltrane and Ornette Coleman, to Charles Lloyd and Cecil Taylor, who have suffered and survived the same tribulations, doesn't so much detract from their parade as enrich it. Parker, alongside a good many of his contemporaries, came up through the loft scene, many of whose progenitors were themselves the progeny of the October Revolutionaries. Without upheavals in jazz, there would be no continuity, no rich heritage... just history. Building on this legacy, the generation at the end of the 20th century blasting open a future for the music, ensuring its passage into the 21st, included players as far apart in age and experience as saxophonists David S Ware and Charles Gayle, multi-reedists Daniel Carter and Sabir Mateen, pianist Matthew Shipp, pianist-percussionist Cooper-Moore, and drummers William Hooker and Susie Ibarra. Collectively, the exhilarating sound of them ripping away from the fabric of tradition has been termed 'ecstatic jazz', a label coined by Steven Joerg, formerly of the hardcore punk Homestead label, and who founded his own free jazz label, AUM Fidelity, out of his enthusiasm for the music. "I started using 'ecstatic jazz' in press releases and advertisements," Joerg explains. "At the time it was a good way to describe the sort of out-of-body experiences that I personally have had listening to the music. 'Avant garde' seemed dead, and the price musicians paid over the years certainly belied the 'free jazz' moniker..." For want of a more marketable tag, ecstatic jazz stuck.

As veterans of the 70s loft revolution, Parker, Ware, Gayle and a few other members of the New York school of ecstatic jazz stuck it out through decades of poverty and public indifference before finally breaking beyond the city boundaries and attaining international recognition. Younger players like pianist Matthew Shipp – who contributes percussive keyboard parts to The David S Ware Quartet when he's not working on his own projects – arrived in the city long after Ayler and the loft scene had passed, but he still spots apparitions. Shipp constantly sails through the Lower East Side, recently living in an apartment Charlie Parker once nested, and frequenting a bar below an old home of Charles Mingus. "This neighbourhood has a very rich tradition," he says. "There's definitely a way of being, a kind of a mode, and it's not narcotics or anything. There's just a very rich tradition of jazz here."

The historical, geographic and personal links to earlier jazz masters can weigh heavily on the current crop of improvisors, who feel forever tethered to their ghostly East River peers. Going up against heroes that large is a losing proposition, some feel, especially as record sales, establishment critics and even a few of their own number favour dead icons over the next big things. "There were more places to play then, and perhaps even the level of playing was higher than it is now," surmises David S Ware, from a perspective informed by three decades of playing. "When you look back, the situation always looks better. We're inspired by that era, but if people listen to the music, there's a million things we do differently as a band."

Younger contemporaries like Shipp take a more positive view of the jazz heritage, asserting that the freewheeling approach of their forebears is only the starting point to journeys elsewhere. "I play universal music," Shipp asserts, "in the sense that John Coltrane played universal music, in that he played jazz-influenced music with spiritual overtones that is influenced by rhythms all over the world but doesn't appropriate those things, it synthesizes them into their endemic jazz sensibility. That's what I do."

So ecstatic jazz isn't Coltrane redux, but a living extension of the saxophonist's transcendentalism.

"They came out of that firsthand," reckons Michael Ehlers, who started the Eremite record label, another key outlet for the music, outside of Boston in 1995 with the writer Byron Coley. "There's no way they wouldn't be influenced by those people. It's kind of a ridiculous argument. Their development of the music is just the natural trajectory." Ehlers records musicians from all over the world, among them Germany's Peter Brötzmann and American expatriate Alan Silva, but most often he finds himself drawing from New York's deep pool of talent.

If ecstatic jazz is romantically characterised by a single image, it could well be that of onetime homeless saxophonist Charles Gayle pouring a decade's worth of suffering and bitterness into long, lungbusting pieces pitched at hyperthyroid intensity and held for infinite duration, with scant pause for breath or contrast. Its denigrators claim the music is all grandstanding bluster and no build-up, launched from peaks that have never been scaled. They argue that it doesn't so much take off from Coltrane as get trapped in his slipstream, bobbing and squalling helplessly in his jet trails. But the very ferocity abhorred by jazz snobs is what's getting the music heard beyond jazz. Support from the rock world and the attendant media attention allows third generation improvisors the freedom to remove musical and marketing straitjackets. Fortunately, the spotlight turned their way just as the players' voices matured after a lifetime of world-weary experience. While the ecstatic jazz scene is still a fringe style that counts CD sales in the low thousands, its audience has been expanding horizontally, picking up listeners and sparring partners along the margins of alt.rock, noise and the John Zorn school of artcore, who discover in ecstatic jazz a level of intensity the match of, say, Sonic Youth at their most frenzied. It is no coincidence that the founders of Eremite and AUM Fidelity have backgrounds in US hardcore rock and noise.

At once adventurous and curious, all the noise fringes are coming together in a rainbow coalition of marginals, sharing audiences and cross-fertilising styles in ad-hoc Improv combinations. New York spots such as Tonic and the Knitting Factory feel like home to ecstatic jazz musicians, and a short circuit of colleges and risk-taking rock and jazz clubs exists for occasional domestic touring. High profile American jazz magazines have put Ware and Shipp on their covers alongside the neo-conservative Wynton Marsalis crowd, and American college radio plays ecstatic jazz artists virtually to the exclusion of all other jazz styles. So much so, in fact, that Shipp is taking a sabbatical from recording to let the rest of the world catch up with his vision and long discography. Even the neo-cons are interested now, with Branford Marsalis signing Ware to a seven record deal with Sony, the first time free improvisation has been backed by major label distribution since the early 70s.

So the New York scene has reached a new stage, more figuratively than literally, since these players still often perform on the same cramped platforms in small clubs. New York living can be tough, forcing historic figures like Gayle on the streets, but it also presents opportunities. "You can do just about anything you want to in New York," says an optimistic William Parker, from a sidewalk cafe below his Lower East Side apartment that's a few blocks away from the homes of Gayle, Shipp, Mateen and Carter. "In Chicago, there's a lot of musicians. There should be more happening in Boston, but there isn't. Philadelphia has its scene, but there's nothing like New York," he contends.

After ceding primacy to Chicago in the late 70s, and to the neo-cons from New Orleans in the conservative 80s, New York's re-emergence as the premier cutting edge jazz domain is due, in part, to some clever marketing. Everyone acknowleges that the term 'ecstatic jazz' is a false construct, but as a marketing device it has undoubtedly paid dividends.

Nevertheless, many musicians prefer to brand the music themselves. William Parker calls it "creative music", Daniel Carter likes to jump-start "functional anarchy" in his life, and Cooper-Moore doesn't think anyone's making music different enough to warrant a new name.

A new label at least helps separate the current musicians from their past and soften comparisons to the 70s loft scene. Figures from the 70s haunt spots such as 501 Canal Street, a five-storey downtown structure that birthed some of the city's current jazz masters 30 years ago. At that time, white flight to the suburbs had emptied out the city, and David S Ware, Cooper-Moore, drummer Tom Bruno and a few others rented an entire building on Canal Street for $550 (today, a single room there would cost twice as much). It would become one of the focal points of a vibrant scene. Just like Ali's Alley and Studio Rivbea, 501 Canal Street was part rehearsal and workshop room, part concert hall and party pad. Cooper-Moore, Ware and Mark Edwards moved to New York together to form the group Apogee, but Ware and Edwards eventually left to study with Cecil Taylor. Cooper-Moore, left to his own devices, began inventing musical instruments and learning their voices, before eventually hightailing it back to Virginia.

It is about here when Charles Gayle re-entered the orbit. He was in at the birth of free jazz in the 60s and got taken up by the 70s loft scene, before the harsh economic realities of the 80s forced him to spend much of that decade homeless. Today, Gayle is a peripheral force on the scene, playing occasionally but keeping a low profile. "I'm a hermit, it's my lifestyle," he says from his East Seventh Street apartment. His concerts frequently include performance pieces drawn from his period of homelessness, in which he presents himself as a character called Streets, a lonely greasepainted mime who clowns around between plaintive wails. "After being in the streets, living like that for so long, I felt like the music, just playing all the time, was not enough for me," he explains.

If Gayle is a hermit, Parker is his opposite: a gregarious presence who organises, inspires and leads a variety of projects: his Little Huey big band; a smaller version that performs with theatre groups; duos with

Matthew Shipp among many others, even including über-fringe figures such as Dorgon (a former member of Dim Sum Clip Job, who has recorded two CDs with Parker); and In Order To Survive, a quartet with Cooper-Moore, Rob Brown and (originally) Susie Ibarra. Parker also puts himself out for occasional all-star work, like his collaboration with Alan Silva and Sun Ra's Marshall Allen. Possibly the best organised of the present ecstatic jazz family, Parker learnt the value, and indeed necessity, of artists becoming self-sufficient from his loft experiences.

While Ware, Gayle and Parker were busy in downtown lofts, 46 year old Roy Campbell Jr spent much of the decade up in the Bronx and Harlem, mixing it up with the city's soul-jazz scene. He studied at Manhattan Community College with Yusef Lateef, met legends such as drummer Sunny Murray, and later formed groups with Kenny Kirkland, Omar Hakim and Charles Neville of The Neville Brothers. He smiles wide and laughs about improvising his way through life in 70s New York. "Wayne Horvitz and some other people had this space, Studio Henry, underneath this exotic pet shop," he remembers. "Every now and then the pets would escape, and you'd come to rehearse and find a snake or a baby alligator crawling around in there."

Eventually, the 70s loft scene dried up as rents soared, and collectives like Apogee disbanded in dispute. Ronald Reagan became the central figure in mainstream American life, and Charles Gayle and his style of playing were literally made homeless. Some of the scene's participants tracked the avant garde pulse to the West Coast and Chicago – where Anthony Braxton was in the ascendant at the AACM (Association for the Advancement of Creative Musicians). Among those who stayed behind, Daniel Carter and others also took to the streets to play for change from passers-by. Cooper-Moore played in Country music cover groups in backwoods Virginia, with an open knife on his Fender Rhodes, where he witnessed bloody barfights ending with women getting tossed headfirst through plate-glass windows.

Players sought different routes out of this bleak period. Around 1983 Daniel Carter began playing with hardcore punk groups such as Frontline (with Gil Evans's son on bass and a Cro-Mag on guitar). "Mingus would have changes of tempo, and in classical music you'd have that, but in most jazz music you establish a tempo and that's kind of the way it goes," says Carter, a greying African-American who almost always wears a flannel shirt when performing, in the tradition of American counterculture icons like ex-Creedence Clearwater Revival leader John Fogerty and Firehose's Mike Watt. "In hardcore punk," he continues, "you had multiple tempos, really starkly different changes in tempo and character all in one piece, kind of like a history of music compacted into one piece." Carter's hardcore experiences are audible in his present music, where he often switches between flute, clarinet and sax, constantly varying expectations.

Things slowly improved for the musicians staying on in Manhattan when John Zorn rose to prominence, and began to engage the jazz scene. The slow recovery across the city's arts was noticed by veterans like Cooper-Moore, who returned from Virginia in 1985 to exercise his dramatic flair by hooking up with dance and theatre companies. The scene was also refreshed by the arrival of young players like Matthew Shipp, who moved in from Delaware, looking to meet William Parker. The two became firm friends and frequent collaborators, creating what could be called the scene's signature sound. Shipp's classically influenced playing carries a heady weight, a counterpoint to Parker's brawny style. Besides his musical talents, Shipp also brought a business acumen to the scene. "Despite the fact that I'm very centred in my vision, I'm a careerist, unapologetically," says Shipp. "I brought an energy, for lack of a better word, a yuppie energy to this scene, about how things should be marketed correctly."

When she came up to the city from Texas in 1988, Susie Ibarra had no particular ambition to become a jazz drummer. Then she had an epiphany while watching The Sun Ra Arkestra, and started studying with Sun Ra drummer Buster Smith. She furthered her studies at Mannes College of Music and Goddard College, and with Vernel Fournier and Milford Graves. However it would be some time yet before she made her own impact on the scene.

To help struggling musicians, the city authorities eventually passed a 'Music in the Subways' programme. A booming economy meant big tips (at least until the Wall Street collapse of 1987). Sabir Mateen, now 48, moved to New York from Philadelphia in 1989, after spending ten years in Los Angeles with pianist and composer Horace Tapscott. In

Philadelphia he had almost joined up with Sun Ra's crew, but instead took a train to New York with a dollar in his pocket. "I immediately began playing in the streets to eat," Mateen says, recalling the year and a half he spent living in a 13th Street squat or wherever he could find a bed. "Those were really rough, hardcore days," he says. "But in that rough period I met a lot of great musicians, most of the musicians I would play with like Jemeel Moondoc and Daniel Carter." Mateen later teamed up with Carter on a variety of projects, most notably Test, with drummer Tom Bruno (the 501 Canal Street veteran), and bassist Matt Heyner, a member of New York's noisenik improvisors The No-Neck Blues Band.

In the midst of this period William Parker seized the initiative and organised the 1984 Sound Unity Festival, a descendent of the 1972 New York Musicians' Festival, which had been co-promoted in a spirit of self-determination by drummer Rashied Ali, and the precursor to the expansive Vision Festival which Parker now organises around Memorial Day every year. Back then, Sound Unity was the only event to gather such diverse musicians as Zorn, Frank Wright, Don Cherry and Billy Bang all under one tent, alongside artists from other disciplines.

By the end of the 80s there was a slight glimmer of better times ahead. The Knitting Factory opened on Houston Street, eventually teaming jazz performers such as Gayle and drummer William Hooker on tag bills with New York's rock avant garde. But jazz was still off limits as far as the music industry was concerned. It was around this time that David S Ware formed his Quartet, with Whit Dickey drumming. He recalls the hard times: "The times that we're living in, you have to figure out a way to keep being a musician. It's another form of improvisation."

However, interest was coming from elsewhere. Shipp and Parker were approached by Rise, a small label from Austin, Texas, to release a duo record, *Zoe*, and William Hooker released *Radiation* on Homestead. Shipp introduced Ware to Homestead's Steven Joerg, who convinced the label's owners to take a chance on avant jazz. The fruits of this new union included Ware's classic *Cryptology*, recorded in the mid-90s as the saxophonist struggled with a severe bout of flu.

With William Hooker hooking up more regularly with rock musicians, and Matthew Shipp releasing work on Henry Rollins's 2.13.61 label, people were soon talking about a new hybrid called punk-jazz. "The way people listen to music has definitely changed," Hooker enthuses, arguing that years of listening to the likes of Sonic Youth and My Bloody Valentine have prepared rock fans for 'difficult' jazz. Undoubtedly, they have also been encouraged by high profile avantists such as Rollins, Thurston Moore (who runs the Ecstatic Peace label with Byron Coley) and Superchunk's Mac McCaughan (who started a label called Wobbly Rail) becoming patrons of Improv. Meanwhile, the romantic tortured artist myth has seduced certain sections of the rock press into writing about the rediscovery of long neglected jazz figures.

Drummer Hooker, for one, welcomes the new energy, collaborating often with Sonic Youth guitarists Moore and Lee Ranaldo, as well as mixing it up with DJ Olive, poets and dancers. "The climate in New York for me is very different than for most jazz musicians because of the exposure I've gotten through Thurston," says Hooker. But other musicians, too, have benefitted from forays into the rock world. So far, The David S Ware Quartet have opened for Sonic Youth; Roy Campbell's Other Dimensions In Music teamed up with Yo La Tengo; and Ibarra has warmed up a Cibo Matto crowd. But the genre-hopping doesn't happen quite as often as the press might make it seem. "It still doesn't mean anything until we can do an actual tour with a band like Sonic Youth," says Ware. "That whole world is yet to be opened up. The Charles Lloyd Quartet used to play in rock 'n' roll venues all the time opening for those bands. That's got to happen now."

Eremite boss Michael Ehlers adds, "There's kind of this fantasy among rock music writers that underground rock has resuscitated free jazz. This music never went away. These guys have been playing it all along and have seen everything come and go twice before."

The 90s crossover of avant rock and free jazz also has its 60s precedent in ESP Records, who released records by The Fugs and The Godz alongside those by Albert Ayler and Patty Waters. Just as fruitful today is the interchange between musicians like Cooper-Moore, Parker and Mateen, and dancers, poets, and artists from other disciplines. Depending on how strictly you define and date it, then, the ecstatic jazz scene is either a tight inner circle of six musicians, or it is a much broader new church that might include Ambient guitar experimentalists like Loren MazzaCane Connors and Dean Roberts alongside jazz figures like saxophonist Rob Brown, former Ware drummer Whit Dickey, out-of-towner Joe McPhee, Susie Ibarra's husband saxophonist Assif Tsahar, and even Boston based guitarist Joe Morris.

"It seems like in the last 20 years a whole lot of people who wouldn't call themselves free jazz musicians have been ushered in to the thing of playing spontaneously," Daniel Carter says. "I've been playing with a lot of younger musicians who aren't so concerned with what they're calling what they're playing. A lot of these players seemed to be interested in free jazz, for want of a better term, and I find myself not wanting to be left in the dust."

The clamour of activity in New York now is sucking newer generations of players into the city, looking to meet their heroes, just like Matthew Shipp 15 years earlier. Boston's Jane Wong and violinist Mat Maneri and Atlanta's Gold Sparkle Band are all recent arrivals, ready to compete with upcoming New Yorkers like Chris Jonas, Ori Kaplan and Neel Murgai.

The trickledown effect from New York's current economic boom has helped finance new clubs and art spaces for the fringe. The Brecht Forum, Tonic, Pink Pony, Roulette, the punk-collective ABC No Rio, The Cooler and Cornelia Street Cafe regularly open their doors to blasts of jazz ecstasy. The loft scene might have long since closed down, but it still occasionally inspires others to take up its initiative. Steven Joerg sometimes opens his Park Slope space (formerly the 19th century wood-lined Brooklyn Republican Club) for music, and The No-Neck Blues Band host events at their Harlem loft. Veterans who have lived through a few turns of free jazz's boom and bust cycle already are only cautiously optimistic about the current state of things, however.

"It's hit and miss," says Charles Gayle. "You have to keep bobbing and weaving. You get an uppercut to the chin, and a couple of left jabs, but you get used to it. It's a lot of work." Especially when those jabs are coming from all sides. Conservative critics complain it's 'just blowing', or that they've heard it all before. Besides, what's so radical about a 30 year old idea like free jazz, anyway?

Nothing, if you believe Cooper-Moore, who calls it a neo-conservative avant garde. "If you listen to the music that was happening 30 years ago, I don't hear much difference in it," he says, from his Spanish Harlem apartment. "There are no new techniques. I stretch to hear new voices.

They've invested in playing a certain way, but art is about pushing ahead, and I don't see any pushing ahead."

Matthew Shipp disagrees: "He's wrong. There was no pianist like me playing in the 60s, there was no guitarist like Joe Morris in the 60s. There are people playing their instruments in ways they've never been played before. They definitely come out of a 60s avant garde tradition, but I think there's some people and group sounds that are very unique and of this time. If there wasn't, I don't think the scene would be as vibrant as it is now."

The music is always changing, always evolving, along with the people who are making it. Charles Gayle, for one, considers he is less brash and more 'sophisticated' these days. "I'm not just playing the energy anymore," he says. "It's not just that cliched sax of the avant garde. I'm starting to use what I've learned over the years. Instead of just playing rough music I'm trying to keep it more personal."

And when the freeway turns out to be a one way street, the truly free-thinking musician is undogmatic enough to check out compositional possibilities for opening up new routes. Composition is favoured by some ecstatisticians, at least as a loose structure for improvisation. "We're thinking of it more as instantaneously composing," says Mateen. "We're thinking of the music as a composition, rather than just playing. You hear some of this music and it sounds like it was written on a piece of paper. That's because there's more spiritual communication now."

Collective endeavours such as Parker's Little Huey Creative Orchestra and Daniel Carter's leaderless ensembles subsume the artist's ego for the good of the music. "It's like what Charles Ives said to his players," Carter explains. "If you don't like these notes, then play your own notes. The idea of individual freedom is very important. Of course, I don't think too many of those cats playing for Charles Ives played different notes."

Where the freeway is signposted with a music stand, William Parker casts a long shadow. As Vision Festival organiser and leader of any number of avant initiatives he wields enormous power and influence. Shipp moved to New York specifically to play with him. Cooper-Moore had a photo of the bassist in his home in Virginia to inspire him to return to Manhattan. But Parker's eminence is more inspiration than obstacle. Younger players like Matt Heyner of The No Neck Blues Band, Test, The

Rashid Bakr Quartet and more, and the 23 year old Guillermo E Brown, the new drummer in The David S Ware Quartet, prove newcomers can quickly penetrate the inner circle.

There is a downside to the family nature of the scene, as Susie Ibarra discovered, when she quit The David S Ware Quartet to pursue her own projects, such as her trio with Cooper-Moore and violinist Charles Burnham. A "political" dispute, she says, led her to quit Parker's In Order To Survive quartet, estranging her from Parker and AUM Fidelity's Steven Joerg. In May 99, a *New York Times* profile of the 28 year old drummer charged the mostly male scene with sexism, which widened the split. In the meantime, Ibarra has morphed from a young jazz talent to a central figure in New York's downtown avant garde, playing often with figures such as Zeena Parkins, Thurston Moore and Ikue Mori. "I have a certain foundation or love for jazz music, but I like to do different things," Ibarra says. "I find it interesting how many genres can connect through improvisation. I like working with Pauline Oliveros because she's very much rooted in improvisation, but as a composer she comes from a whole other tradition." Ibarra used that expanding Rolodex to curate programming one month at Tonic, and appeared on rock group Yo La Tengo's 2000 album *And Then Nothing Turned Itself Inside Out*. It is salutary to remember that all this hullabaloo is about a music so marginal that sales breaking 5000 copies are the equivalent of the gold or platinum discs elsewhere. Pianist Shipp counts his listeners one by one, literally tracking sales several times each week in downtown Manhattan record stores, where he also starts the buzz about his next show or project. "It's sale by sale now, but it's going to create an envelope for successive generations. When they discover jazz, they'll discover us first," Shipp says. The scene's influence is wider than sales figures can convey, like that old chestnut about The Velvet Underground's original poor album sales. At this point most people who buy a CD from AUM Fidelity, No More Records or Eremite are either in a group, write for a fanzine or Website, or are otherwise personally engaged with the music. Supporters volunteering to help each year at the artist-organised Vision Festival share the collective idea; new labels seem to sprout up with each passing season; and hundreds of players still make the same pilgrimage to meet William Parker that Shipp made 15 years ago.

So the future is bright, right? For now, at least, a generation of avant garde jazz musicians is in its prime, and a successive generation is being groomed to take over. In the early 90s it discovered how to regenerate the music through its merger with rock's left wing. More recently, Matthew Shipp and William Parker have recorded with DJ Spooky, opening other possible futures through digital collaborations. Daniel Carter has publicly experimented with programmers, and Cooper-Moore has a secret stash of his own computer generated compositions. "My interest for myself musically is basically electronic," the 53 year old says. "That's where my ears are, with music that would disturb a lot of other people. It settles me down so I can focus the next day."

Steven Joerg can also imagine a Techno future for his extreme champions. "The beats and waves crowd could certainly appreciate this music," he says. "If you take the metaphor that music is a drug, then this is the ultimate fix. If you're really down with rhythm, harmony and melody at a super high level and polyrhythms and multiple directions at once, then this is it."

BIBLIOGRAPHY/DISCOGRAPHY

Print sources followed by recordings are listed here chapter by chapter. All recordings are CD editions unless stated otherwise. Multiple CD sets are indicated as '2xCD' (double), etc.

THE HIDDEN WIRING

Joel Chadabe Electric Sound: The Past And Promise Of Electronic Music. New Jersey: Prentice Hall 1997

RECORDING ANGELS

Jonathan Cott Stockhausen: Conversations With The Composer. New York: Simon & Schuster 1973
Carolyn Marvin When Old Technologies Were New. New York: Oxford University Press 1988
Marshall McLuhan Understanding Media. Cambridge, Mass: MIT Press 1992
Avital Ronell The Telephone Book. Lincoln: University Of Nebraska Press 1989

Various The Ghost Orchid: An Introduction To EVP. PARC 1999
— Mesmer. Ash International LP 1995
— Mesmer Variations. Ash International 1996

ON THE MIC

Hilton Als "No Respect" in *The New Yorker* (2 November 1998)
William Dufty & Billie Holiday Lady Sings The Blues. London: Penguin 1984
Frances Dyson "Circuits Of The Voice: From Cosmology To Telephony". www.soundculture.org/words/dyson_circuits.html

The Beach Boys Pet Sounds. Capitol 1966
Peter Brötzmann Machine Gun. FMP 1968
Jeff Buckley Grace. Columbia 1994
Bob Dylan The Basement Tapes. Columbia 2xCD 1975
Diamanda Galas Plague Mass. Mute 1991
Billie Holiday Lady Day: The Complete Billie Holiday On Columbia, 1933 44.

Columbia/Sony 2001
Mississippi John Hurt Complete Studio Recordings. Vanguard 3xCD 2001
Robert Johnson The Complete Recordings. CBS/Sony 2xCD 1996
Nirvana In Utero. Geffen 1993
Elvis Presley The Sun Sessions. RCA 1976
Frank Sinatra Songs For Swingin' Lovers. Capitol 1955
Various (rec by Maya Deren). Divine Horsemen: The Voodoo Gods Of Haiti. Lyrichord Discs 1980
Scott Walker Tilt. Fontana 1995

THE JERRYBUILT FUTURE

Robert Ashley The Wolfman. Source 4xLP 1966
David Behrman Wave Train, Runthrough, et al. Alga Marghen 1959-68
John Butcher & Phil Durrant Secret Measures. Wobbly Rail 1997
— Requests And Antisongs. Erstwhile 2000
Alvin Lucier Music For Solo Performer. Lovely Music LP 1982
— Vespers (1968) from Electronic Sound. Mainstream LP 1971
MEV (Musica Elettronica Viva) Spacecraft (1966). Alga Marghen 2001
— The Sound Pool (1970). BYG Actuel LP 2002
Mimeo (Music In Movement Orchestra) Electric Chair + Table. Grob 1998
— **& John Tilbury** The Hands Of Caravaggio. Erstwhile 2001
Gordon Mumma Studio Retrospect. Lovely Music 2000
— Megaton For Wm Burroughs from The Dresden Interleaf 13 February 1945. Lovely Music LP 1979
Supersilent Supersilent 4. Rune Grammofon 1998
David Tudor Rainforest (Versions I & IV). Mode 1998

— Three Works For Live Electronics.
Lovely Music 1996

WORSHIP THE GLITCH

Jacques Attali Noise: The Political Economy
Of Music. Minneapolis: University Of
Minnesota Press 1985
Francis Bacon New Atlantis. London:
Harlan Davidson 1989
William S Burroughs The Job. London:
Penguin 1989
Henry Edwards "A Deeply Emotional Man"
(interview with Bryan Ferry) in Raygun 21
(November 1994)
Denise Sullivan "Survival Research
Laboratories" in Raygun 5 (April 1993)

Aphex Twin "Bucephalus Bouncing Ball"
from I Care Because You Do. Warp 1995
Autechre Chiastic Slide. Warp 1997
— LP5. Warp 1998
Kim Cascone bluecube []. Noton 1998
Christophe Charles Undirected 1986-1996.
Mille Plateaux 1997
Coil Musick To Play In The Dark Vol 1.
Chalice 1999
ELpH vs Coil Worship The Glitch.
Eskaton 1995
Farmers Manual Explorers_We. OR 1998
— fsck. Tray 1997
— No Backup. Mego 1996
Fennesz Endless Summer. Mego 2001
— Fennesz Plays EP. Moikai 1999
— Hotel Paral.lel. Mego 1997
— Plus Forty Seven Degrees 56' 37"
Minus Sixteen Degrees. 51' 08".
Touch 2000
Fenn O'Berg The Magic Sound Of Fenn
O'Berg. Mego 1998
— The Return Of Fenn O'Berg. Mego 2002
General Magic Frantz! Mego 1997
— Rechenkönig. Mego 1999
Bernhard Günter Un Peu De Neige Salie.
Table Of The Elements 1993
— Slow Gestures/Cérémonie Désir
(For Heike). trente oiseaux 1999
Ryoji Ikeda +/-. Touch 1996
Microstoria Init Ding. Mille Plateaux 1996
— _snd. Mille Plateaux 1996
Neina Subconsciousness.
Mille Plateaux 2000
Non Pagan Muzak. Mute 1978-79 (7")
Oval 94 Diskont. Mille Plateaux 1995
— Systemisch. Mille Plateaux 1994

Pan Sonic Kulma. Blast First 1995
Pita Seven Tons For Free. Mego 1996
— Get Out. Mego 1999
Pole Pole1. Kiff SM 1998
Pure The End Of Vinyl. Mego 3" CD 1999
Akira Rabelais Elongated Pentagonal
Pyramid. Ritornell 1999
Rehberg & Bauer ballt. Touch 1999
— Faßt. Touch 1997
Dean Roberts All Cracked Medias.
Mille Plateaux 1998
snd Makesnd Cassette. Mille Plateaux 1999
Yasunao Tone Solo For Wounded CD.
Tzadik 1997
Various Clicks + Cuts. Mille Plateaux
2xCD 2000
— Clicks + Cuts Vol 2. Mille Plateaux
2xCD 2001

THE ETERNAL DRONE

Lester Bangs Psychotic Reactions And
Carburetor Dung. London: Heinemann 1988
Georges Bataille Formless In Visions Of
Excess: Selected Writings 1927-1939.
Minnesota: Minneapolis University 1985
Joachim-Ernst Berendt Nada Brahma: The
World Is Sound. Rochester, VT: Destiny
Books/Inner Traditions 1988
Marcus Boon "Ocean Of Sound (Ocean Of
Silence)" (interview with Sri Karunamayee) in
Ascent 14 (Summer 2002)
Alan Cummings "When The Music's Over"
(interview with Keiji Haino) in The Wire 221
(July 2002)
Rene Daumal "A Fundamental Experiment:
Roger Shattuck" in The Drug User:
Documents 1840-1960. New York:
Blast 1991
Kyle Gann In Sound And Light: La Monte
Young And Marian Zazeela. Lewisburg,
PA: Bucknell University Press 1996
Peter Hamel Through Music To The Self.
Tisbury: Compton Press 1978
Hazrat Inayat Khan The Mysticism Of Music,
Sound And Word.
New York: Shambhala 1996
David Reck Music Of The Whole Earth.
New York: Macmillan 1977
David Toop Ocean Of Sound.
London: Serpent's Tail 1995

**John Cale/Tony Conrad/Angus MacLise/La
Monte Young/Marian Zazeela** Inside The
Dream Syndicate: "Day Of Niagara" April 25,

1965. Table Of The Elements 2001
Catherine Christer Hennix The Electric Harpsichord. Etymon 2002
Keiji Haino The 21st Century Hard-y-Guide-y Man: Even Now, Still I Think. Tokuma 1998
— **(aka Nijiumu)** Era Of Sad Wings. PSF 1993
Ustad Abdul Karim Khan "Raga Malkauns" from Classic Gold. HMV India MC 1933-34
Ustad Bade Ghulam Ali Khan Gunkali/Malkauns. HMV India MC 1960s
Alvin Lucier Music On A Long Thin Wire. Lovely Music 1980
Pandit Ram Narayan Raga Lalit. Nimbus 1992
Pandit Pran Nath Midnight Raga/Raga Malkauns. Just Dreams (forthcoming)
Pérotin Vocal Works (The Hilliard Ensemble). ECM 1989
Lou Reed Metal Machine Music. RCA 1975
Various Driftworks. Big Cat 4xCD 1996
— Isolationism. Virgin 2xCD 1994
The Velvet Underground Peel Slowly And See. Polydor 5xCD 1995

SLAPPING PYTHAGORAS

Joscelyn Godwin Harmonies Of Heaven And Earth. London: Thames & Hudson 1987
Stuart Isacoff Temperament. London: Faber & Faber 2002
Jamie James The Music Of The Spheres. London: Abacus 1995
Thomas Levenson Measure For Measure: A Musical History Of Science. London: Simon & Schuster 1994
Harry Partch Genesis Of A Music. New York: Da Capo 1975
Arnold Schoenberg Fundamentals Of Musical Composition. London: Faber & Faber 1999

Tony Conrad Early Minimalism Vol 1. Table Of The Elements 4xCD 1998
— Slapping Pythagoras. Table Of The Elements 1996
Charles Dodge Earth's Magnetic Field. Nonesuch LP 1970
Arnold Schoenberg Moses Und Aron (1932). Decca 2xCD (cond Georg Solti) 1984

THE RAGGED TROUSERED ANTHOLOGIST

Manly P Hall The Secret Teachings Of All Ages: An Encyclopedic Outline Of Masonic, Hermetic, Cabbalistic, And Rosicrucian Symbolical Philosophy. Los Angeles: Philosophical Research Society 1989
Paola Igliori (ed) American Magus. New York: Inanout Press 1996
Carl Jung Man And His Symbols. London: Pan 1978
David Keenan CD review of *Harry Smith Anthology Volume 4* in The Wire 195 (May 2000)
Harry Smith, Allen Ginsberg, Rani Singh, et al Think Of The Self Speaking: Harry Smith, Selected Interviews. Seattle: Elbow/Cityful Press 1998

Various The Anthology Of American Folk Music (compiled by Harry Smith, 1952). Smithsonian Folkways 6xCD 1997
— Harry Smith's Anthology Of American Folk Music Volume 4. Revenant 2xCD 1999

THE SOLAR MYTH APPROACH

Anonymous The Urantia Book. New York: Uversa Press 2002
Jill Purce The Mystic Spiral. London: Thames & Hudson 1974
Robert G Temple The Sirius Mystery. London: Sidgwick & Jackson 1976

Amiri Baraka A Black Mass. Son Boy 2001
Hawkwind Doremi Fasol Latido. United Artists 1972
— Space Ritual Alive In London. United Artists 1972
Attilio Mineo Man In Space With Sounds. Subliminal Sounds 1962
Parliament Mothership Connection. PolyGram 1976
Karlheinz Stockhausen Dienstag Aus Licht. Stockhausen Verlag 2xCD 1977-91
— Donnerstag Aus Licht. Stockhausen Verlag 4xCD 1978-81
— Hymnen. Stockhausen Verlag 4xCD 1966
— Montag Aus Licht. Stockhausen Verlag 5xCD 1984-88
— Samstag Aus Licht. Stockhausen Verlag 4xCD 1981-83
— Sirius. Stockhausen Verlag 2xCD 1977
Sun Ra Space Is The Place. Impulse! 1972

HUMANS, ARE THEY REALLY NECESSARY?

John Bird Percy Grainger.
London: Faber & Faber 1982
Erik Davis Techgnosis.
London: Serpent's Tail 1995
Jean Gimpel The Medieval Machine:
The Industrial Revolution Of The Middle
Ages. New York: Penguin 1977
Joscelyn Godwin Athanasius Kircher:
A Renaissance Man And The Quest For Lost
Knowledge.
London: Thames & Hudson 1979
Percy Grainger "Free Music" (1938).
www.obsolete.com/120_years/machines/
free_music_machine/
Hermann Helmholtz On The Sensations Of
Tone As A Psychological Basis For The
Theory Of Music. Bristol: Thoemmes 1988
Mary Hillier Automata & Mechanical Toys.
London: Bloomsbury 1988
FT Marinetti "Multiplied Man And The Reign
Of The Machine" from War, The World's Only
Hygiene (1911-15), in RW Flint (ed),
Marinetti: Selected Writings.
New York: Farrar, Straus And Giroux 1972
Michael Nyman Experimental Music:
Cage And Beyond. Cambridge: Cambridge
University Press 1999
Michael Parsons Interview with Alvin Lucier
in Resonance Volume 4 # 1 (1995)
Harry Partch Genesis Of A Music.
New York: Da Capo 1975
Chris Rice Interview with Harry Bertoia in
Halana issue 1 (winter 1996)
EG Richardson Sound: A Physical Textbook.
London: E Arnold & Co 1927
Raymond Roussell Impressions d'Afrique.
London: Calder 1983
Sonic Boom: The Art Of Sound (exhibition
catalogue). London: Hayward Gallery 2000
Calvin Tomkins The Bride And The
Bachelors: Five Masters Of The Avant-Garde.
Harmondsworth: Penguin 1976
Benjamin Woolley Virtual Worlds.
Oxford: Blackwell 1992

Pierre Bastien Mecanoid. Rephlex 2001
— Musiques Machinales. SMI 1993
— Musiques Paralloïdres. Lowlands 1998
Harry Bertoia Unfolding. PSF 1993
Maxime De La Rochefoucauld Automates
Ki. Plastique 1998
Mauricio Kagel Acustica.
Deutsche Grammophon 2xLP 1971
— Staatstheater.
Deutsche Grammophon 6xLP 1981
Christina Kubisch Dreaming Of A Major
Third. Edition RZ 1998
Alan Lamb Primal Image. Dorobo 1995
Alvin Lucier Music On A Long Thin Wire.
Lovely Music 1992
Conlon Nancarrow Studies For Player Piano.
Wergo 5xCD 1999
Evan Parker & Paul Lytton Three Other
Stories (1971-74). Emanem 1995
— Two Octobers (1972-75). Emanem 1996
Harry Partch Delusion Of The Fury.
Innova 2001
Karlheinz Stockhausen Tierkreis (for 12
music boxes). Stockhausen Verlag 1975
David Toop & Max Eastley New And
Invented Instruments. Obscure 1975
Various A New Guide To Sound Sculpture
And Invented Instruments Vol 1. FMR 2001

AUTOMATING THE BEAT

Theodor W Adorno Philosophy Of Modern
Music. New York: Continuum 1994
Walter Hughes "In The Empire Of The Beat:
The Discourse Of Disco" in Andrew Ross &
Tricia Rose (eds), Microphone Fiends:
Youth Music & Youth Culture.
London: Routledge 1994

MC ADE Bass Rock Express. 4-Sight 1985
Hamilton Bohannon Foot Stompin' Music.
Diablo 1998
James Brown Live At The Apollo.
Polydor 1962
Candido Jingo. Charly 1979
Chic C'est Chic. Atlantic 1978
Bo Diddley His Best. Chess/Universal 1997
A Guy Called Gerald Black Secret
Technology. Juice Box 1996
Eddie Kendricks People... Hold On.
Motown 1972
Kraftwerk Trans Europe Express. EMI 1977
Latin Rascals Mixmasters Vol 1.
Max Music 1999
The Meters The Very Best Of The Meters.
Rhino 1997
Earl Palmer Backbeat – The World's
Greatest Rock 'N' Roll Drummer. Ace 1999
Huey 'Piano' Smith & His Clowns This Is
Huey 'Piano' Smith. Music Club 1998
The Stooges The Stooges. Elektra 1969
Donna Summer "I Feel Love" from I

Remember Yesterday. Casablanca 1977
The Temptations "Law Of The Land" from
Masterpiece. Motown 1973
Various Rhythms Of Rapture: Sacred Musics
Of Haitian Vodou.
Smithsonian Folkways 1995
The Young Tuxedo Brass Band Jazz Begins.
Atlantic LP 1959

THE AUTOBAHN GOES ON FOREVER

Peter Handke Falsche Bewegung
(Wrong Movement). Frankfurt Am Main:
Suhrkamp 1975
Paul Virilio Speed And Politics.
New York: Semiotext(e) Foreign Agents 1977
— War And Cinema: The Logistics Of
Perception. London: Verso 1989
Wim Wenders Emotion Pictures: Reflections
On The Cinema. London: Faber 1989

Basic Channel Basic Channel. Basic
Channel 1996
Frieder Butzmann Das Mädchen Auf Der
Schaukel. Zensor 2xLP 1984
Ciccone Youth The Whitey Album.
Blast First 1988
Einstürzende Neubauten Ende Neu.
Mute 1999
Harmonia Musik Von Harmonia.
Metronome 1974
Kraftwerk Autobahn. Parlophone 1974
— The Mix. EMI 1991
— Tour De France (single). EMI 1983
La Düsseldorf La Düsseldorf.
Captain Trip 1976
La! Neu? Year Of The Tiger.
Captain Trip 1998
Malaria! Compiled. Moabit LP 1991
Moebius & Beerbohm Double Cut. Sky 1983
Moebius & Plank Zero Set. Sky 1982
Neu! Neu! 1. Grönland/EMI 1971
— Neu! 2. Grönland/EMI 1972
— Neu! 75. Grönland/EMI 1975
Iggy Pop Lust For Life. Virgin 1977
The Ramones Anthology. Sire/Warner
Archives 2xCD 1999
Michael Rother Radio: Singles 1977-93.
Random 1993
Bruce Springsteen Born To Run. CBS 1975
Sonic Youth "Expressway To Yr Skull" from
Evol. Blast First 1986
3 Phase Straight Road. Tresor 1994
Various Easy Rider (Original Soundtrack).
MCA 1969

ROCK CONCRÈTE

Thomas B Holmes Electronic And
Experimental Music.
New York: Routledge 2002
Vernon Joynson Fuzz, Acid And Flowers:
A Comprehensive Guide To American Garage,
Psychedelic And Hippie Rock (1964-1975).
Leeds: Borderline Productions 1993
Robin Maconie The Works Of Karlheinz
Stockhausen. Oxford: Oxford University
Press 1976
Greg Russo Cosmik Debris: The Collected
History And Improvisations Of Frank Zappa.
New York: Crossfire Publications 1998
Oliver Trager The American Book Of
The Dead. New York: Fireside/Simon &
Schuster 1997

The Beach Boys Pet Sounds. Capitol 1966
The Beatles The Beatles (aka The White
Album). Apple 2xCD 1968
— Magical Mystery Tour. Parlophone 1967
— Revolver. Parlophone 1966
— Sgt Pepper's Lonely Hearts Club Band.
Parlophone 1967
The Box Tops The Letter/Neon Rainbow.
Sundazed 1967
Holger Czukay & Rolf Dammers Canaxis V.
Spoon 1969
Fifty Foot Hose Cauldron Plus.
Big Beat 1968
The Grateful Dead Anthem Of The Sun.
Warner Brothers 1968
Pierre Henry Messe Pour Le Temps Présent.
Philips 1967
— Symphonie Pour Un Homme Seul/Le
Voyage. Philips 1962
Jefferson Airplane After Bathing At Baxter's.
RCA 1968
— Jefferson Airplane Loves You.
RCA 4xCD 1992
John Lennon & Yoko Ono Unfinished Music
No 1: Two Virgins. Rykodisc 1968
— Unfinished Music No 2: Life With The
Lions. Rykodisc 1969
Love Da Capo. Elektra 1967
The Lovin' Spoonful Greatest Hits.
Buddha 2000
The Mothers Of Invention Freak Out!
Rykodisc 1966
— We're Only In It For The Money.
Rykodisc 1968
John Oswald Grayfolded 1969-1996.
Swell/Artifact 2xCD 1996

Spooky Tooth/Pierre Henry Ceremony.
A&M 1970
Steppenwolf Early Years. MCA 1969
Karlheinz Stockhausen Gesang Der
Jünglinge. Stockhausen Verlag 1955-56
The United States Of America The United
States Of America. Edsel 1968
Edgard Varèse The Complete Works (cond
Ricardo Chailly). London/Decca 2xCD 1998
Various OHM: The Early Gurus Of Electronic
Music. Ellipsis Arts 3xCD 2000
Frank Zappa Lumpy Gravy. Rykodisc 1967

DECK WRECKERS

John Cage "The Future Of Music: Credo"
in Silence. London: Marion Boyars 1995
David Toop The Rap Attack.
London: Serpent's Tail 1984/2000

Afrika Bambaataa Death Mix.
Winley 12" 1983
Bebe & Louis Barron Forbidden Planet
(Original Soundtrack). GNP Crescendo 1956
John Cage The 25 Year Retrospective.
Wergo 3xCD 1958
DJ Ca$h Money & Marvelous "The Music
Maker" from Where's The Party At?
Sleeping Bag 1988
Gang Starr No More Mr Nice Guy.
Wild Pitch 1989
Grand Master Flash & The Furious Five
Adventures On The Wheels Of Steel.
Sequel/Sugar Hill 3xCD 1999
Grand Wizard Theodore
Can I Get A Soul Clap? Tuff City 1980
Ground Zero Ground Zero.
God Mountain 1993
Herbie Hancock "Rockit" from Future Shock.
Columbia 1983
Invisibl Skratch Piklz Invisibl Skratch Piklz
Versus Da Klamz Uv Deth.
Asphodel 12" 1998
DJ Jazzy Jeff & The Fresh Prince
He's The DJ – I'm The Rapper. Jive 1988
Philip Jeck Loopholes. Touch 1995
— Surf. Touch 1999
Diane Labrosse/Ikue Mori/Martin Tétreault
Île Bizarre. Ambiances Magnétiques 1998
René Lussier & Martin Tétreault Dur Noyau
Dur. Ambiances Magnétiques 1998
Christian Marclay Records 81-89.
Atavistic 2000
Project DARK. Excited By Gramophones
Vol 4. Invisible 1999

Q-Bert Demolition Pumpkin Squeeze Music.
No label MC 1994
Various Old School Rap To The Beat Y'All:
The Sugar Hill Story. Sequel 3xCD 1994
— Return Of The DJ Vol 1.
Bomb Hip-Hop 1995
— Return Of The DJ Vol 2.
Bomb Hip-Hop 1997
West Street Mob Back To The Old School.
Sequel 1999
The X-ecutioners Built From Scratch.
Loud 2002
Otomo Yoshihide The Night Before The
Death Of The Sampling Virus. Extreme 1993

DESTROY ALL MUSIC

Rosa Trillo Clough Futurism: The Story Of A
Modern Art Movement – A New Appraisal.
New York: Greenwood Press 1961
Luigi Russolo Art Of Noises.
New York: Pendragon Press 1986

Georges Antheil Ballet Mecanique (1923-
25). Electronic Music Foundation 2000
— Airplane Sonata (1921, Herbert Henck,
piano). ECM New Series 2001
Pierre Schaeffer/Pierre Henry
L'Oeuvre Musicale. INA/GRM 4xCD 1998
Edgard Varèse Amériques (1917-21, cond
Pierre Boulez). Sony Classical 1991
Various Futurism And Dada Reviewed.
Sub Rosa 1989

THE LIMITS OF LANGUAGE

Hans (Jean) Arp Dadaland.
London: Calder 1948
William S Burroughs "The Cut-Up Method Of
Brion Gysin" in The Third Mind.
London: Calder 1978
Bob Cobbing & Peter Mayer Concerning
Concrete Poetry. London: Writers
Forum 1978
Richard Kostelanetz (ed) Text-Sound Texts.
New York: William Morrow 1980
Tom Leonard Reports From The Present.
London: Jonathan Cape 1995
Greil Marcus Lipstick Traces.
London: Faber & Faber 2002
Marshall McLuhan Counterblast.
London: Rapp & Whiting 1969
Melody Sumner, Kathleen Burch, Michael
Sumner (eds) The Guests Go In To Supper.
Oakland/San Francisco: Burning Books 1986

Antonin Artaud Pour En Finir Avec Le Jugement De Dieu (1947). Sub Rosa 1996
John Cage Sixty-Two Mesostics Re Merce Cunningham. Hat Hut 2xCD 1991
— Empty Words (Parte III). Cramps 2xCD 1990
Henri Chopin Les 9 Saintes-Phonies: A Retrospective. Staalplaat 1994
— Revue OU. Alga Marghen 4xCD 2002
Paul Dutton Mouth Pieces. OHM Editions 2000
Brion Gysin The Pool K III. Alga Marghen 1998
Åke Hodell Verbal Brainwash And Other Works. Fylkingen 3xCD 2001
Kurt Schwitters Ursonate. Wergo 1930
Various Futurism And Dada Reviewed 1912-59. Sub Rosa 1989
— Lunapark 0.10. Sub Rosa 2000
— Miniatures (compiled by Morgan Fisher). Voiceprint 1994
— Surrealism Reviewed. LTM 2002

THE MUSIC OF CHANCE

John Cage Silence: Lectures And Writings. London: Marion Boyars 1978
Andy Hamilton "Change Of The Century": interview with Christian Wolff in The Wire 202 (December 2000)
Nouritza Matossian Xenakis. London: Kahn & Averill 1990
Jean-Jacques Nattiez (ed) The Boulez-Cage Correspondence. Cambridge: Cambridge University Press 1993
Leeonard Ratner "Ars Combinatoria: Chance And Choice In The Eighteenth Century" in Landon Robbins, HC (ed), Studies In Eighteenth Century Music. London: Allen & Unwin 1970
Mark Sinker & James Nye "Uncaged" in The Wire 104 (October 1992)

Ross Bolleter "Nallan Void" from Various, Austral Voices. New Albion 1990
— Crow Country. Pogus Productions 2001
Pierre Boulez Structures I & II (Alfons and Aloys Kontarsky, pianos). Wergo 1951-52
John Cage Music Of Changes (Joseph Kubera, piano). Lovely Music 1951
— Fontana Mix. Hat Hut 1958
Witold Lutoslawski Venetian Games. EMI Matrix 1960-61
Karlheinz Stockhausen Ylem. Stockhausen Verlag 1973

John Zorn Cobra. Hat Hut 1987
— Cobra Live At The Knitting Factory. Knitting Factory Works 1995

SMILING FACES SOMETIMES

The Four Tops "Are You Man Enough?" from Shaft In Africa (Original Soundtrack). ABC 1973
The O'Jays Back Stabbers. Columbia 1972
— Ship Ahoy. Columbia 1973
The Persuaders Thin Line Between Love And Hate. Atlantic 1971
Public Enemy "Fight The Power" from Fear Of A Black Planet. Def Jam 1990
Sly & The Family Stone There's A Riot Goin' On. Edsel 1971
The Staple Singers "I'll Take You There" from Be Altitude: Respect Yourself. Stax 1972
The Temptations Sky's The Limit. Motown 1971
The Undisputed Truth "Smiling Faces Sometimes" from The Undisputed Truth. Gordy 1971
War All Day Music. United Artists 1971

FRAMES OF FREEDOM

Bruno Bartolozzi New Sounds For Woodwind (trans/ed Reginald Smith Brindle). London: ??? 1967.
David W Bernstein & Christopher Hatch Writings Through John Cage's Music, Poetry, + Art. Chicago/London: University Of Chicago Press 2001
John Cage Musicage: Cage Muses On Words, Art, Music. Hanover/London: Wesleyan University Press Of New England 1996
Aimé Césaire "Solar Throat Slashed" from Aimé Césaire: The Collected Poetry (trans Clayton Eshleman & Annette Smith). Berkeley: University Of California Press 1983
Timothy Day A Century Of Recorded Music: Listening To Musical History. London: Yale University Press 2000
Albert Glinsky Theremin: Ether Music & Espionage. Urbana and Chicago: University Of Illinois Press 2000
Felicitas D Goodman Speaking In Tongues.Chicago: University Of Chicago Press 1972
Robert Sherlaw Johnson Sleevenote to Olivier Messiaen, Les Corps Glorieux.

Argo LP 1970
Steven Johnson Emergence.
London: Allen Lane 2001
Douglas Kahn Noise, Water, Meat:
A History Of Sound In The Arts.
London: MIT Press 1999
Bettina L Knapp Antonin Artaud, Man Of
Vision. Chicago: Swallow Press 1980
Jean Marcel The History Of Surrealist
Painting. London: Weidenfield &
Nicholson 1960
Franklin Rosemont André Breton And The
First Principles Of Surrealism.
London: Pluto Press 1978
Spare, Austin Osman The Book Of Pleasure
(Self-Love): The Psychology Of Ecstasy.
Private printing 1913
Toru Takemitsu "A Single Sound"
in Confronting Silence.
Berkeley: Fallen Leaf Press 1995
Gennifer Weisenfeld Mavo: Japanese Artists
And The Japanese Avant Garde, 1905-1931.
Berkeley: University Of California Press 2002
Alan S Weiss Breathless: Sound Recording,
Disembodiment and The Transformation of
Lyrical Nostalgia. Middletown, CT: Wesleyan
University Press 2002

Albert Ayler Bells. ESP 1965
— Spirits. Debut 1964
— Spirits Rejoice. ESP 1965
— Spiritual Unity. ESP 1964
Han Bennink Solo. ICP 1972
John Cage Sonatas And Interludes For
Prepared Piano Vol 1 (Yuji Takahashi, piano).
Fylkingen 1965
Ornette Coleman Free Jazz. Atlantic 1960
— Something Else! Atlantic 1959
Henry Cowell "The Banshee" from Piano
Music Folkways 1963
Claude Debussy Syrinx (Severino Gazzelloni,
flute). Heliodor Wergo 1969
Baby Dodds Talking And Drum Solos.
Folkways 1959
Milford Graves Percussion Ensemble With
Sunny Morgan. ESP 1965
Olivier Messiaen "Oraison" from Various,
OHM: The Early Gurus Of Electronic Music.
Ellipsis Arts 3xCD 2000
Spontaneous Music Ensemble
Karyobin. Chronoscope 1968
— Withdrawal. Emanem 1966-67
Cecil Taylor Jazz Advance. Blue Note 1955
Edgard Varèse Density 21.5 & Ecuatorial
from The Complete Works. Decca 2xCD 1998

GENERATION ECSTASY

Valerie Wilmer As Serious As Your Life.
London: Quartet 1977

Guillermo E Brown Soul At The Hands Of
The Machine. Thirsty Ear 2002
Dorgon & William Parker Broken Circle.
Jumbo Recordings 1999
Charles Gayle Homeless. Silkheart 1988
Milford Graves Grand Unification.
Tzadik 1998
William Hooker & Lee Ranaldo Envisioning.
Knitting Factory Works 1995
Susie Ibarra Radiance. Hopscotch 1999
Sabir Mateen Trio Divine Mad Love.
Eremite 1997
Other Dimensions In Music Now!
AUM Fidelity 1998
— Special Quintet with Matthew Shipp
Time Is Of The Essence Is Beyond Time.
AUM Fidelity 2000
William Parker & In Order To Survive
Compassion Seizes Bed-Stuy.
Homestead 1996
— The Peach Orchard. AUM Fidelity 1998
**William Parker & The Little Huey Creative
Music Orchestra** Sunrise In The Tone World.
AUM Fidelity 1997
Matthew Shipp The Flow Of X. 2.13 1997
— The Multiplication Table. Hatology 1998
— Points. Silkheart 1994
Test Live/Test. Eremite 1998
— Test. AUM Fidelity 1999
David S Ware Cryptology. Homestead 1995
— Third Ear Recitation. DIW 1993

CONTRIBUTORS

Marcus Boon grew up in London, spent most of the last 20 years in New York, and recently moved to Toronto where he writes and teaches literature. His first book, *The Road Of Excess: A History Of Writers On Drugs*, will be published by Harvard in the UK in January 2003. His work has appeared in *NME*, *The Face*, *Fringeware Review*, *Signal To Noise* and *21C*, and more can be found at his Website: www.hungryghost.net.

Julian Cowley has published widely on literature and on music. At the end of the 1970s he regularly played improvised music with guitarist Hugh Metcalfe (who later formed BirdYak with sound poet Bob Cobbing and dancer Jennifer Pike). Throughout the 1980s Cowley worked closely with Eric Mottram, poet, professor and champion of radical poetics. During the 1990s Cowley became a regular contributor to *The Wire*. He currently lives in Hertfordshire.

Christoph Cox teaches philosophy at Hampshire College in Amherst, Massachusetts and writes about contemporary music and art for *The Wire*, *Cabinet*, *Artforum*, *Pulse!*, and other magazines. His book *Nietzsche: Naturalism And Interpretation* was published by the University of California Press in 1999. With Daniel Warner, he is currently editing an anthology on theories and practices in music from Russolo to DJ culture.

Erik Davis is a writer based in San Franciso, a charming if somewhat provincial locus of weirdness. His 1998 book, *TechGnosis: Myth, Magic, And Mysticism In The Age Of Information* is currently being translated into six languages. Davis serves as a contributing editor for *Wired* and *Trip*, and has contributed essays to a number of journals and book anthologies on topics ranging from Descartes to dub. Some of his work can be accessed at www.techgnosis.com.

Andy Hamilton teaches philosophy at Durham University. He has been writing for *The Wire* since 1985 – he started very young – *and writes for Jazz Review*, and for *Classic CD* before its untimely demise. He has published articles on Aesthetics and Philosophy of Psychology, including "The Art Of Improvisation' in *British Journal Of Aesthetics* (January 2000). He is currently collaborating with saxophonist Lee Konitz on a volume of conversations and reminiscences, provisionally titled *A Word From Lee*.

Ken Hollings is a writer based in London. His work has appeared regularly in *The Wire*, *Sight & Sound*, *Bizarre* as well as in *Frieze*, *Gargoyle*, *CTHEORY* and the St Martin's Press anthologies *Digital Delirium* and *The Last Sex*. He has presented texts at the ICA in London, the Transmediale Festival in Berlin, Sónar in Barcelona and the Sydney Biennale. He has also edited books by John Cage, Georges Bataille, Jean Cocteau and Hubert Selby. His novel *Destroy All Monsters* – described by *The Scotsman* as "a mighty slab of trippy, cult, out-there fiction. Mind-bending reading" – is available from Marion Boyars Publishers.

Biba Kopf has been writing about German music for *The Wire* and other music publications since before the fall of West Berlin. Other than that he'll only own up to scripting a Slovenian TV documentary about Laibach, called *Bravo*.

Ian Penman is a freelance writer and critic.

Edwin Pouncey is a regular contributor to *The Wire* where he has written about, amongst others, Alice Coltrane; John Fahey; John Cale; Merzbow; Amon Düül 2; and The Boredoms. As Savage Pencil he provides the illustration for the magazine's regular Primer feature, together with his *Trip Or Squeek* comic strip. He is currently researching material for a monograph about the art of minimalist musician Charlemagne Palestine. He lives in Streatham, South London with his partner Jill and continues to hunt down rare free jazz records; books relating to witchcraft and Restoration Theatre historian Montague Summers; art ephemera; and Japanese vinyl toys.

Tom Roe is a sound and text manipulator who has written for *The New York Post*, *The New York Times*, *Newsday*, *Signal To Noise*, *Billboard*, *Detour*, *Magnet* and many other publications. He also co-founded the Brooklyn micro-radio station and multimedia collective free103point9, with which he often performs in New York.

Mark Sinker is writing *The Electric Storm*, a critical history of music and technology, to be published by Quartet Books.

Peter Shapiro is one of the world's leading air guitar experts. He is currently assistant editor of *The Wire* and has contributed to *Spin*, *The Independent*, *Time Out*, *Uncut*, *Urb*, *Sleaze Nation* and is the author of four books.

Philip Smith, the former Boo Hoo of Mahagonny in the Neo-American Church (Kleps was puzzled), lives in Berkeley, California, where he edits digital reproductions of rare books for Octavo and is a witting participant in the antiquarian book trade.

David Toop is a composer, author, critic and sound curator. He has published three books: *Rap Attack* (first published in 1984,

now in its third edition), *Ocean Of Sound*, and *Exotica* (a winner of the Before Columbus Foundation American Book Award 2000). He has written for many publications, including *The Wire*, *The Face*, *The Times*, *The New York Times*, *Urb* and *Bookforum*. In 2000, he curated Sonic Boom, the UK's biggest exhibition of sound art, for the Hayward Gallery in London and in 2001 he curated sound for Radical Fashion at the Victoria & Albert Museum. His first album was released on Brian Eno's Obscure label in 1975 and since 1995 he has released six solo CDs. At Lisbon Expo 98 he composed the music for the nightly spectacular, *Acqua Matrix*, and in 2002, his composition *Siren Space* was performed on the Thames at the close of the Thames Festival. Currently a Visiting Research Fellow at the London Institute, he is writing a new book on technology and performance.

Rob Young was born in 1968, joined *The Wire* in 1993 and has been editing the magazine since March 2000. He has published work in a variety of books, magazines and newspapers.

INDEX

THE WIRE 20 1982-2002: AUDIO ISSUE

Mute 3xCD Released: 18 November 2002

A triple CD box set compiled to mark *The Wire*'s 20th anniversary in 2002. Contains more than 40 tracks covering the magazine's 20 year history and beyond, including:

Steve Lacy "The Wire"
Ennio Morricone (with Gruppo Di Improvvisazione Nuova Consonanza) "Seguita"
Coil "Wrong Eye"
Hands To "Egress (excerpt)"
David Toop & Max Eastley "Buried Dreams"
Vivian Jackson & King Tubby "Tubby's Vengeance"
Fennesz "Don't Talk (Put Your Head On My Shoulder)"
Derek Bailey "M 5"
Traditional Musicians, Bali "Cockfight – Trance In Paksabali And Kesiman – Gamelan Beleganjur"
Einstürzende Neubauten "Pygmäen"
AMM "After Rapidly Circling The Plaza"
Mars "11,000 Volts"
Cabaret Voltaire "Breathe Deep"
Tony Conrad with Faust "The Death Of The Composer Was In 1962"
Designer "Vandal"
Torture "Soaking Bodies In Dub"
Fela Kuti "Shenshema"
The Art Ensemble Of Chicago "Illistrum"
Sonic Youth "Expressway To Yr Skull"

Spring Heel Jack/The Blue Series Continuum "Salt"
This Heat "Paper Hats"
Stereolab & Nurse With Wound "Simple Headphone Mind"
Jac Berrocal "Rock 'N' Roll Station"
Sun Ra & His Solar-Myth Arkestra "Ancient Ethiopia"
Christian Marclay "Jukebox Capriccio"
John Cage "Williams Mix"
Yoshihide Otomo "Cathode #4: Soundcheck Version"
Bjork "Headphones"
Keith Hudson "Satan Side"
Terry Riley "Music For The Gift Part 1"
William S Burroughs (with Ian Sommerville) "Silver Smoke Of Dreams"
Supersilent "4.2"
Suicide "Rocket USA"
Larry Young "Khalid Of Space Part 2 – Welcome"
Fushitsusha "The Caution Appears Part 5"
John Coltrane (with Alice Coltrane) "Living Space"
John Fahey "Some Summer Day"
Diamanda Galas "25 Minutes To Go"

www.mute.com www.mutebank.co.uk www.thewire.co.uk